THiS FASHiON SKETCHBOOK BELONGS TO:

....

....

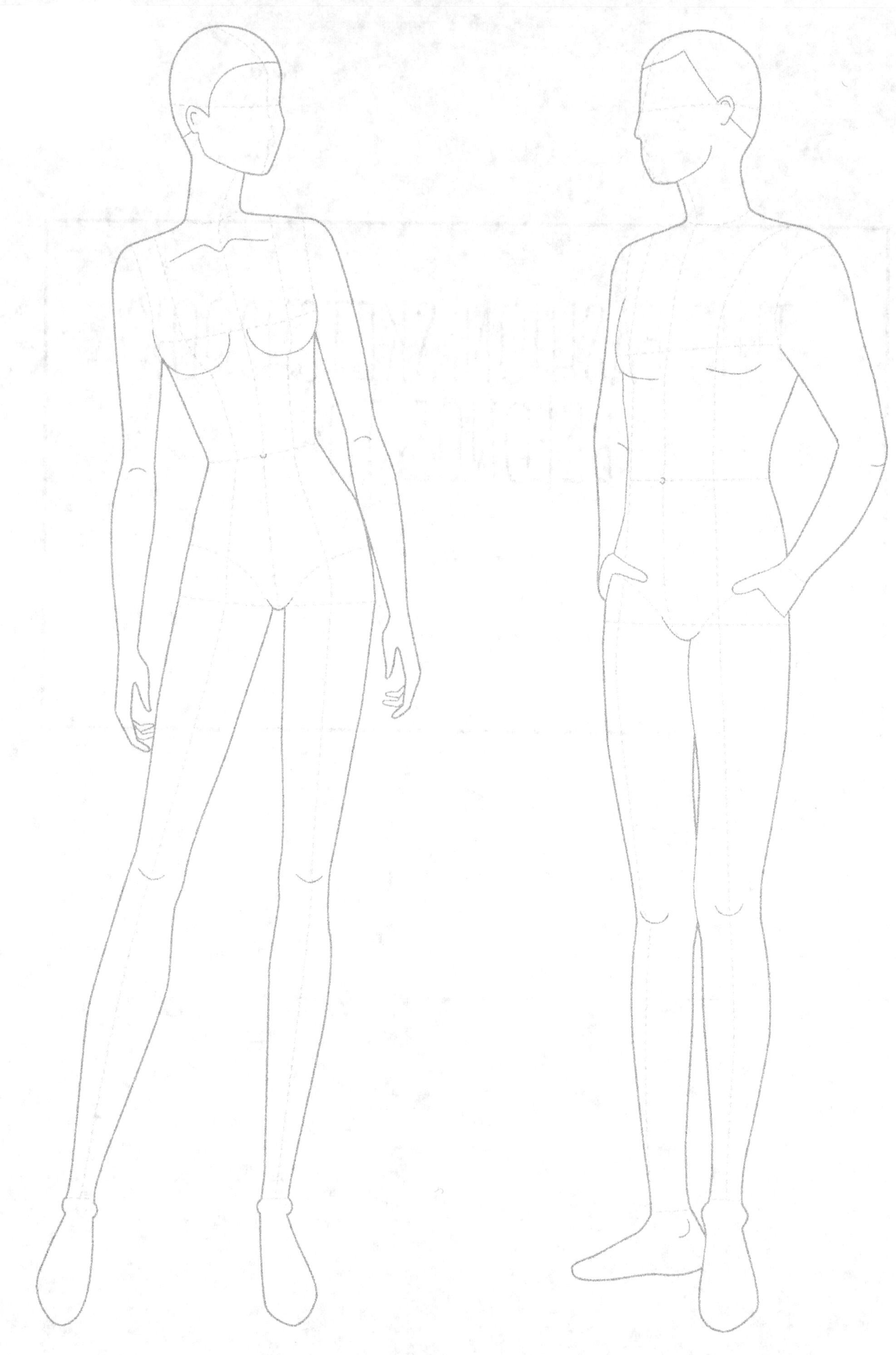

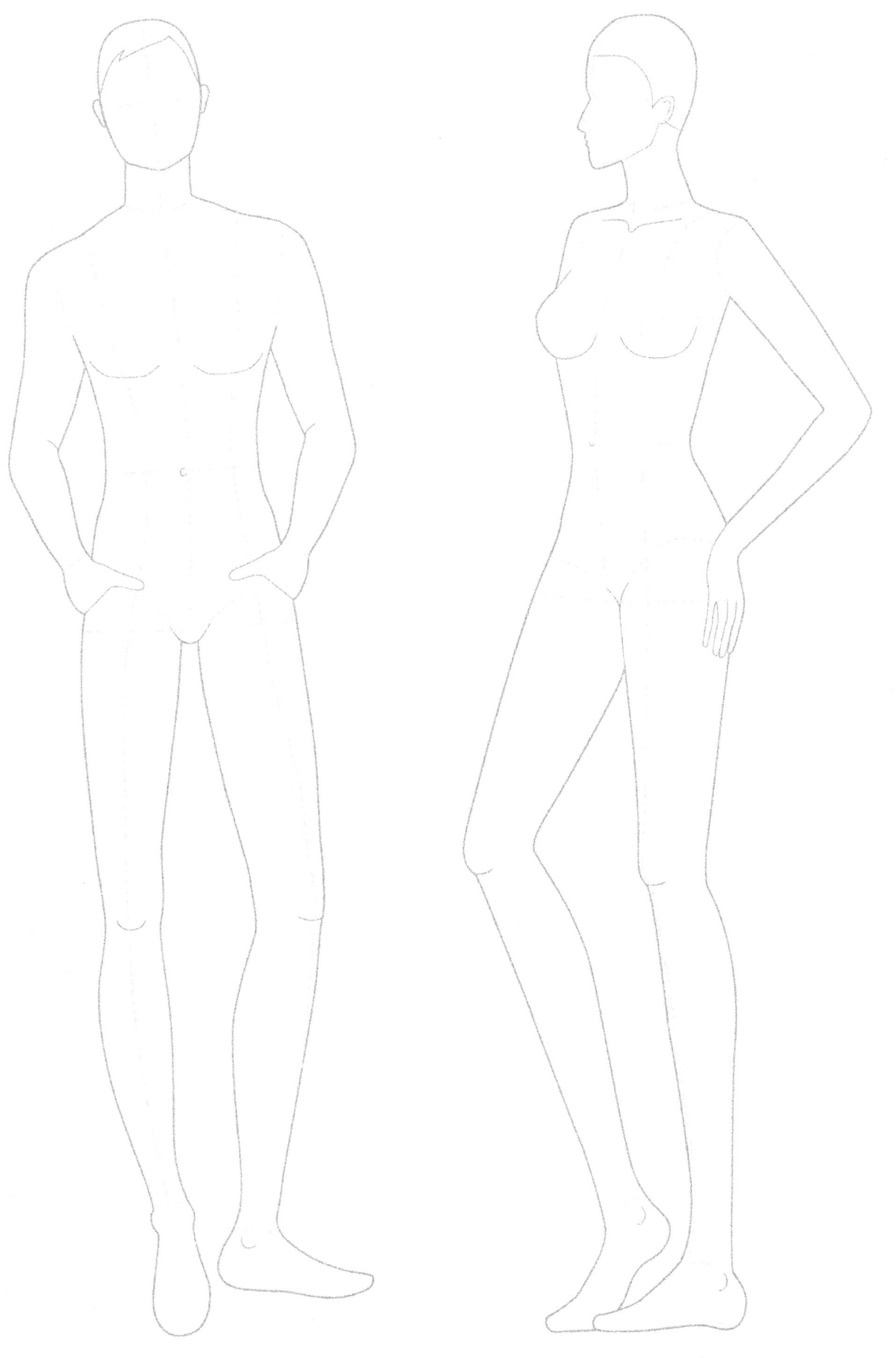

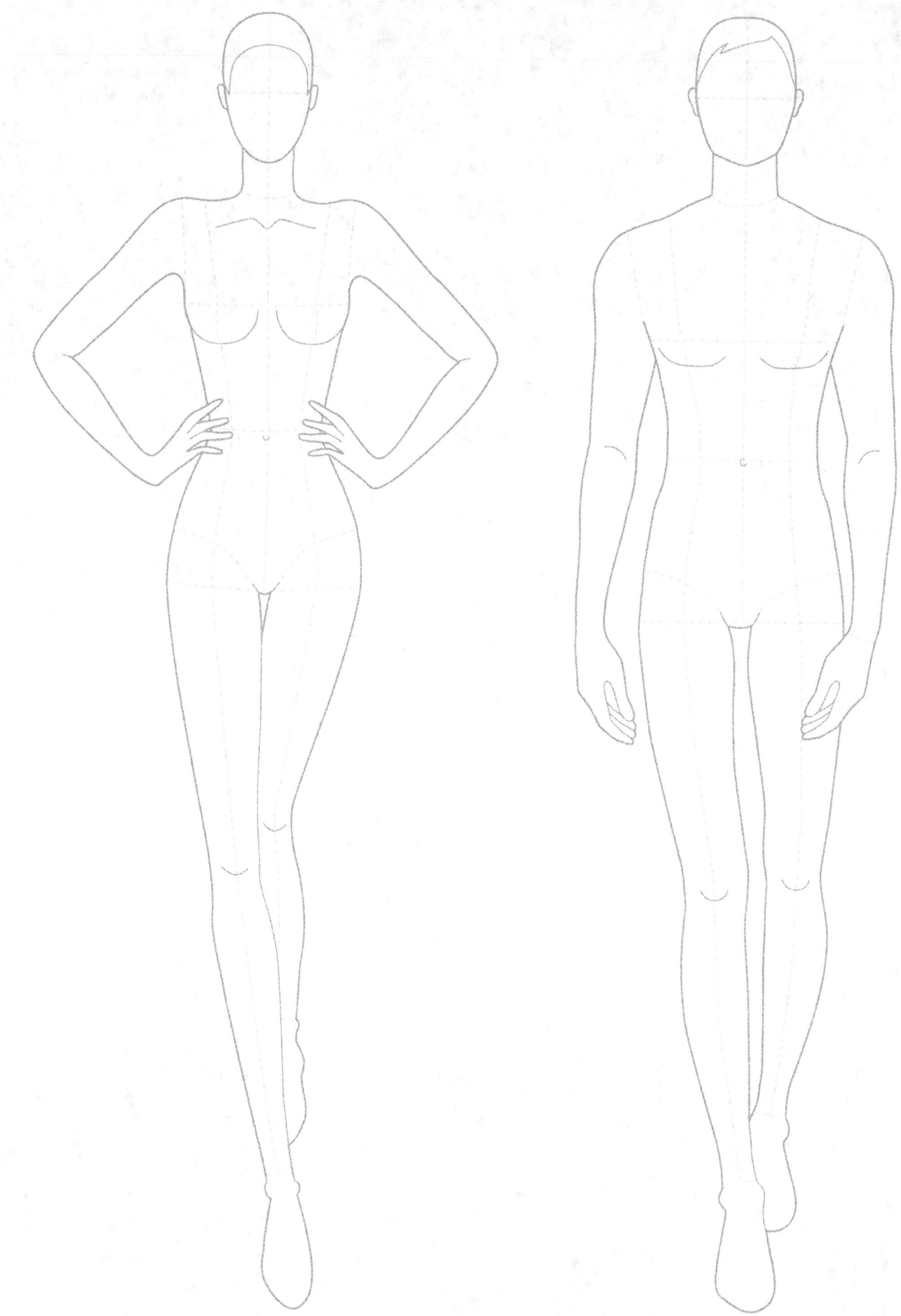

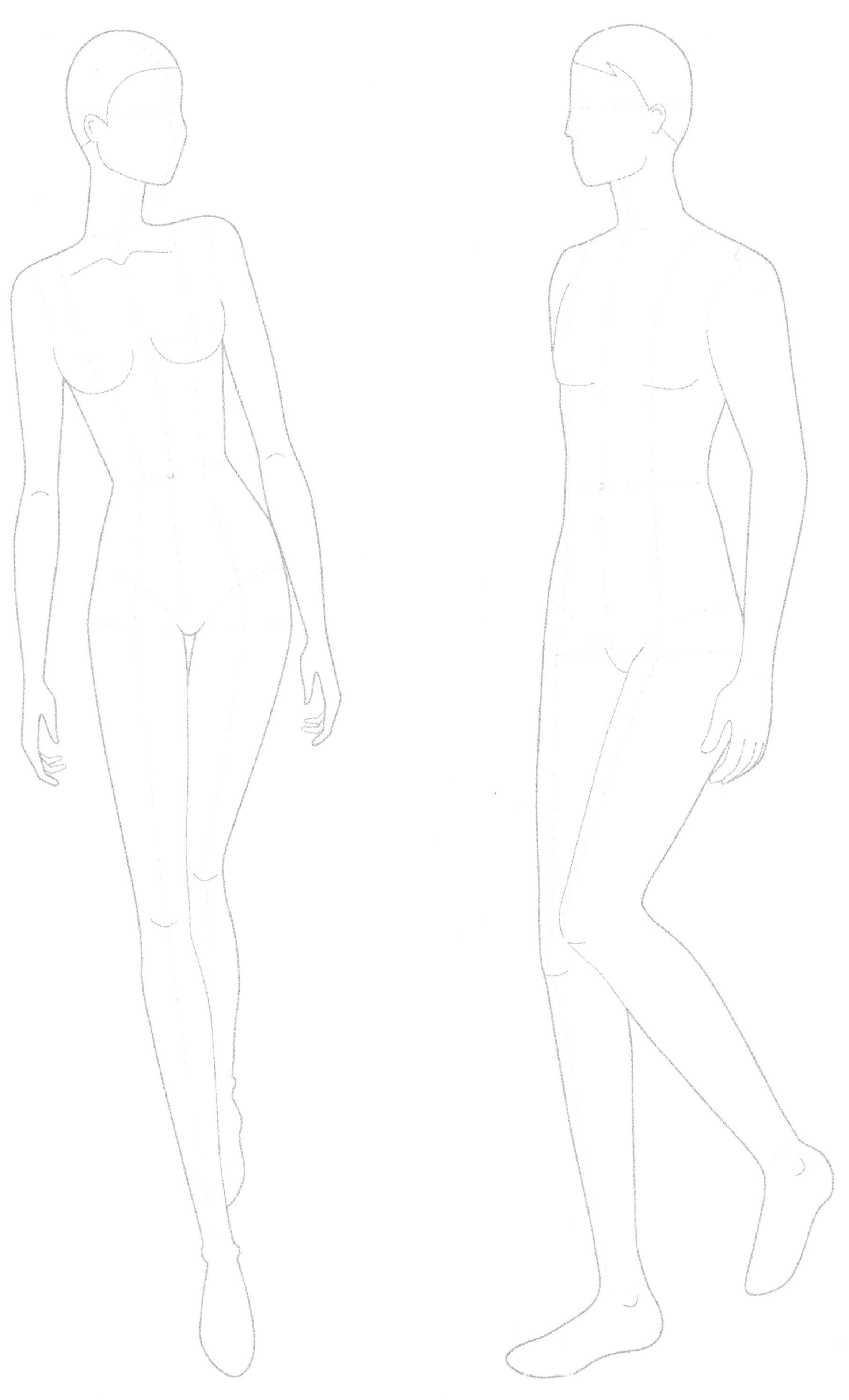

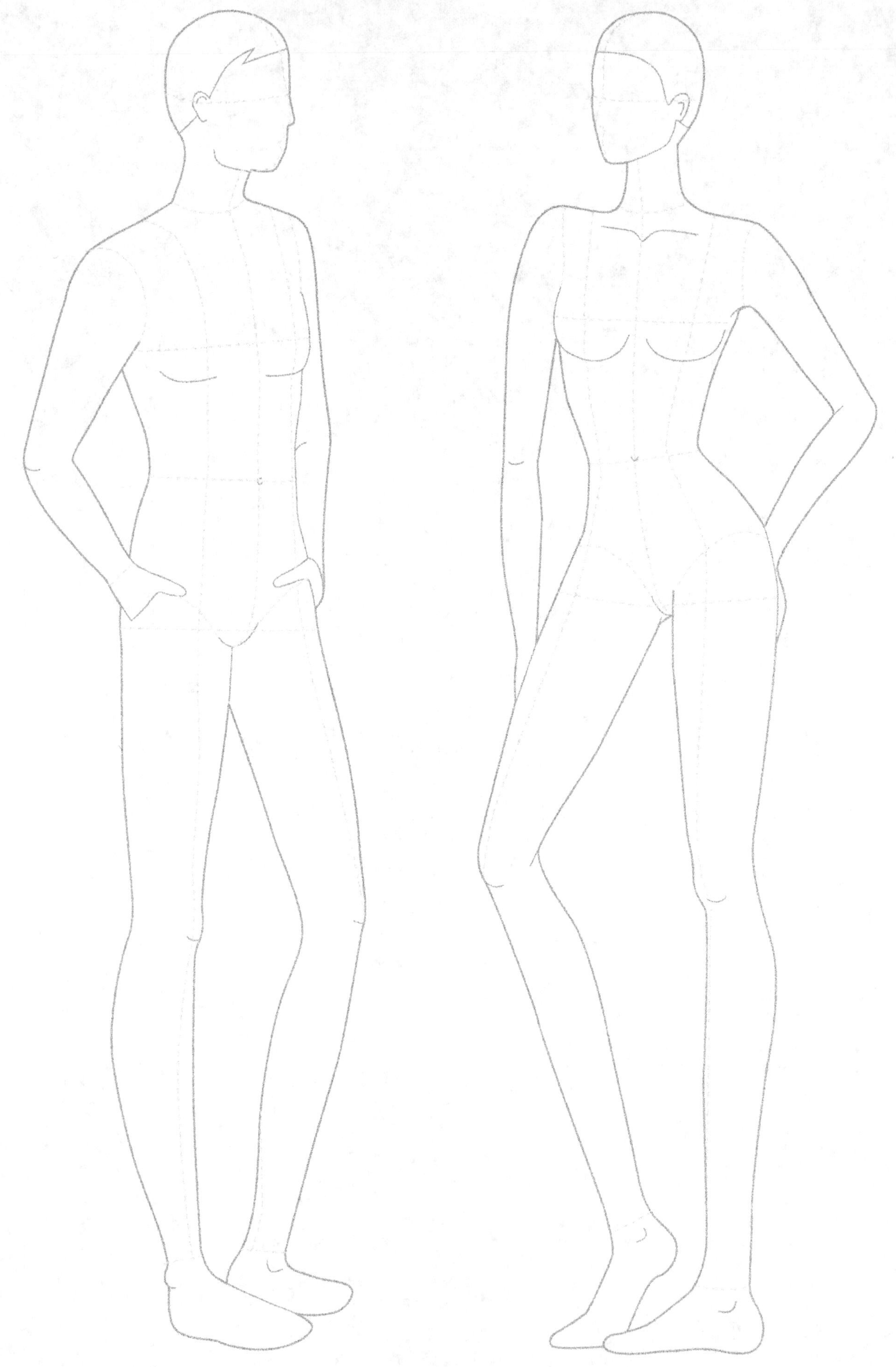

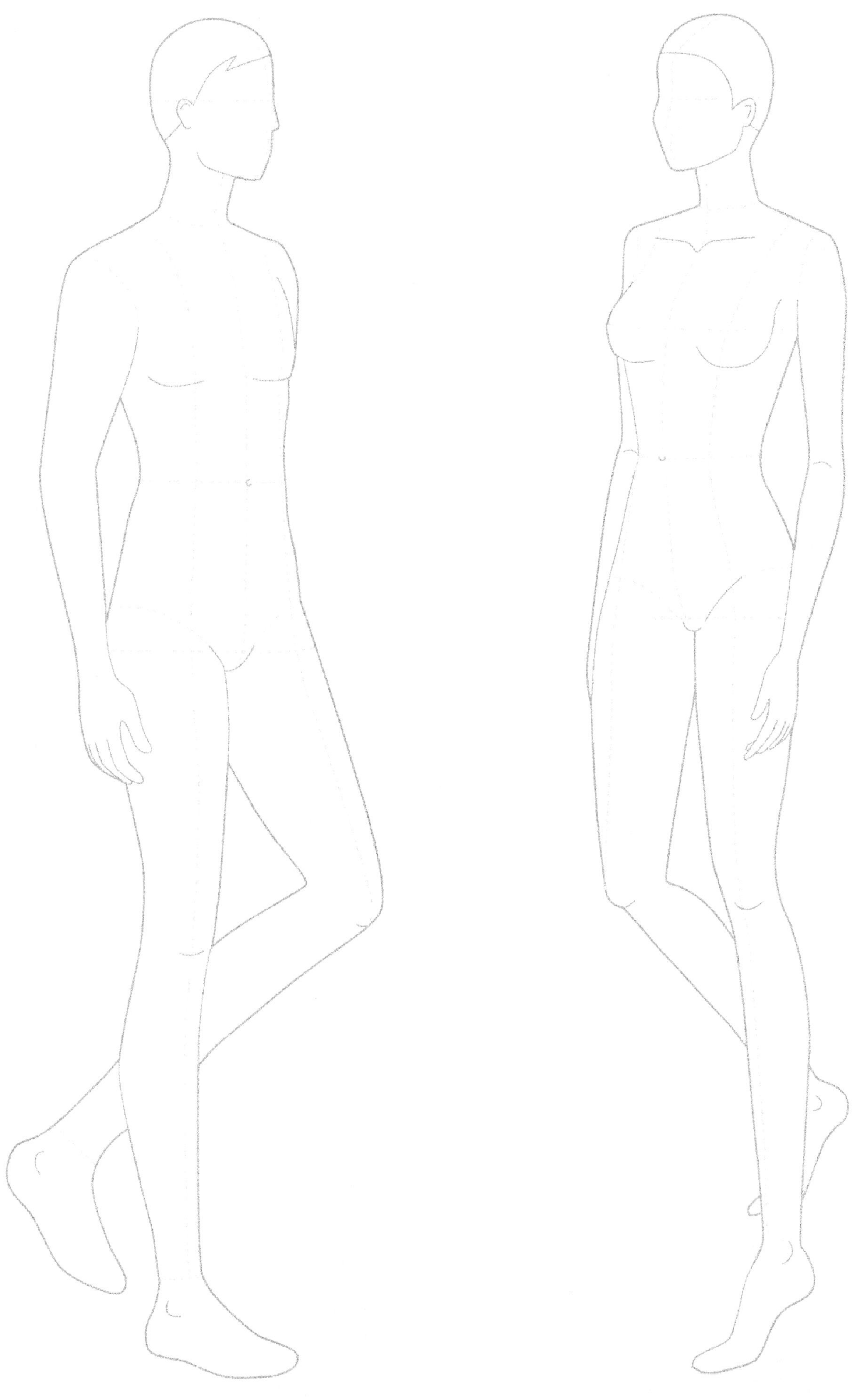

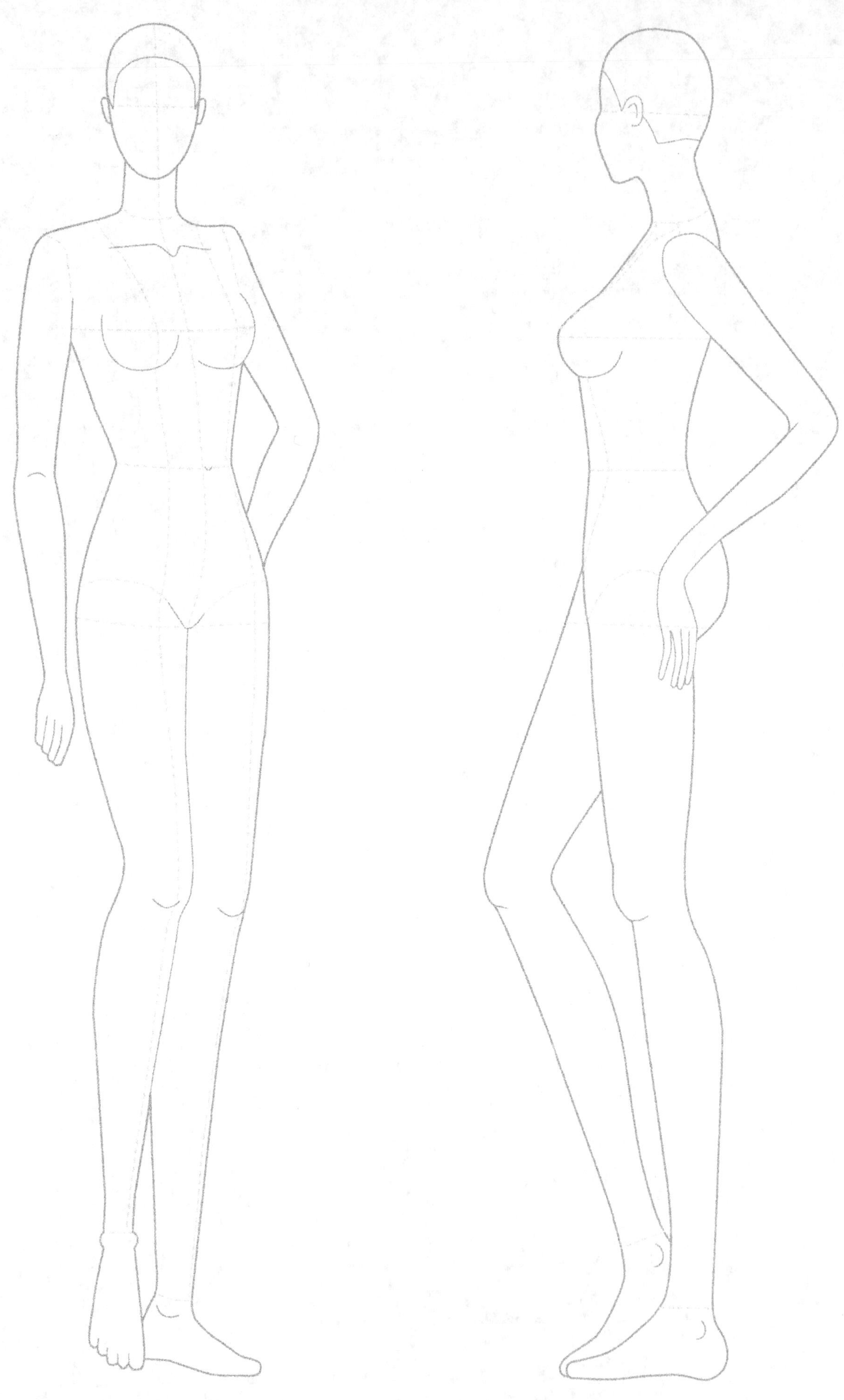

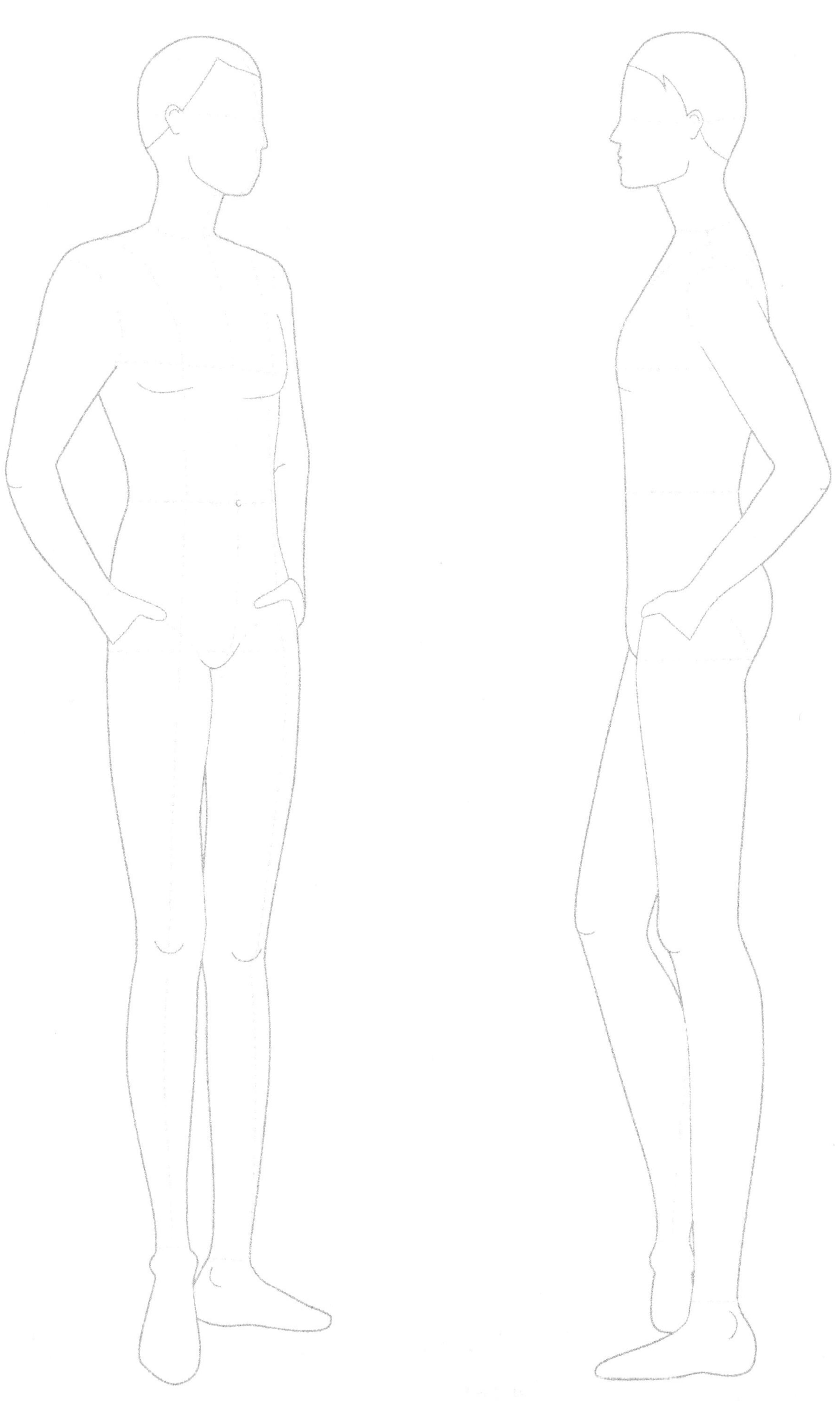

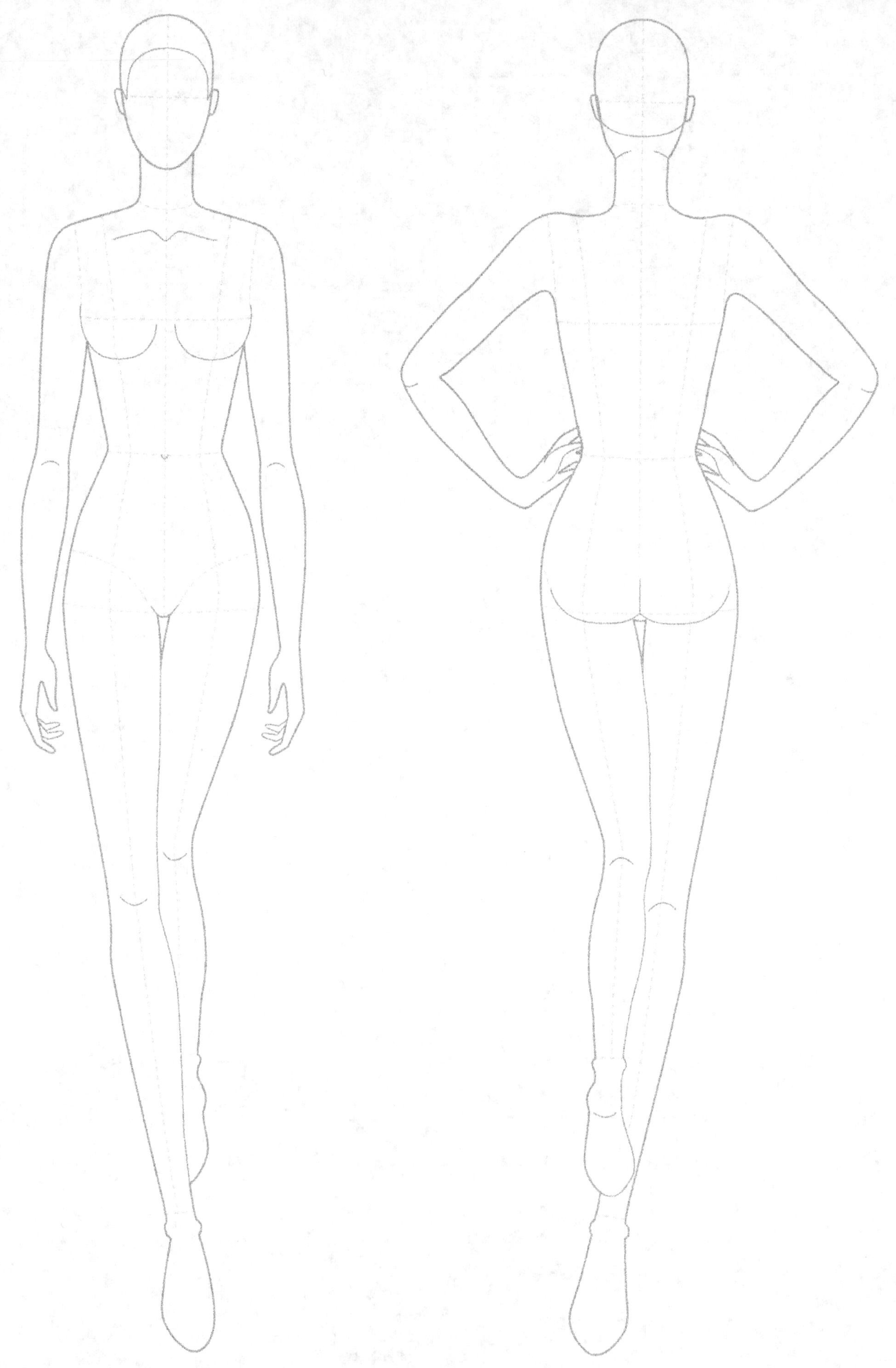

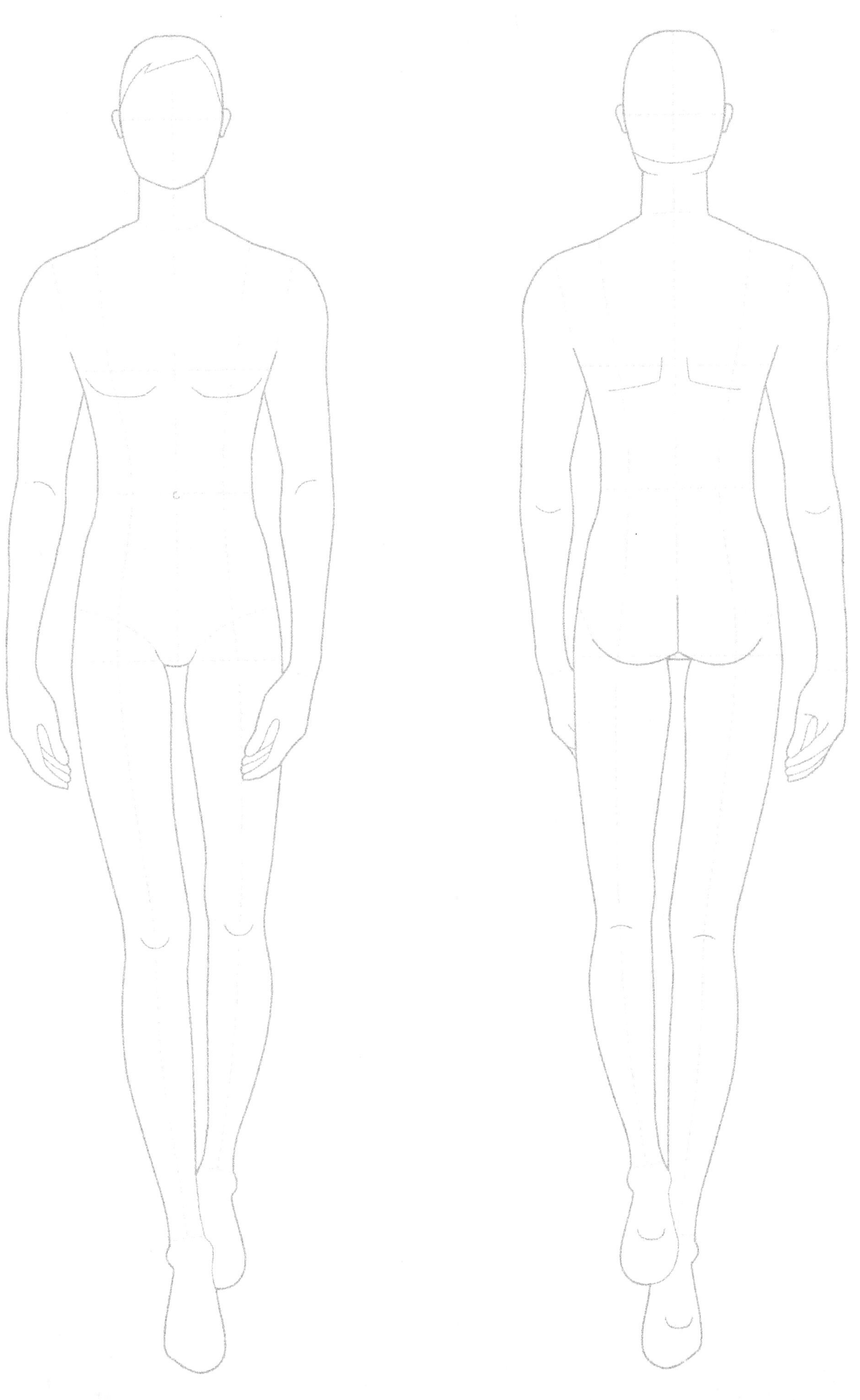

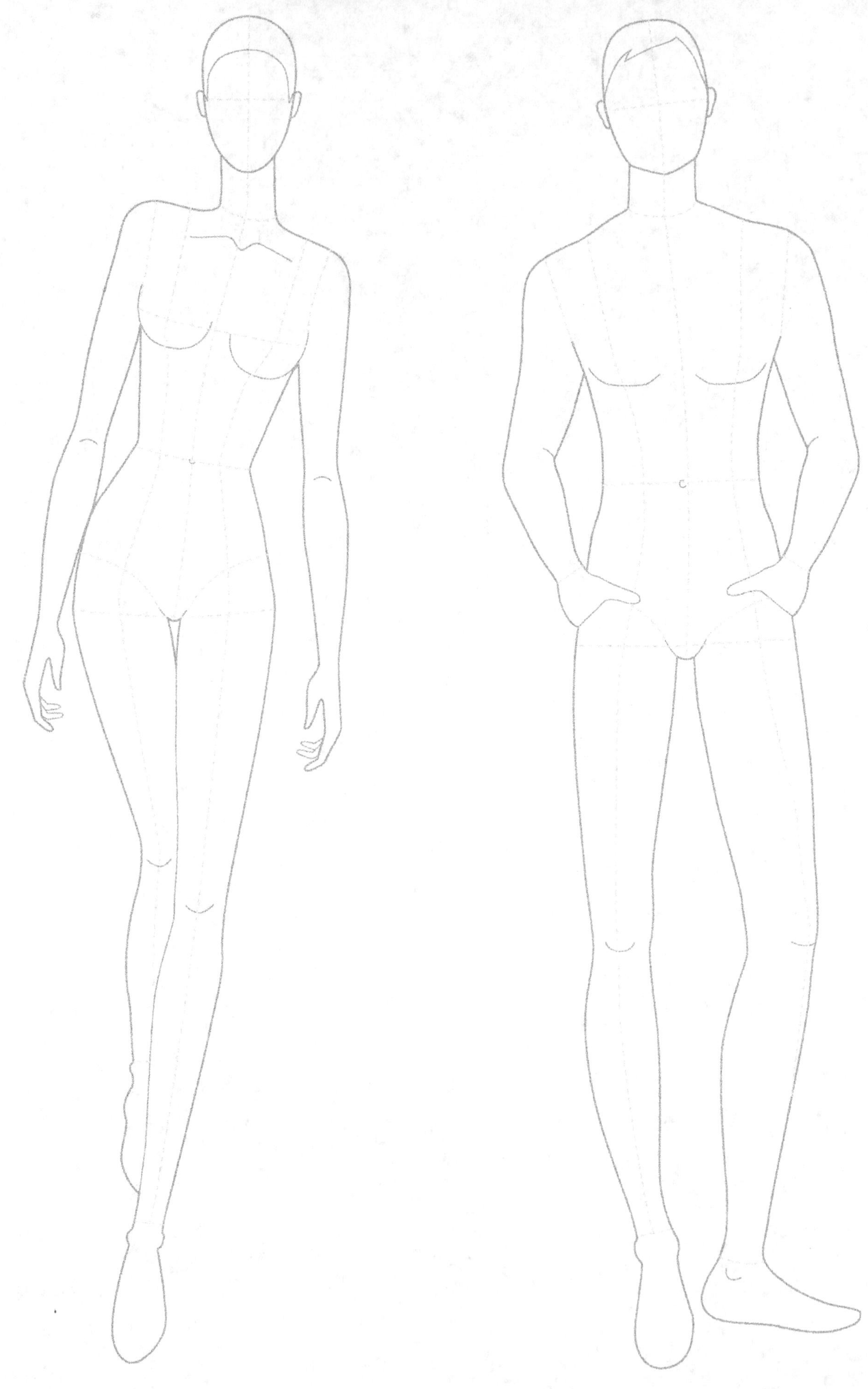

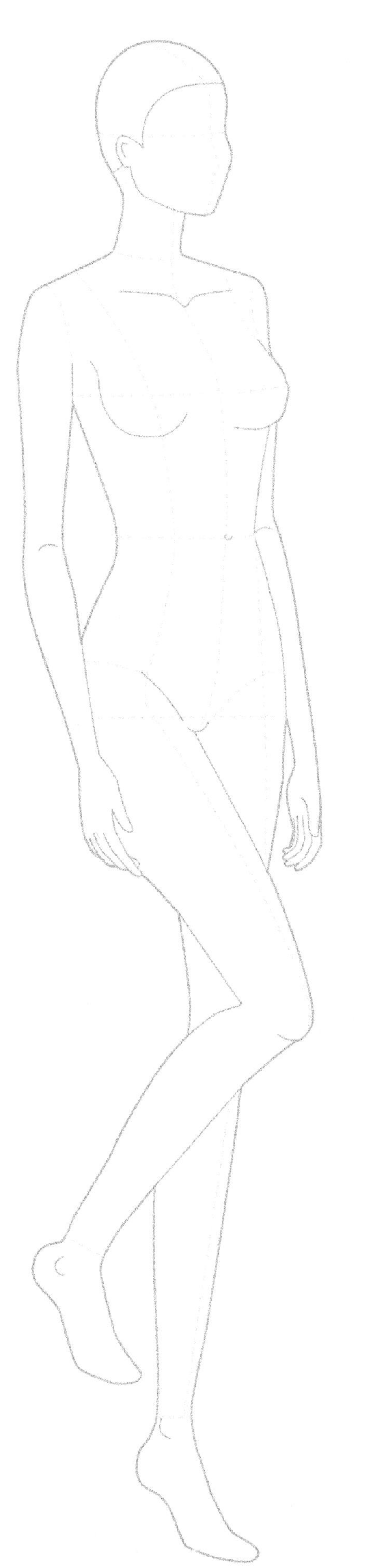
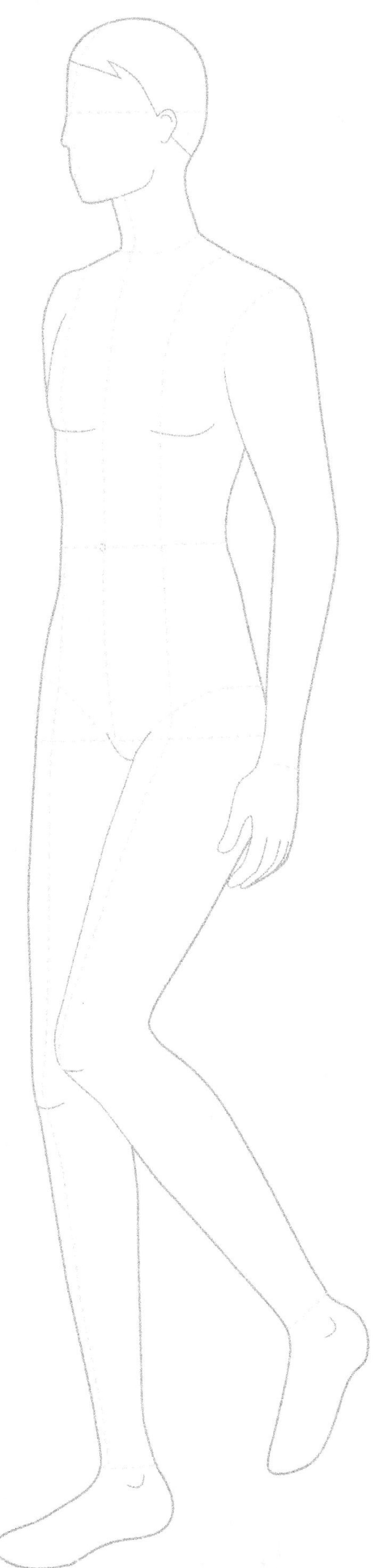

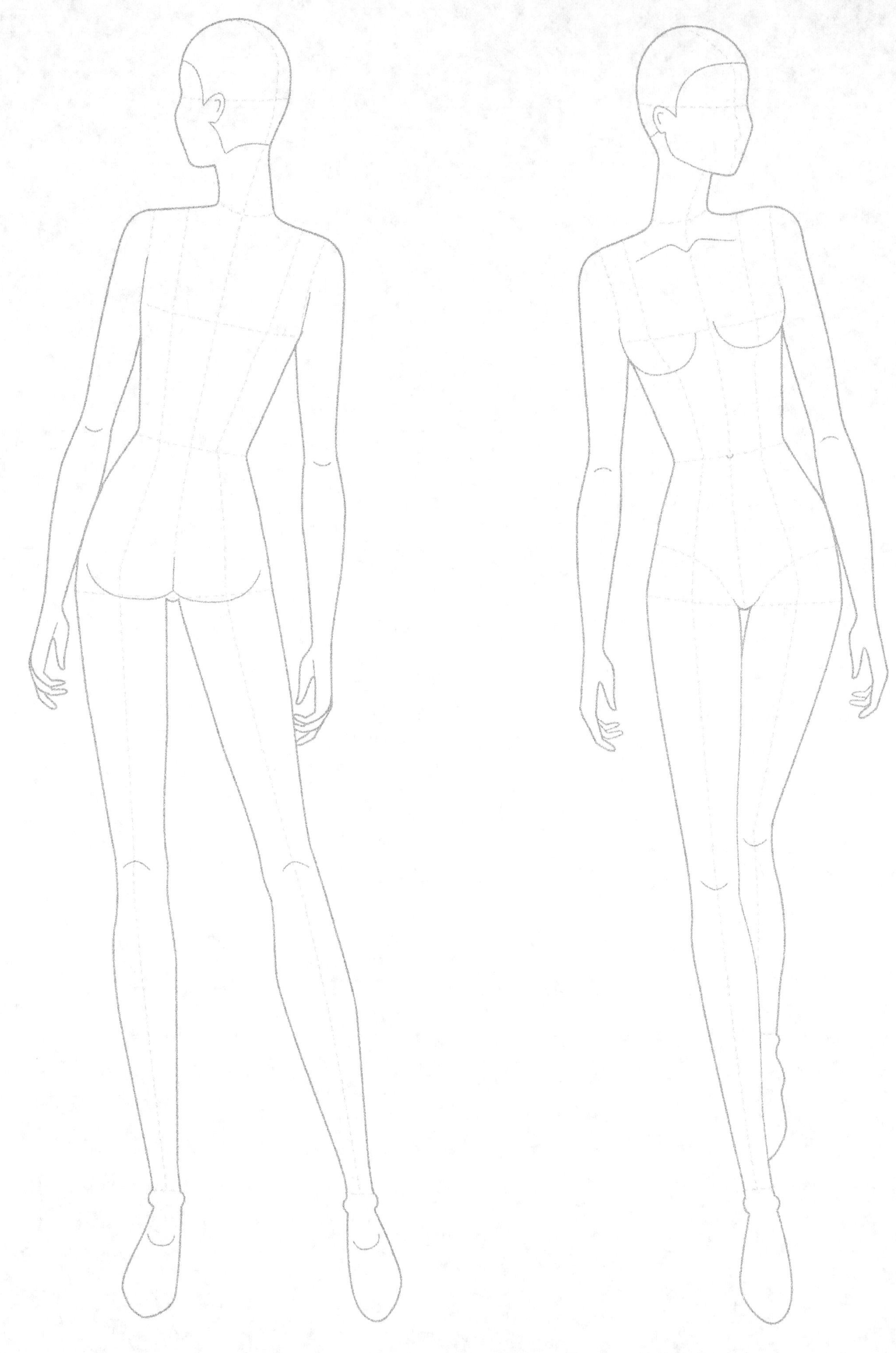

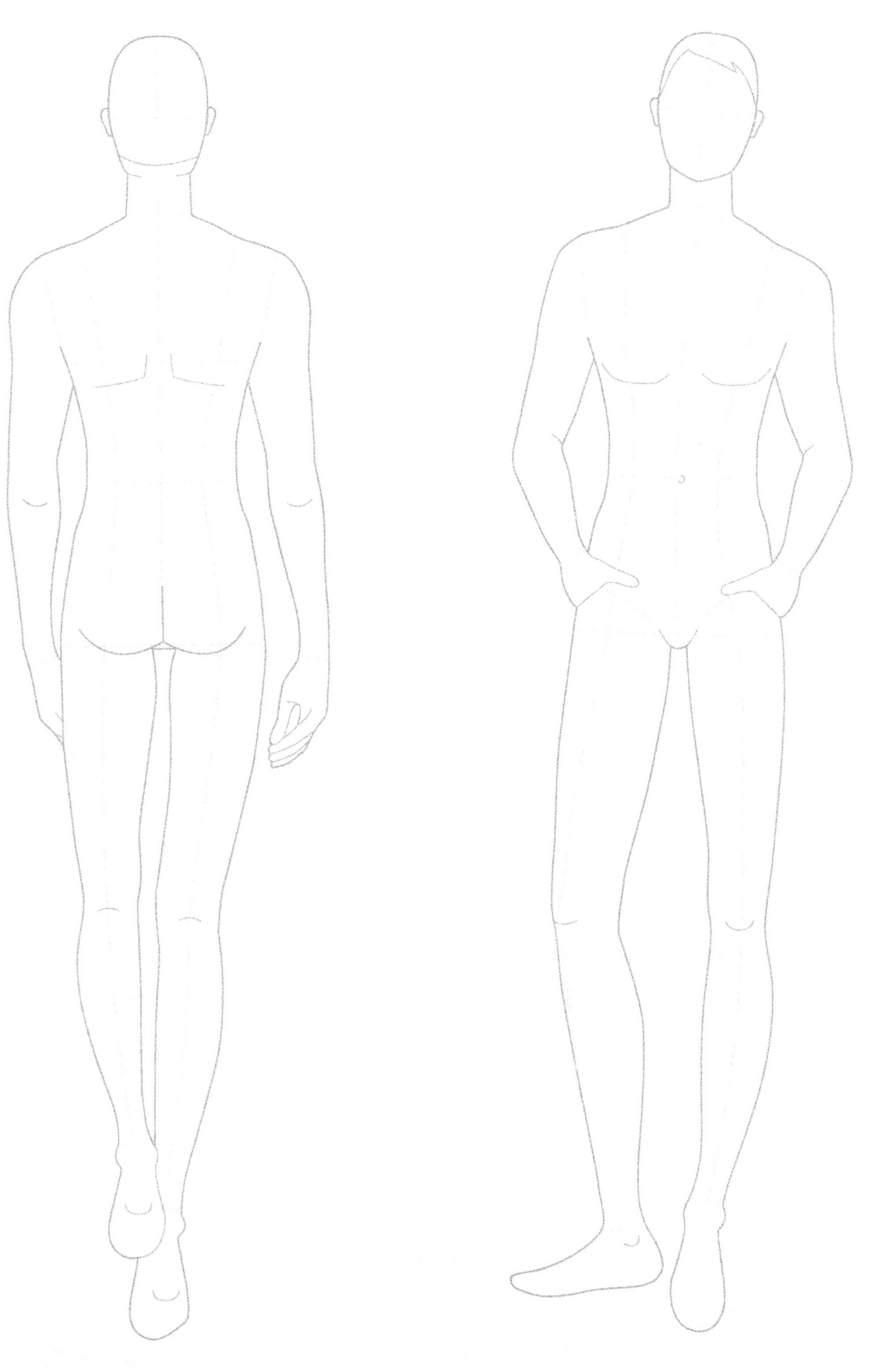

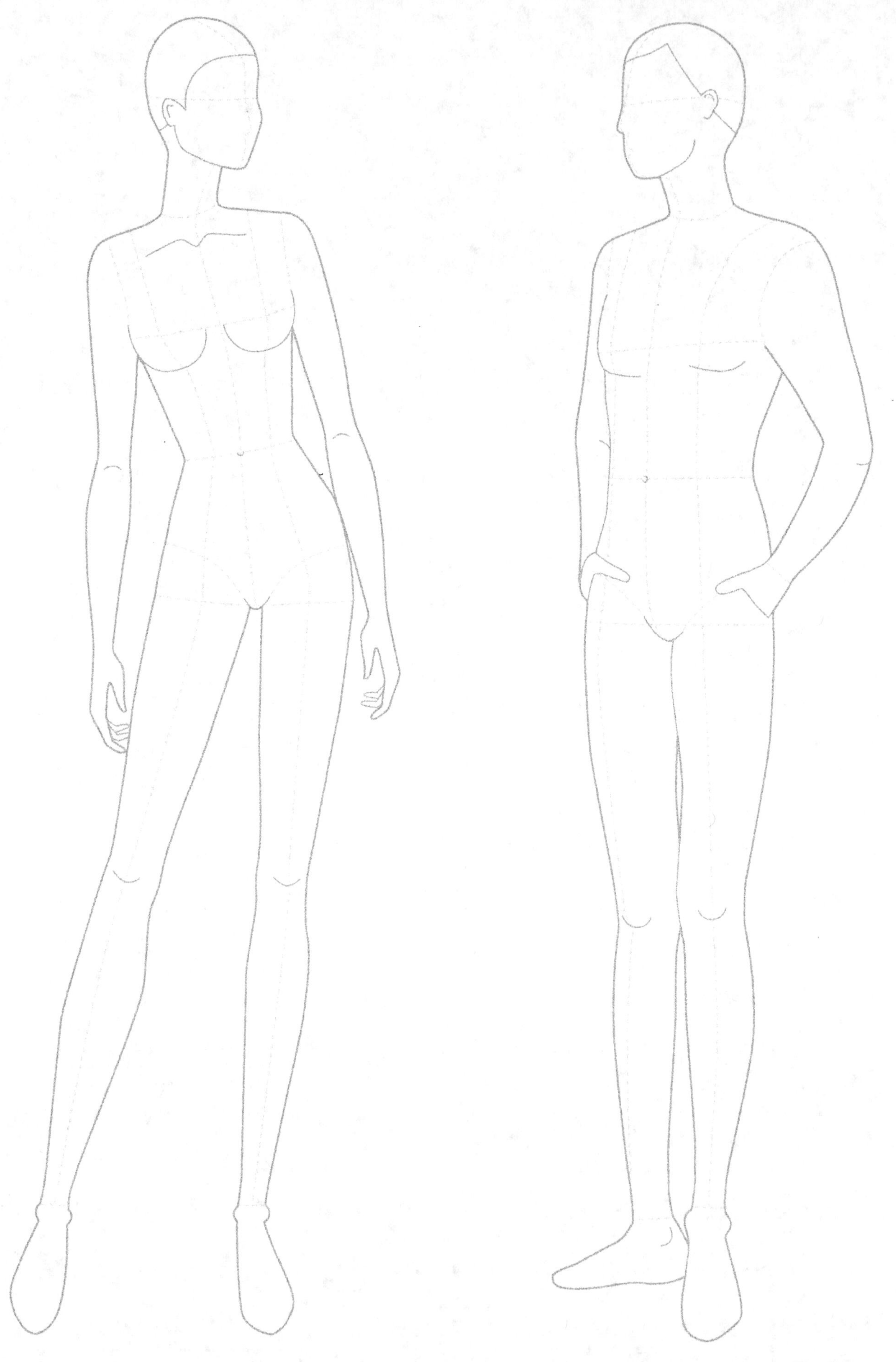

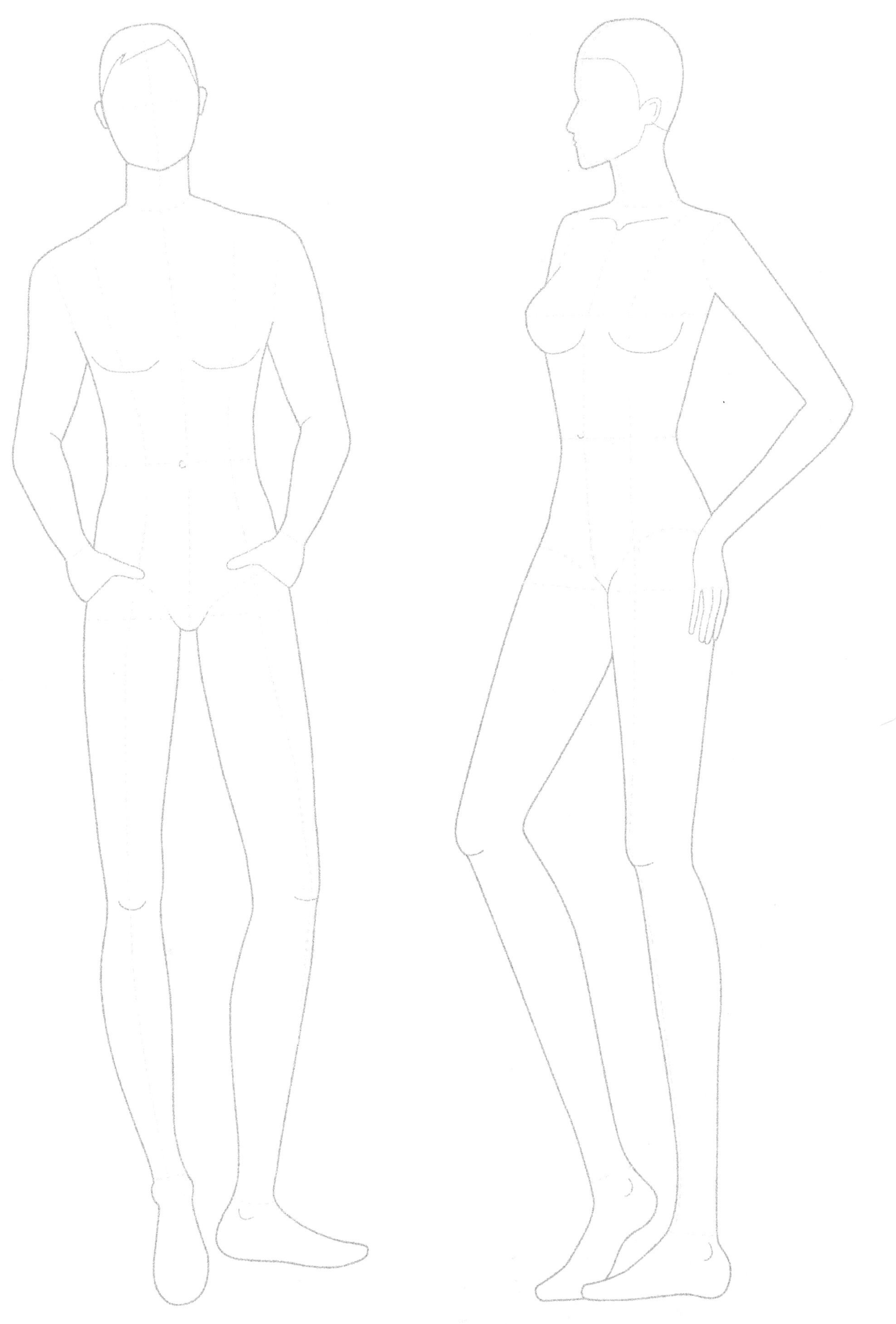

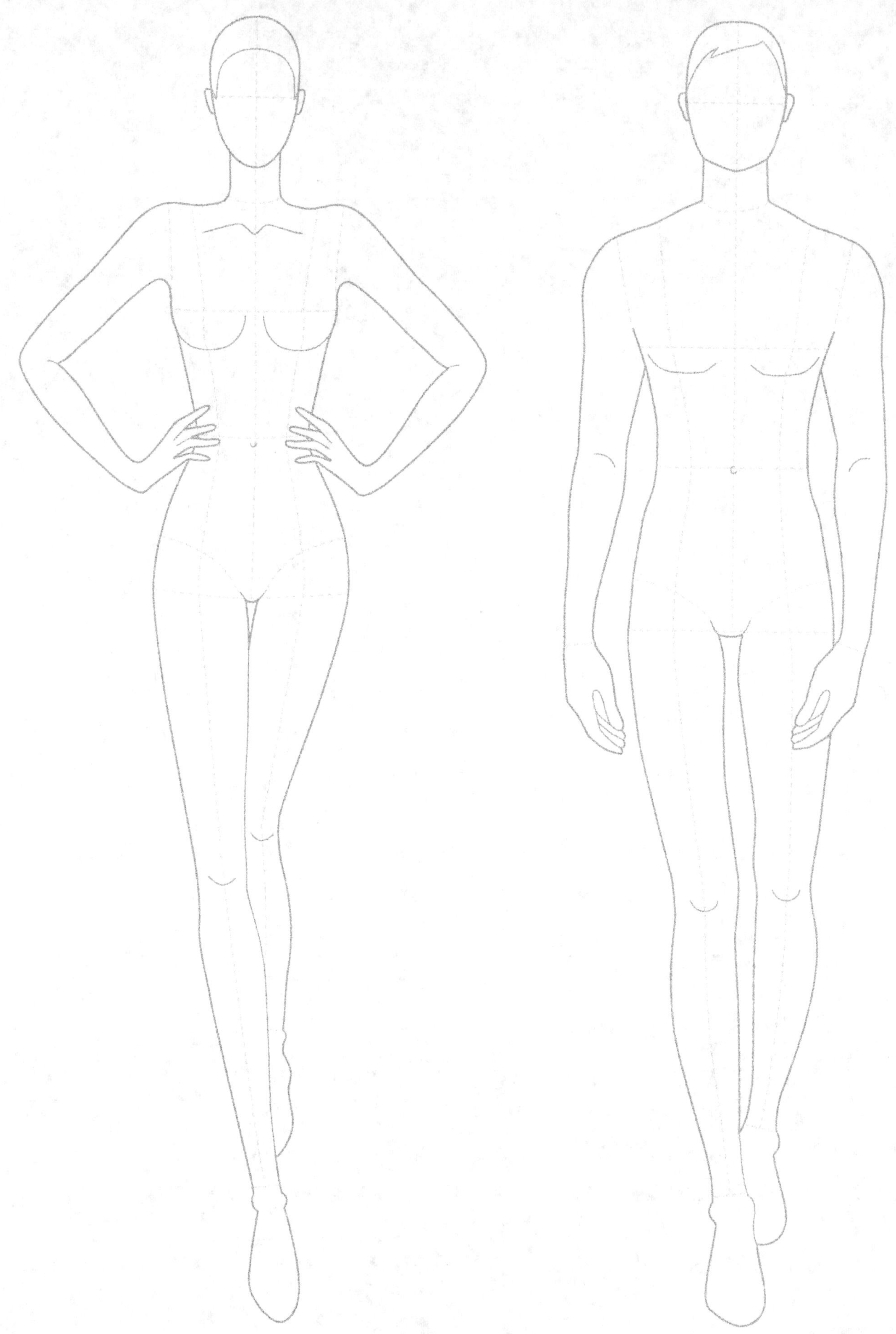

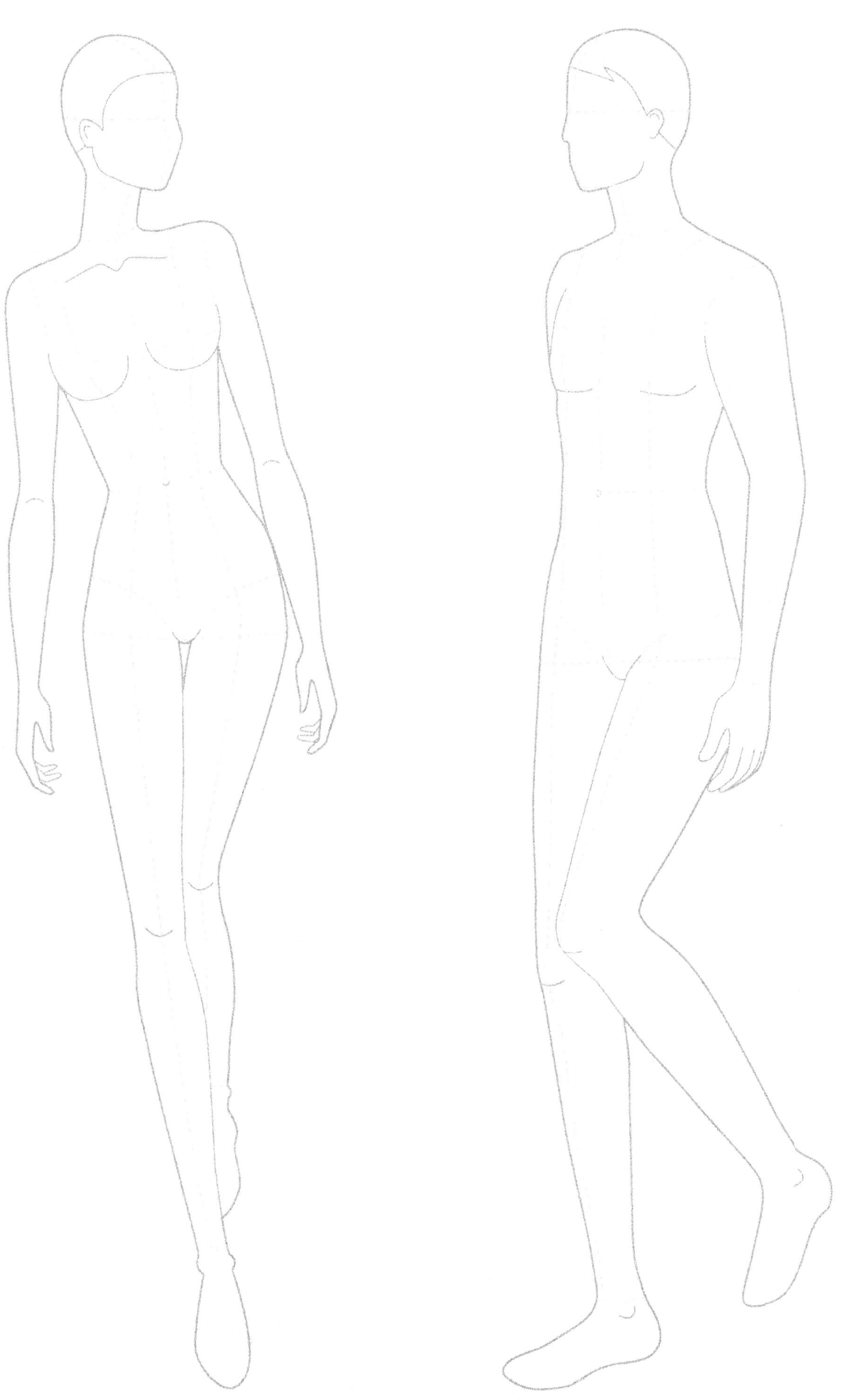

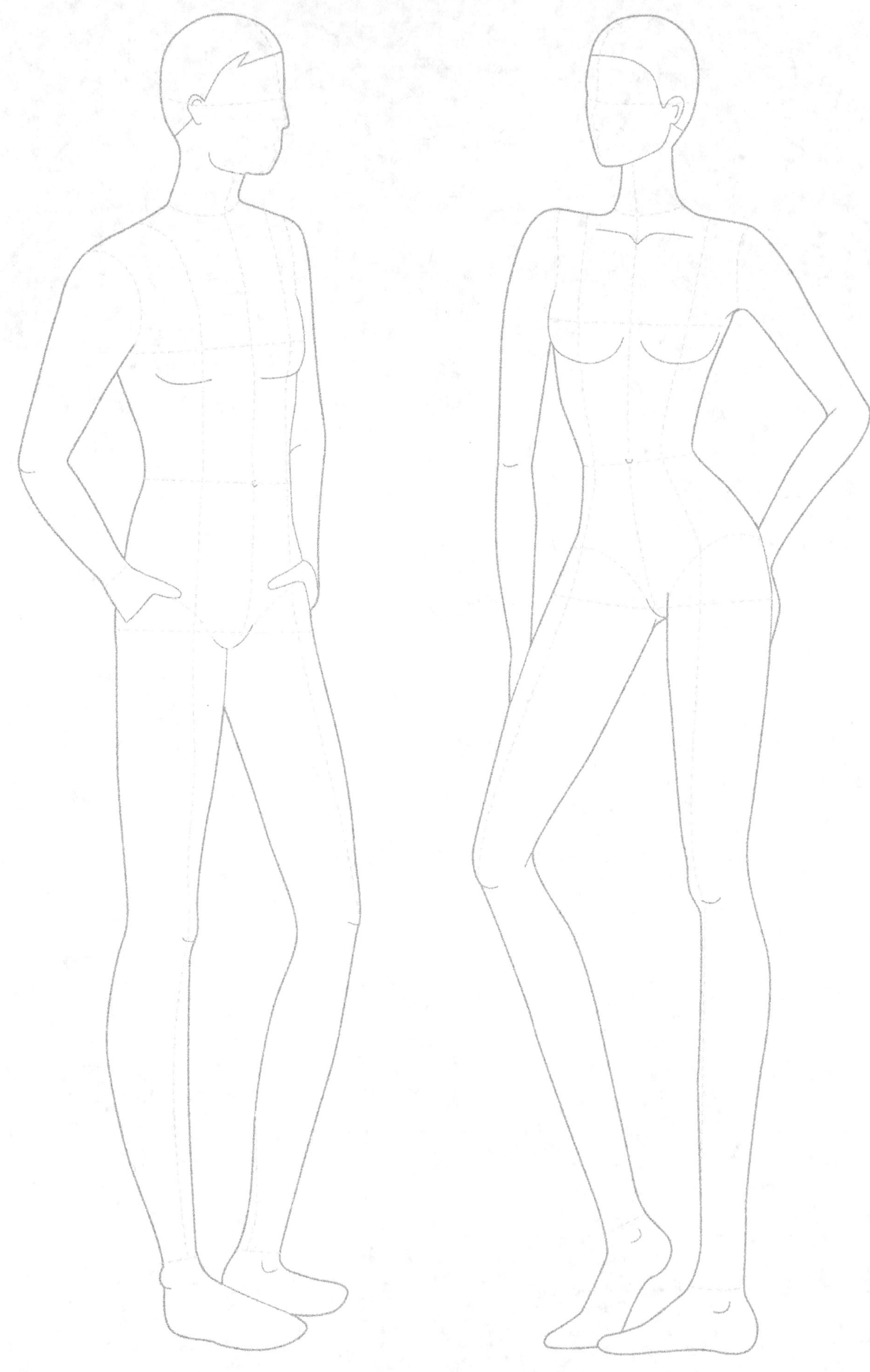

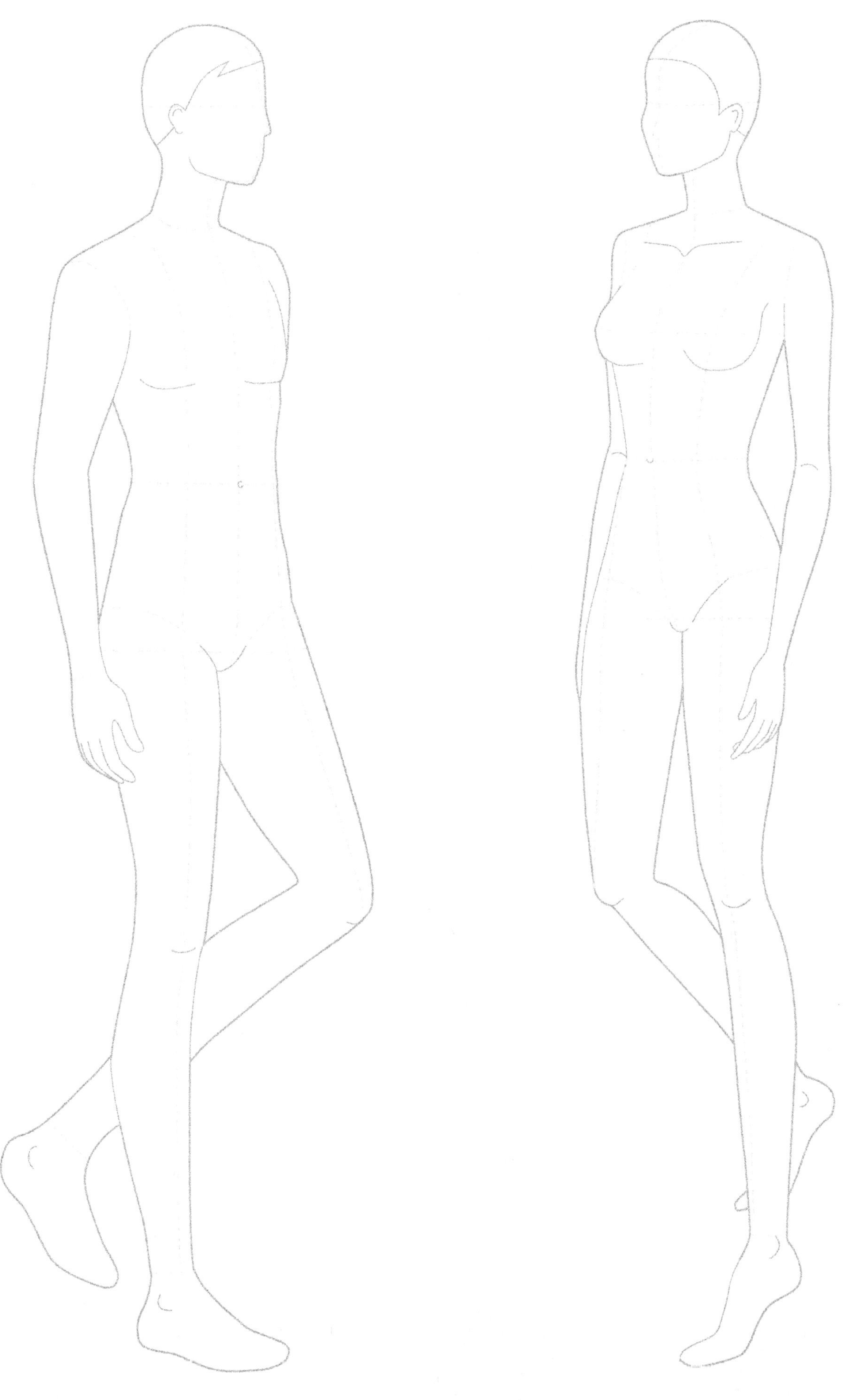

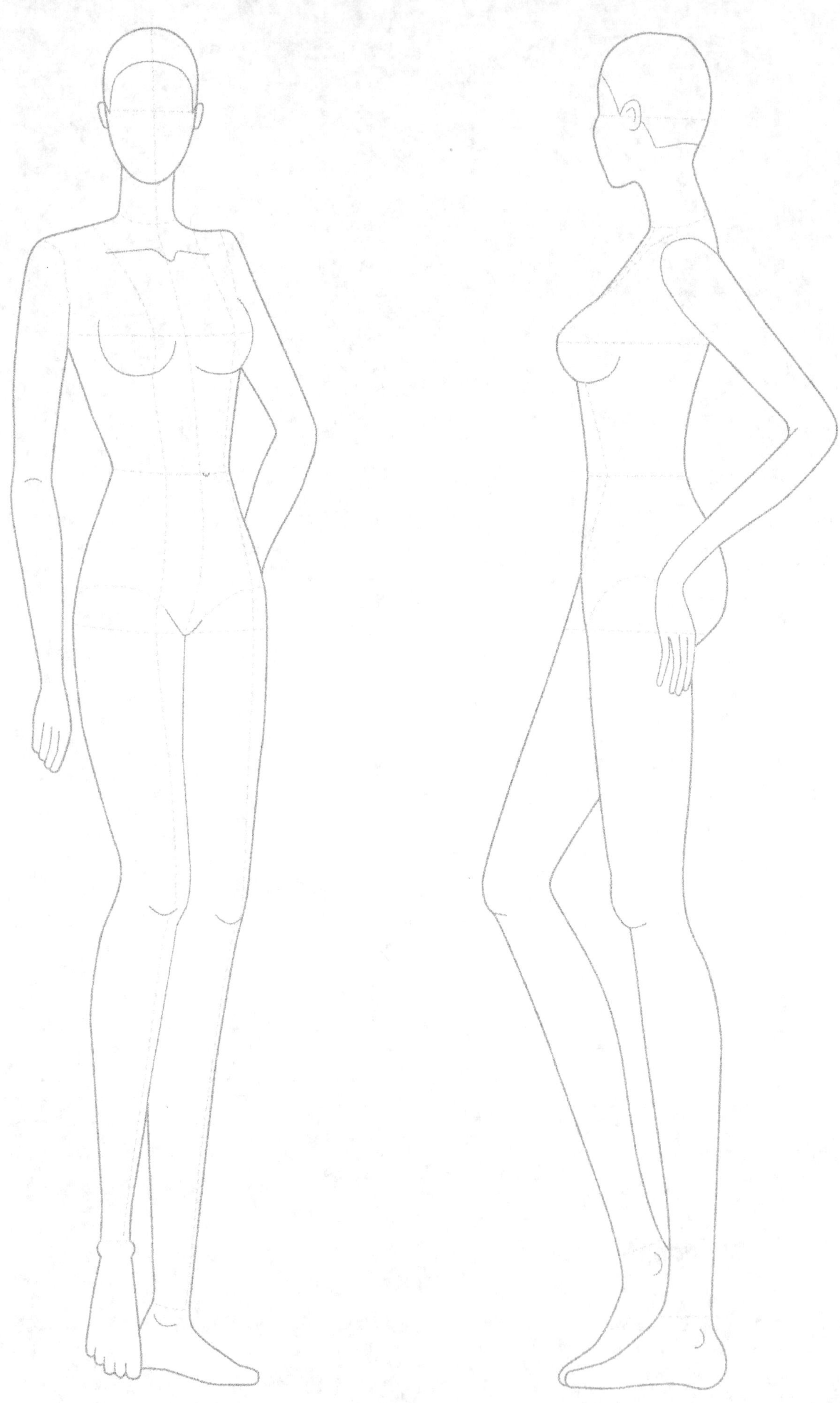

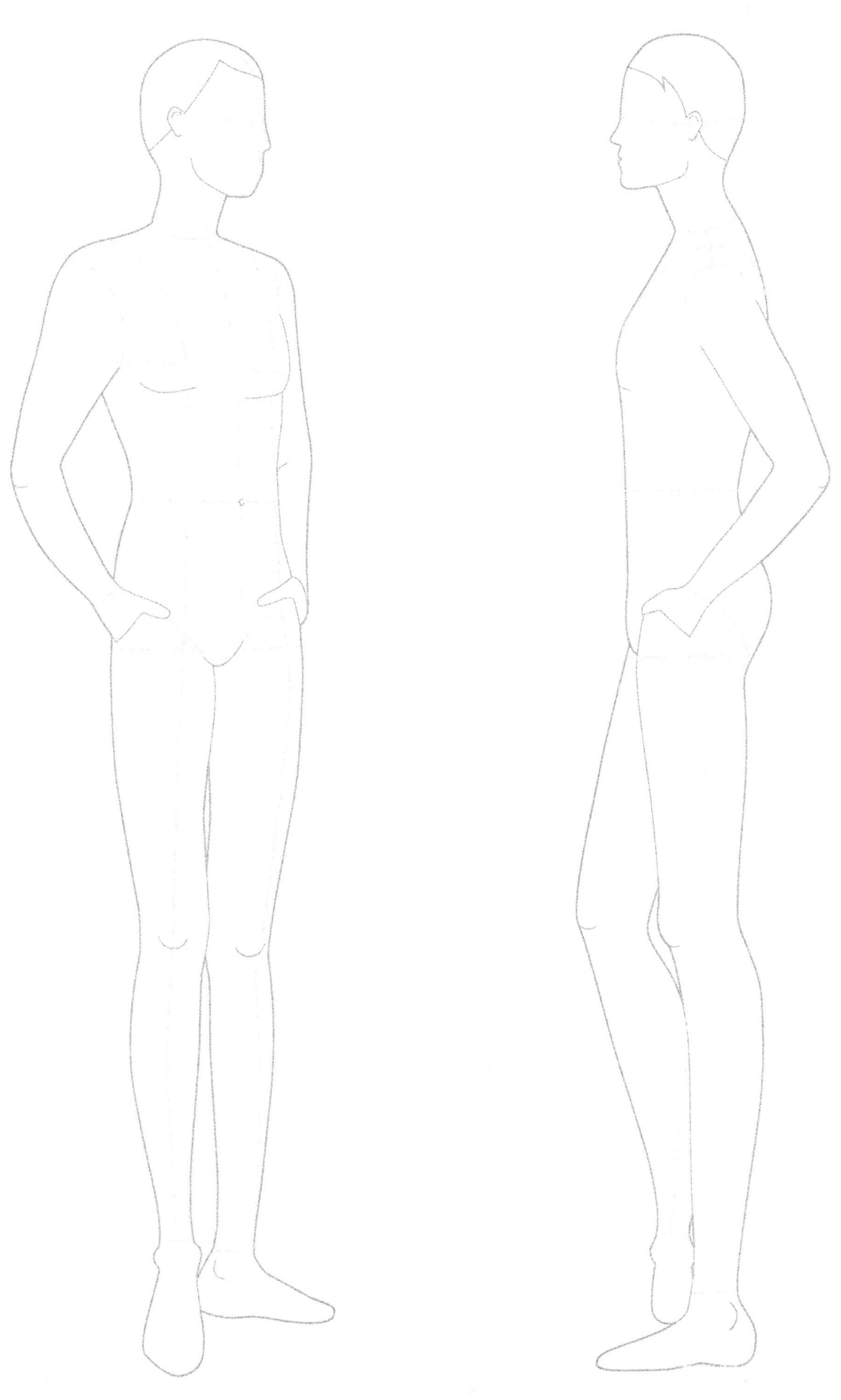

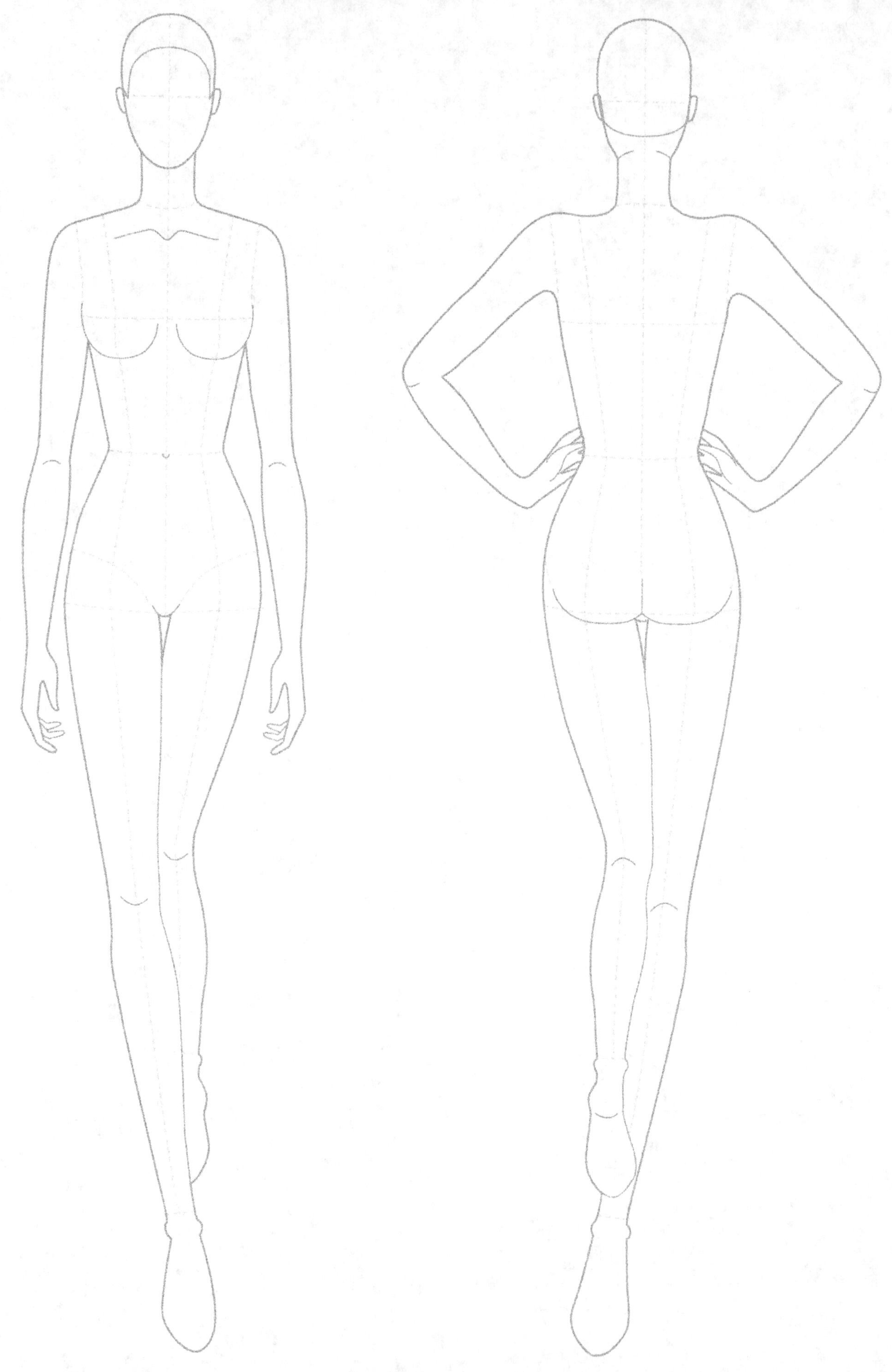

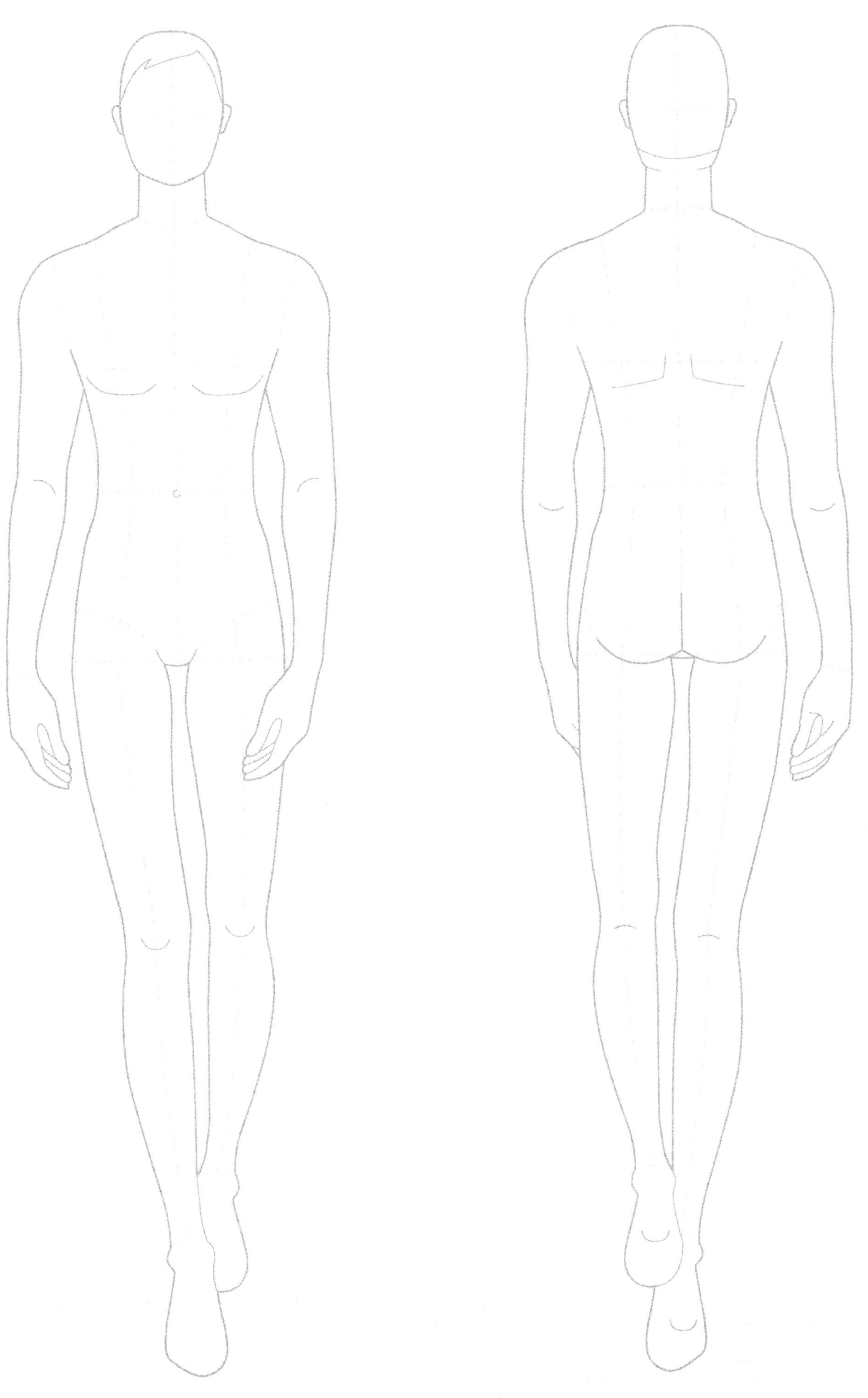

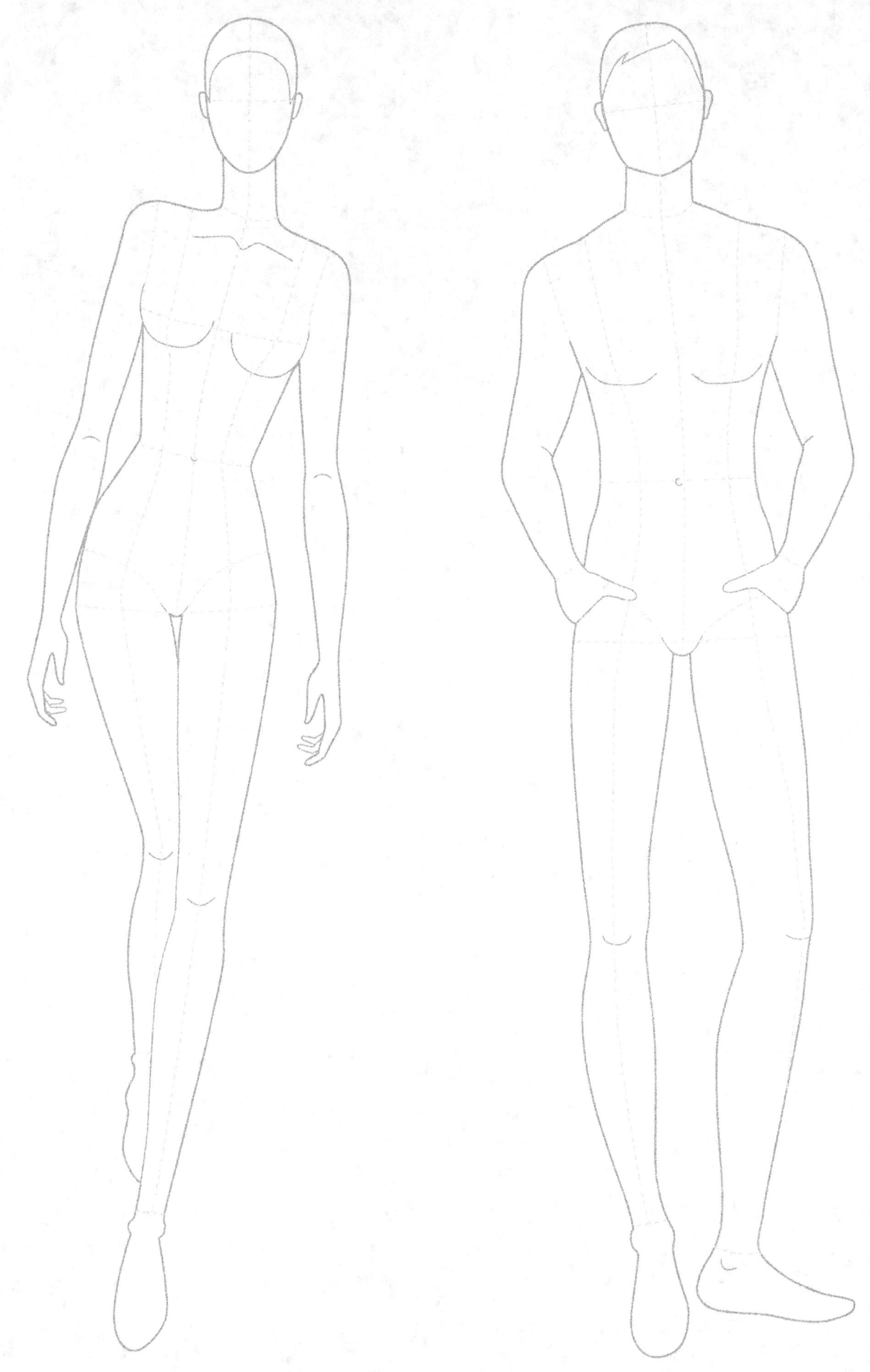

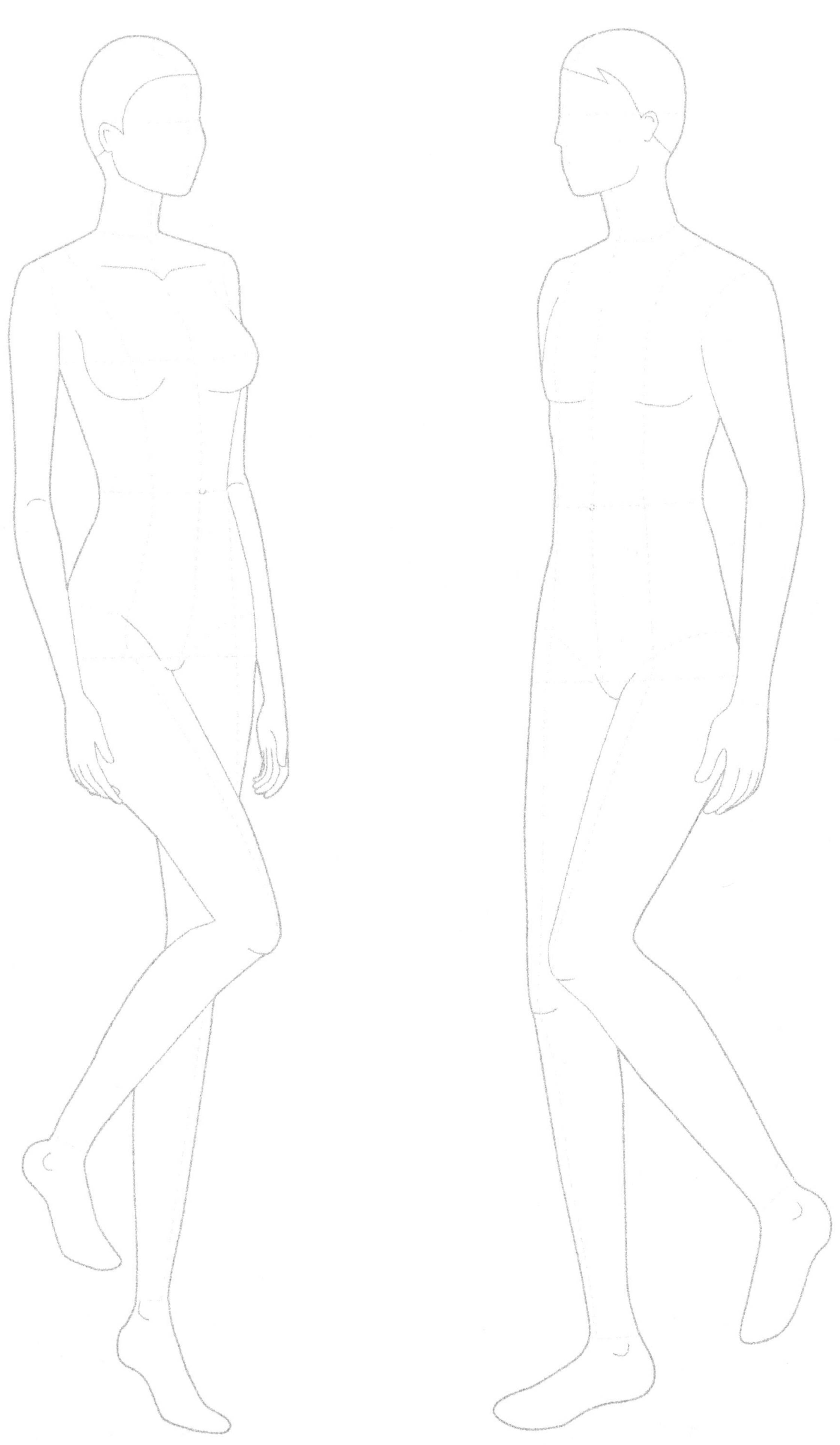

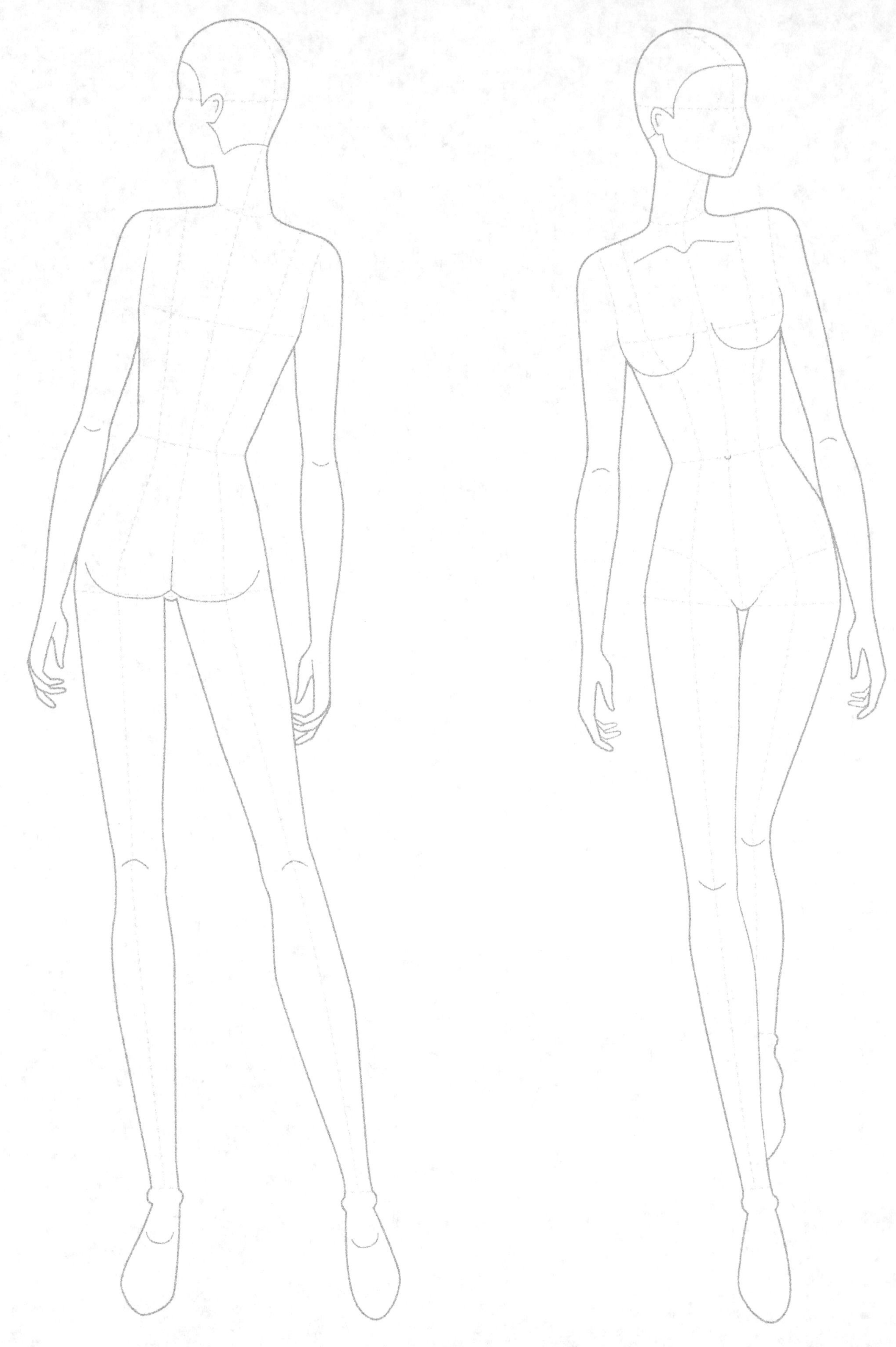

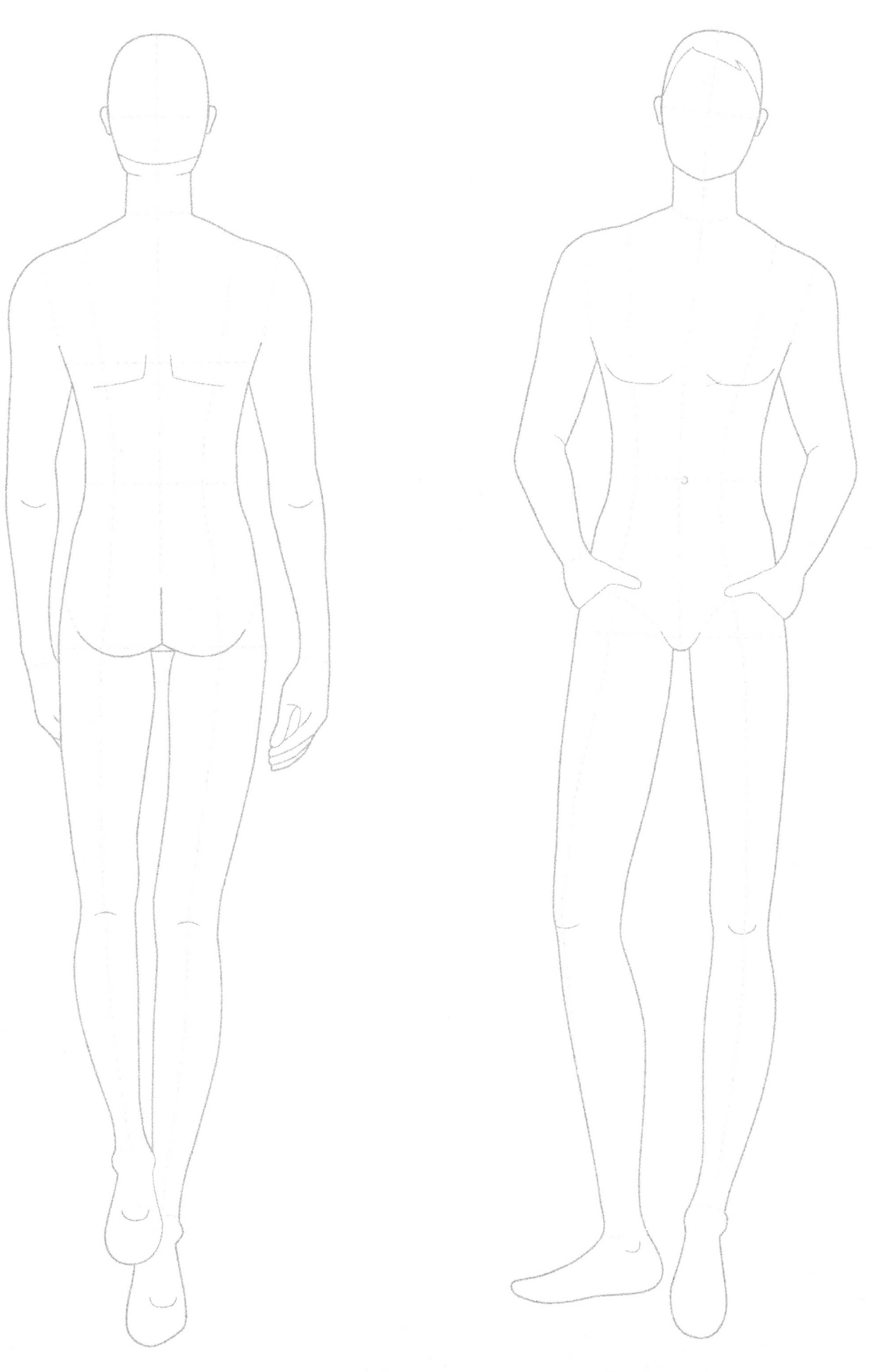

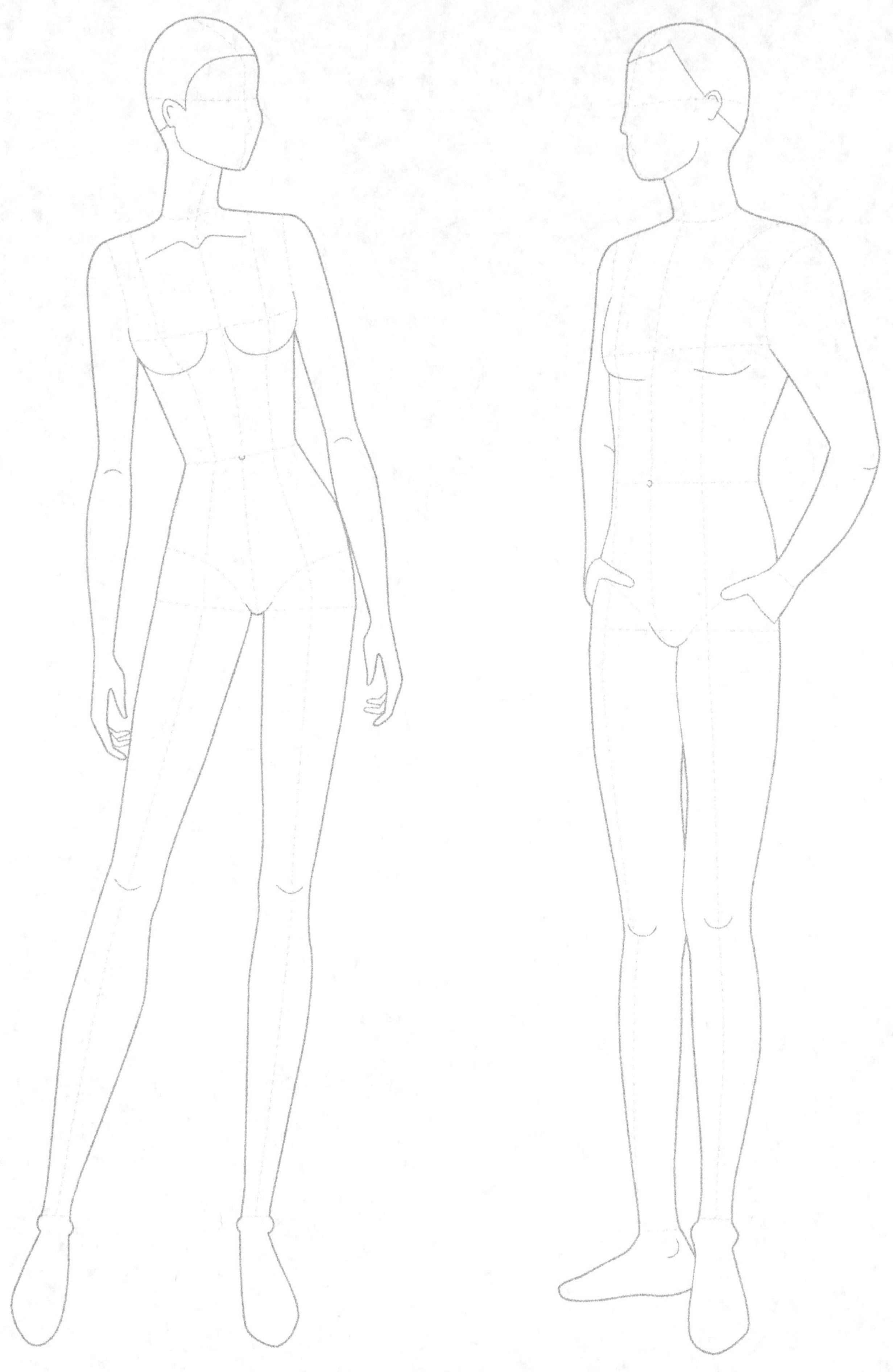

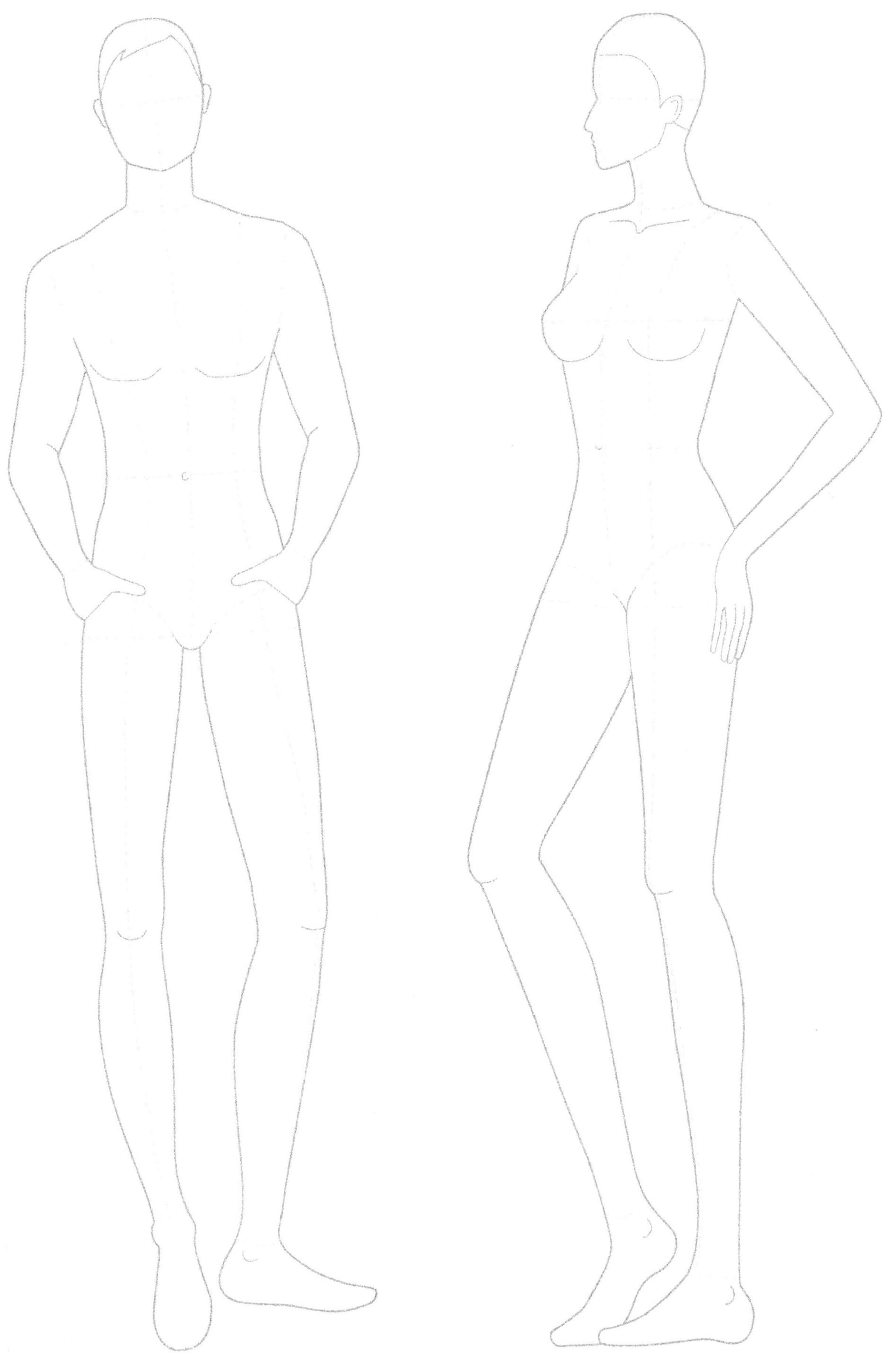

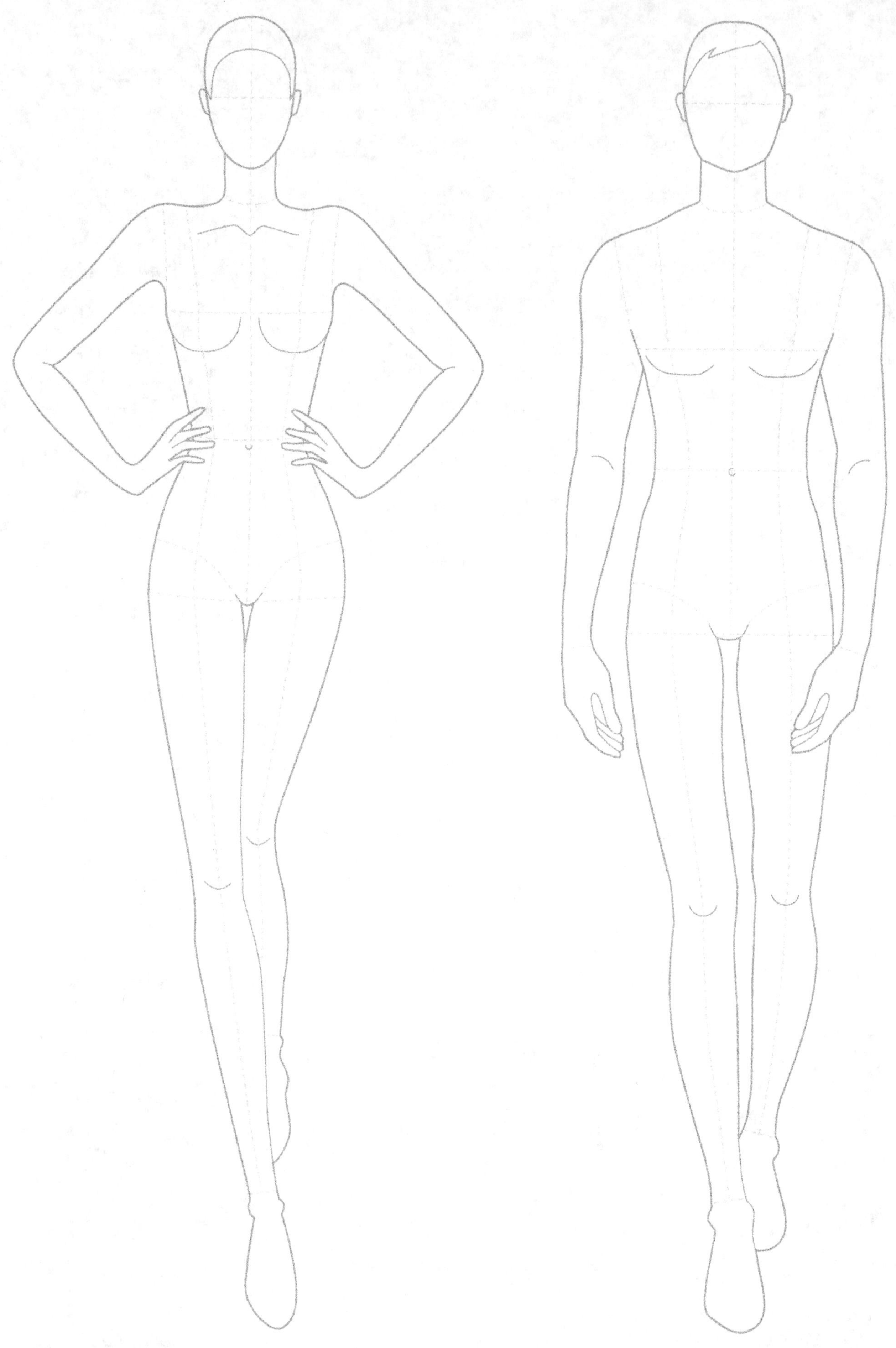

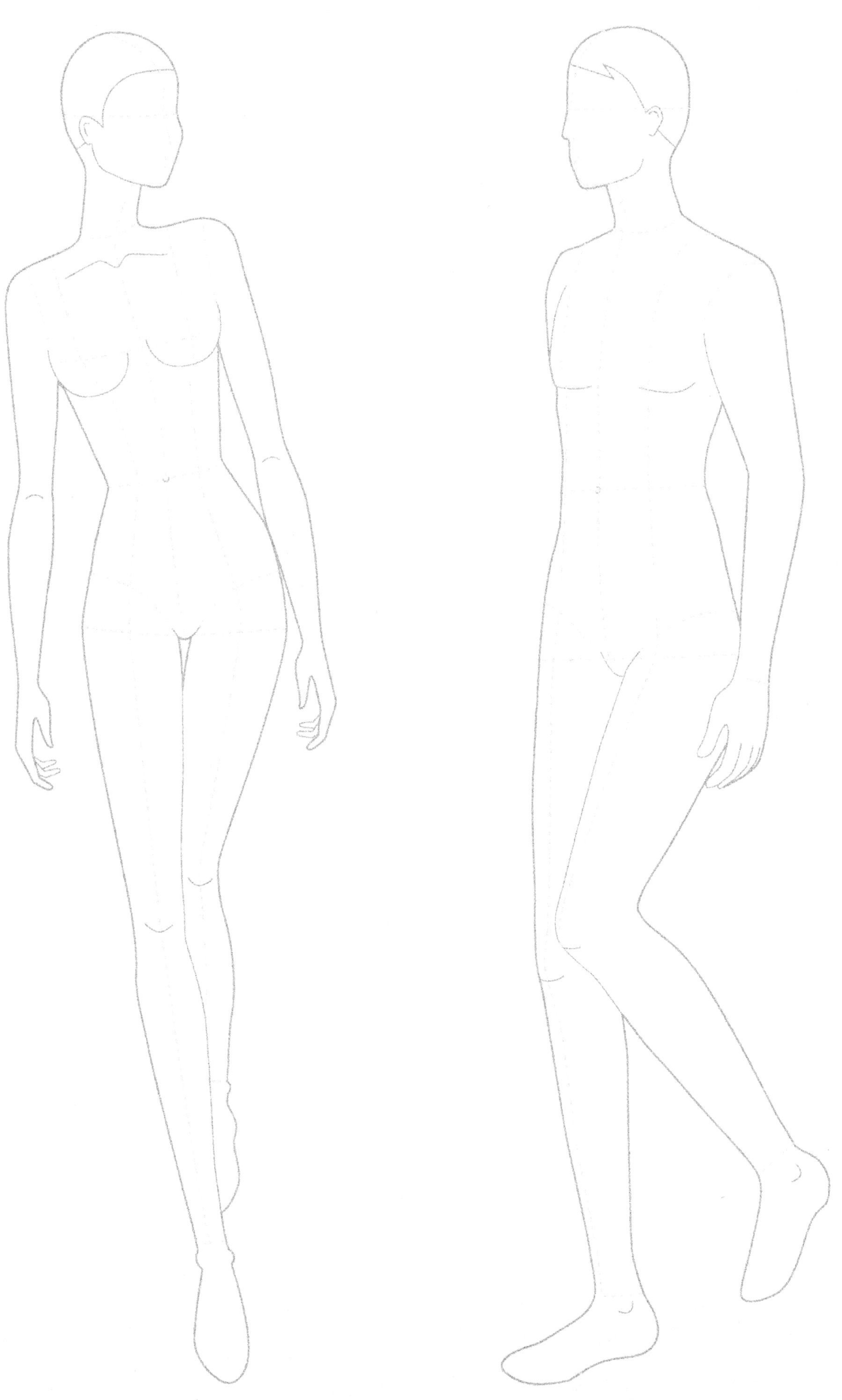

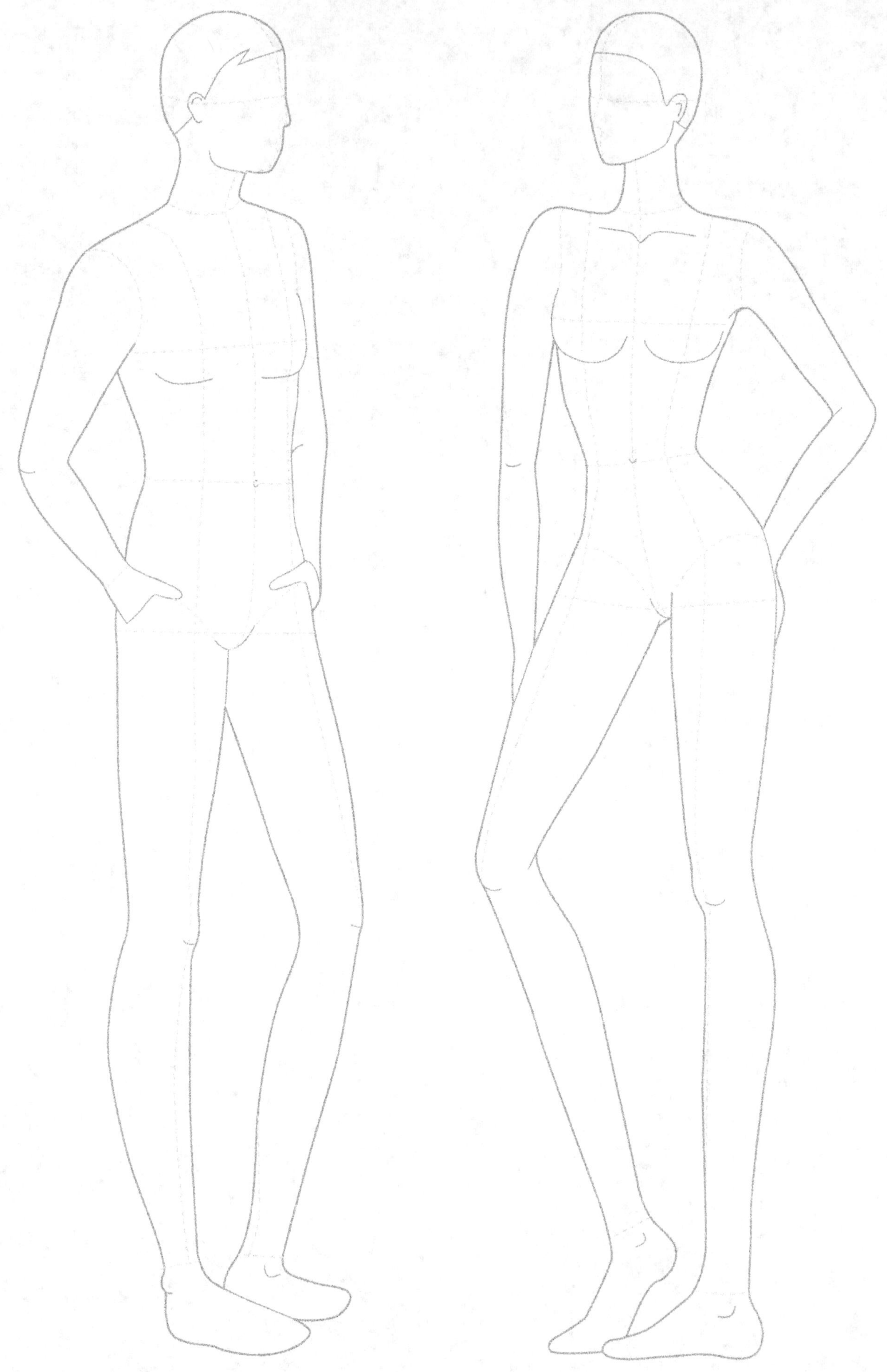

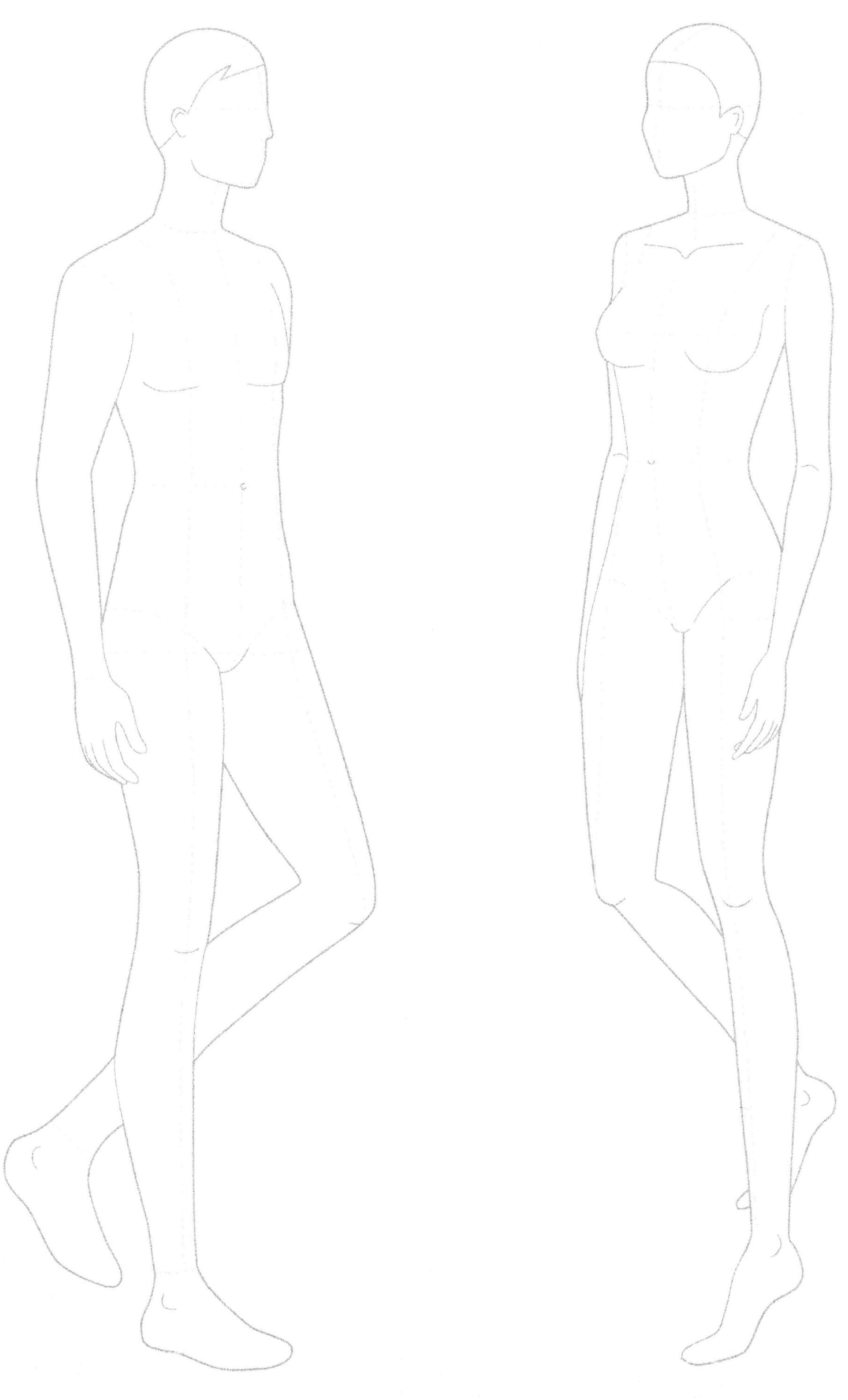

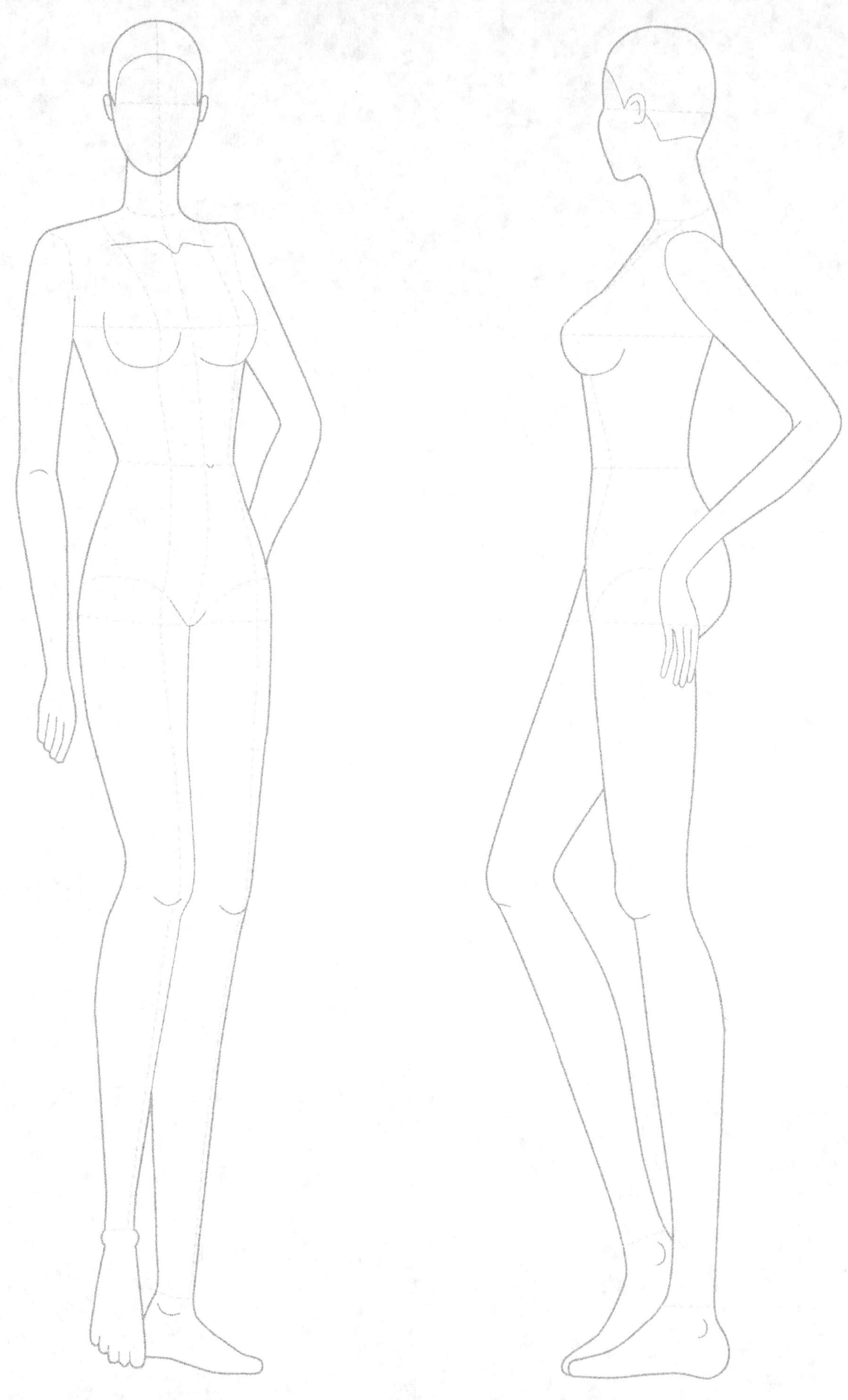

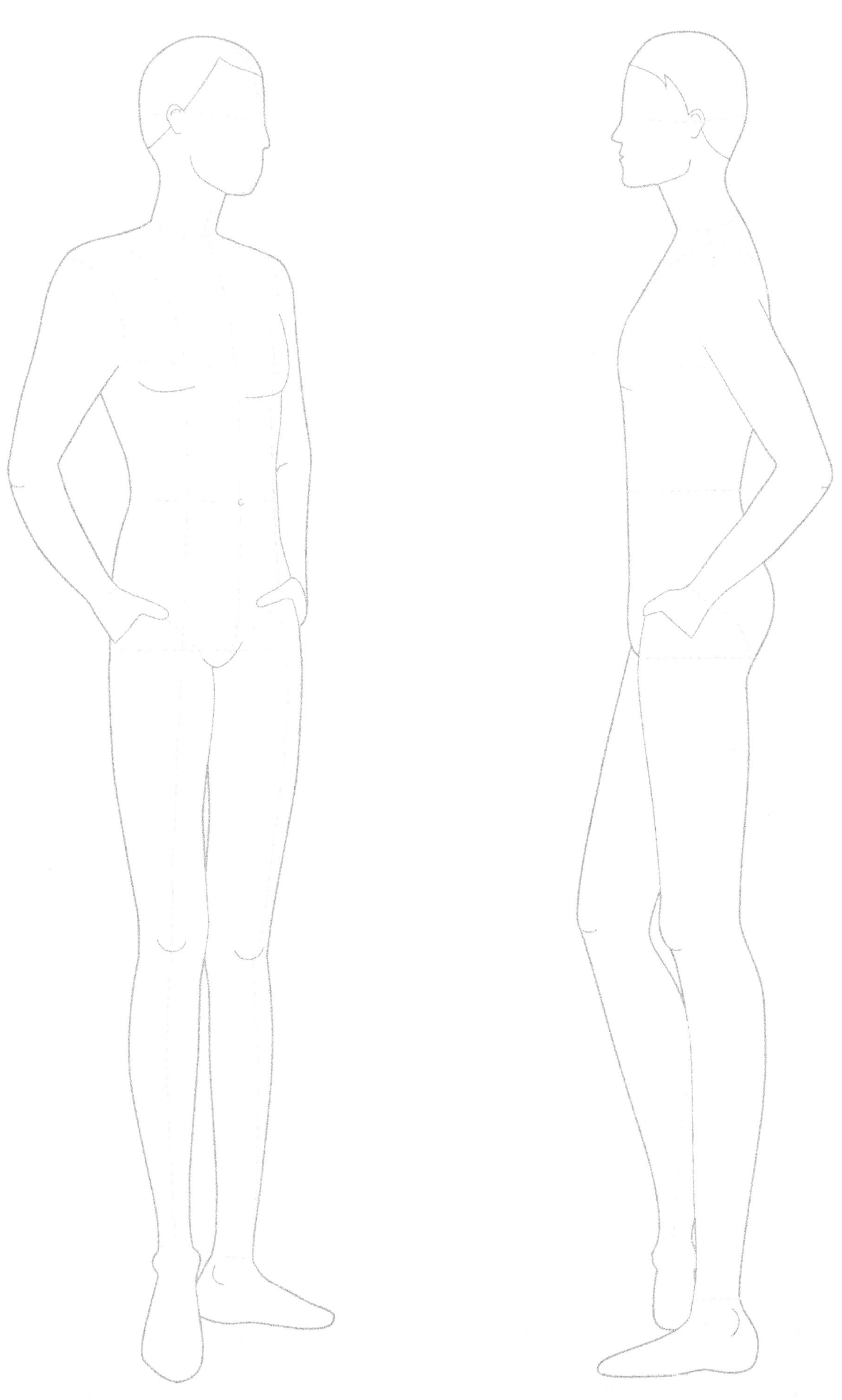

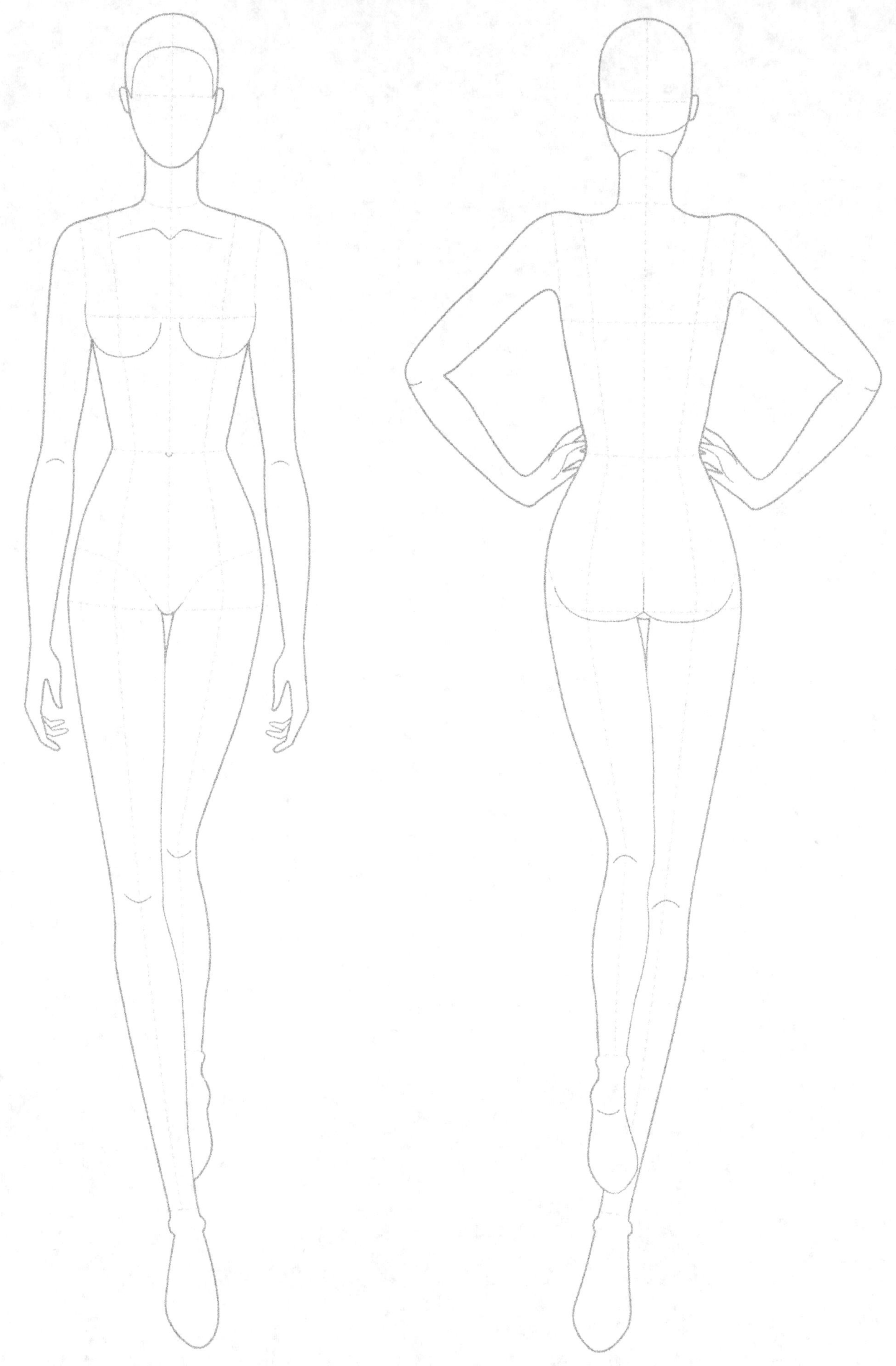

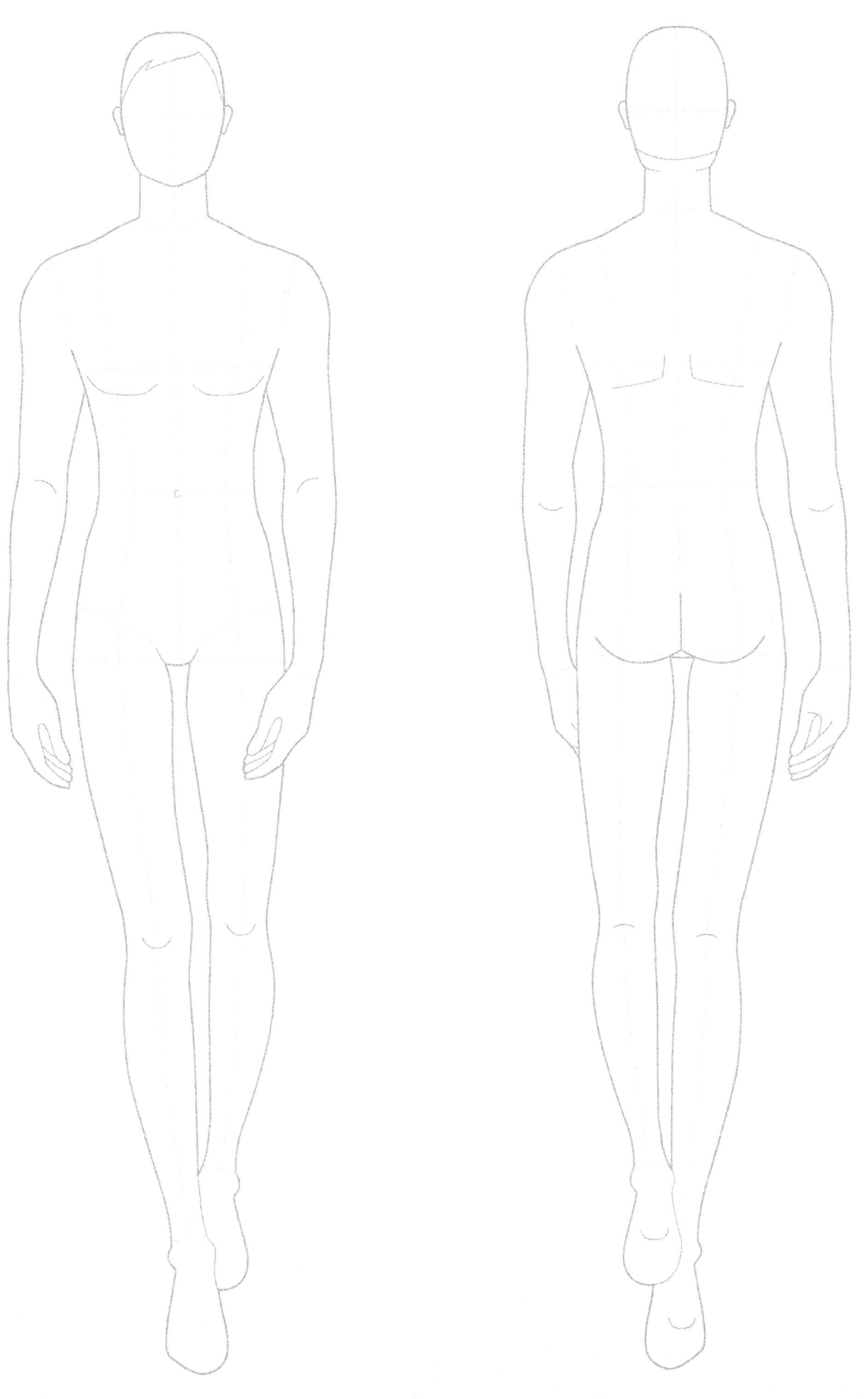

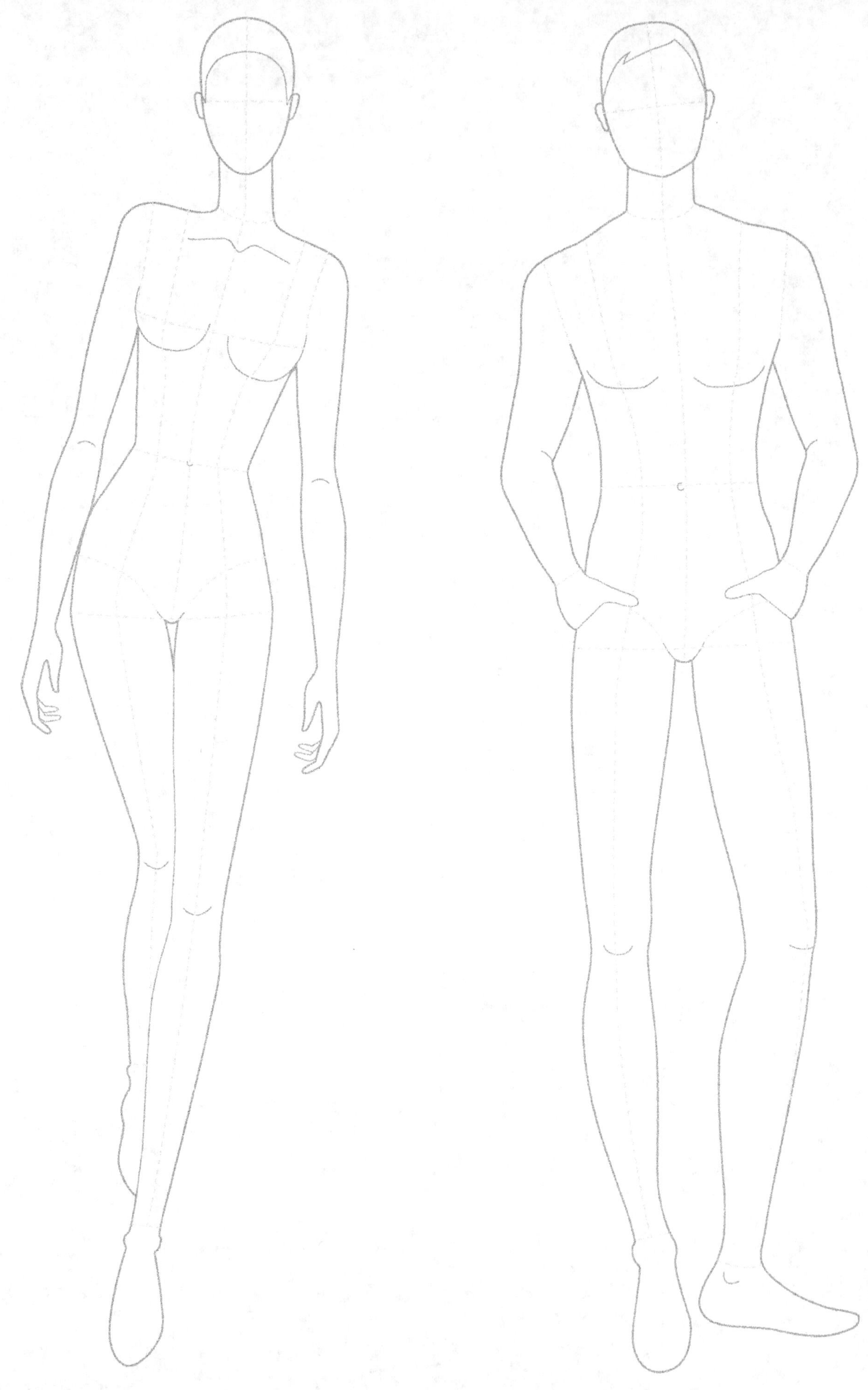

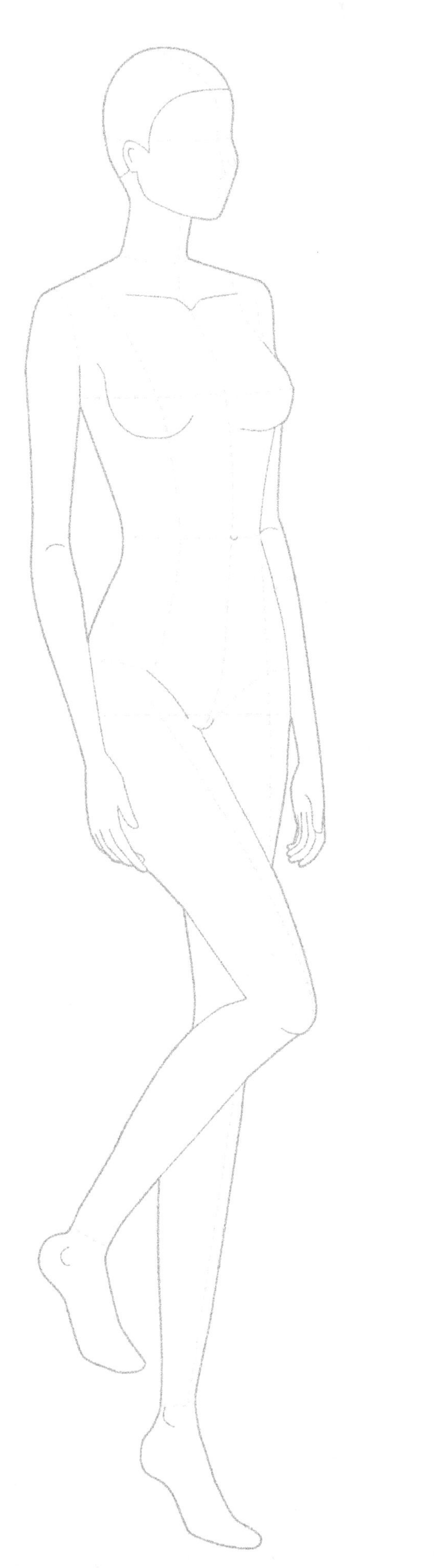
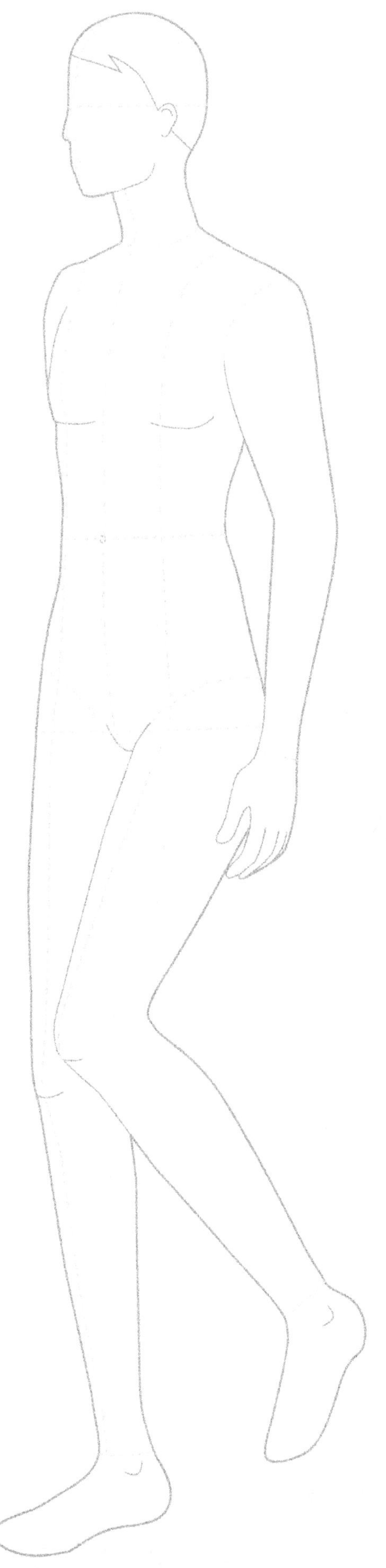

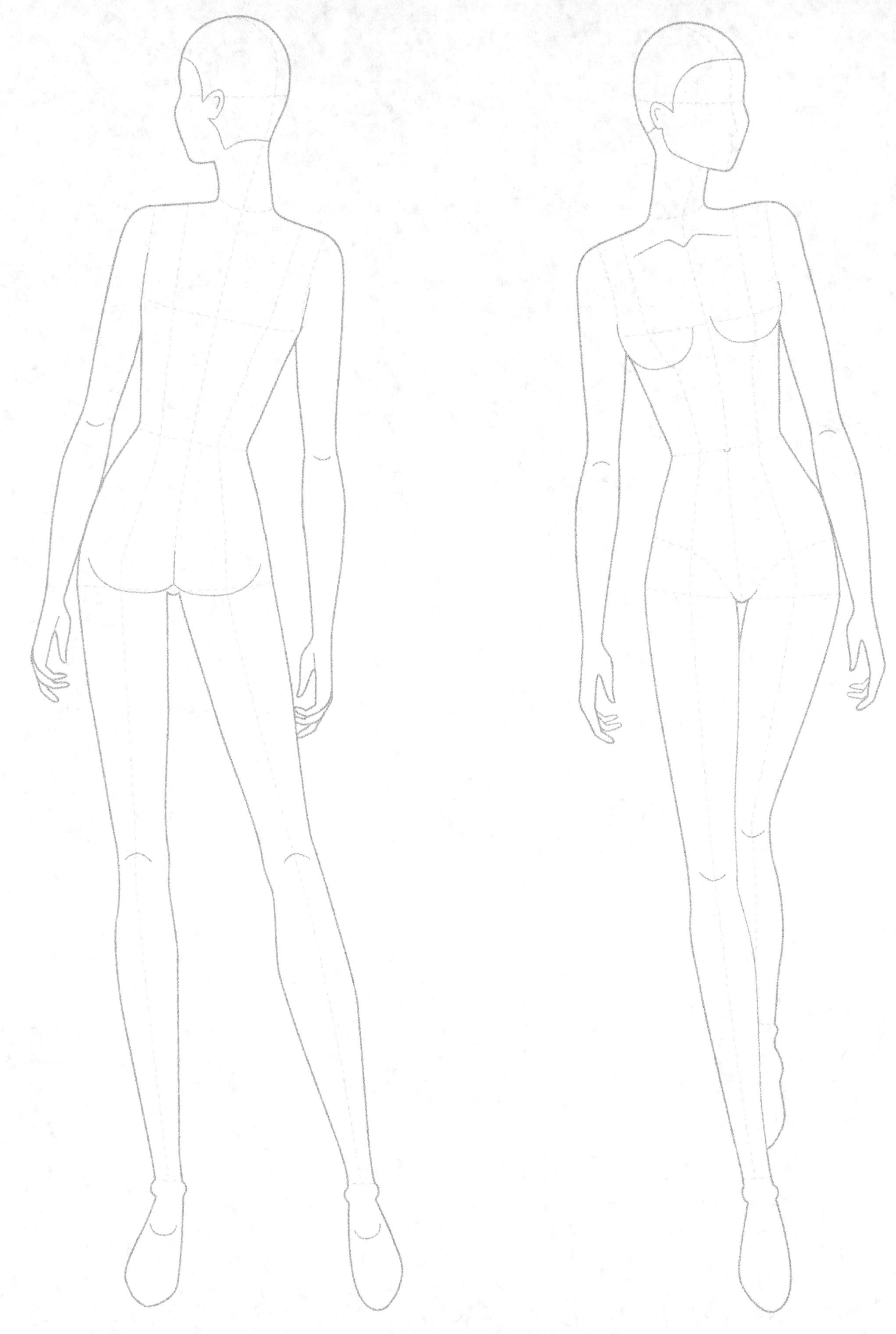

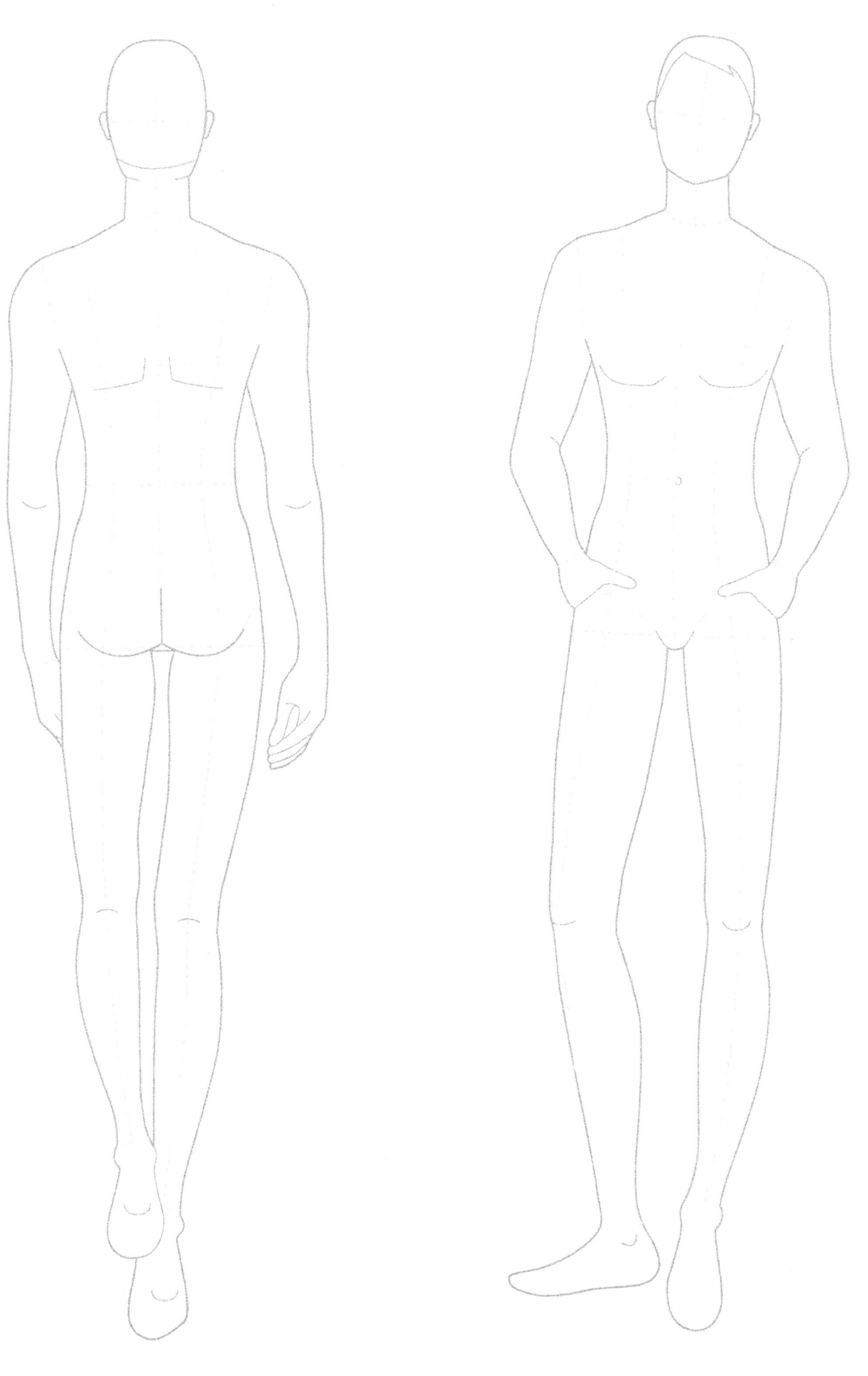

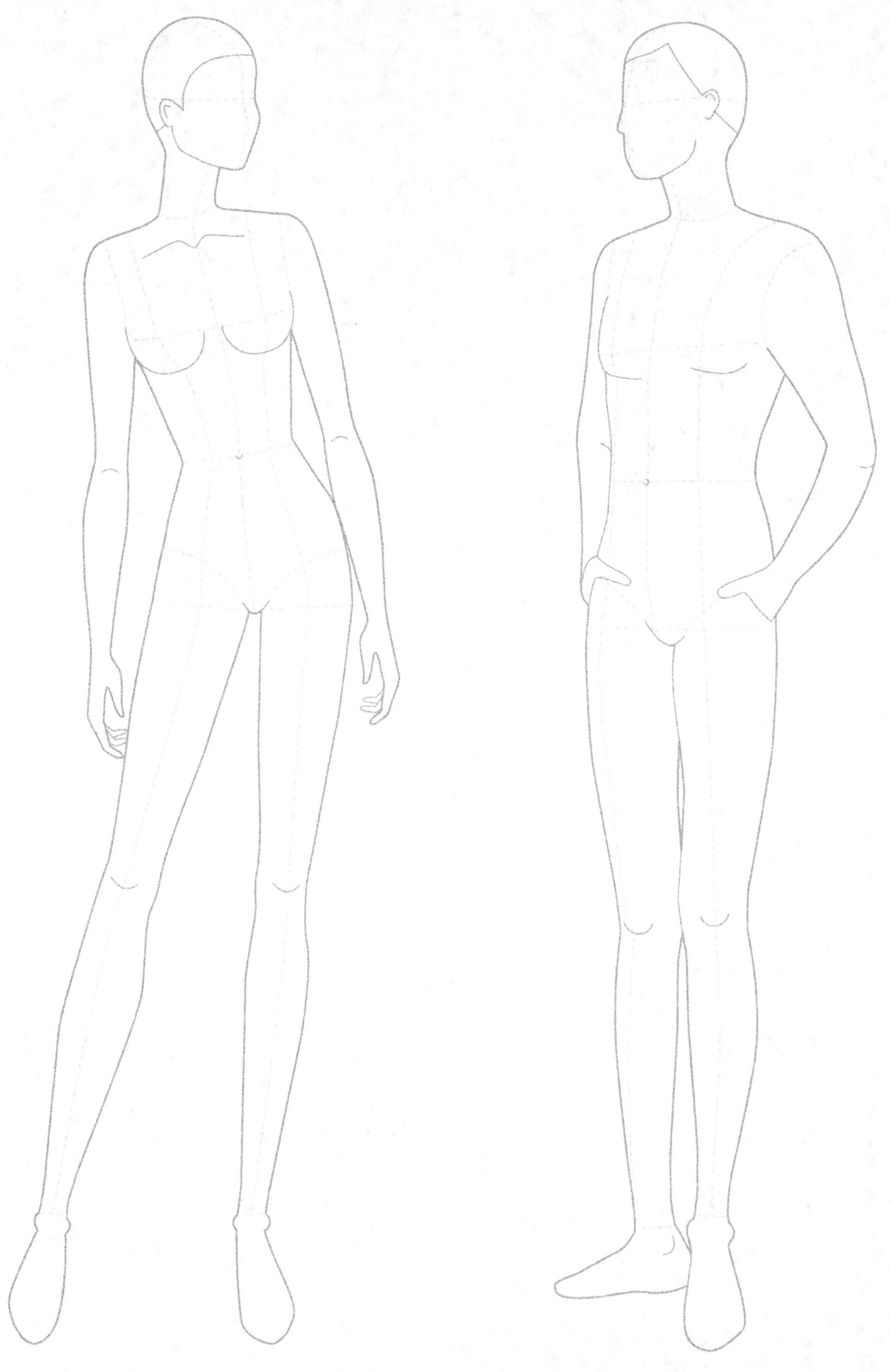

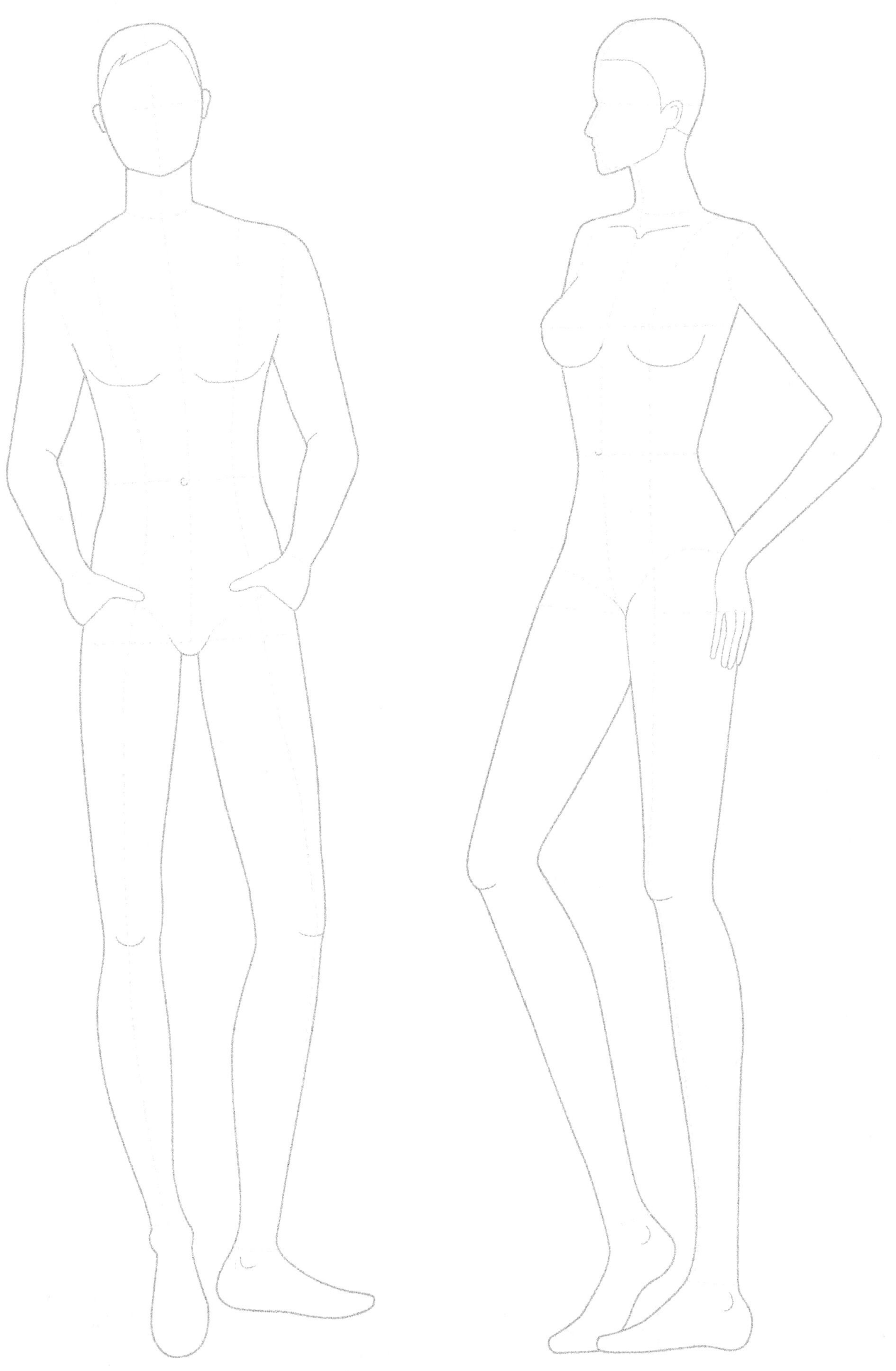

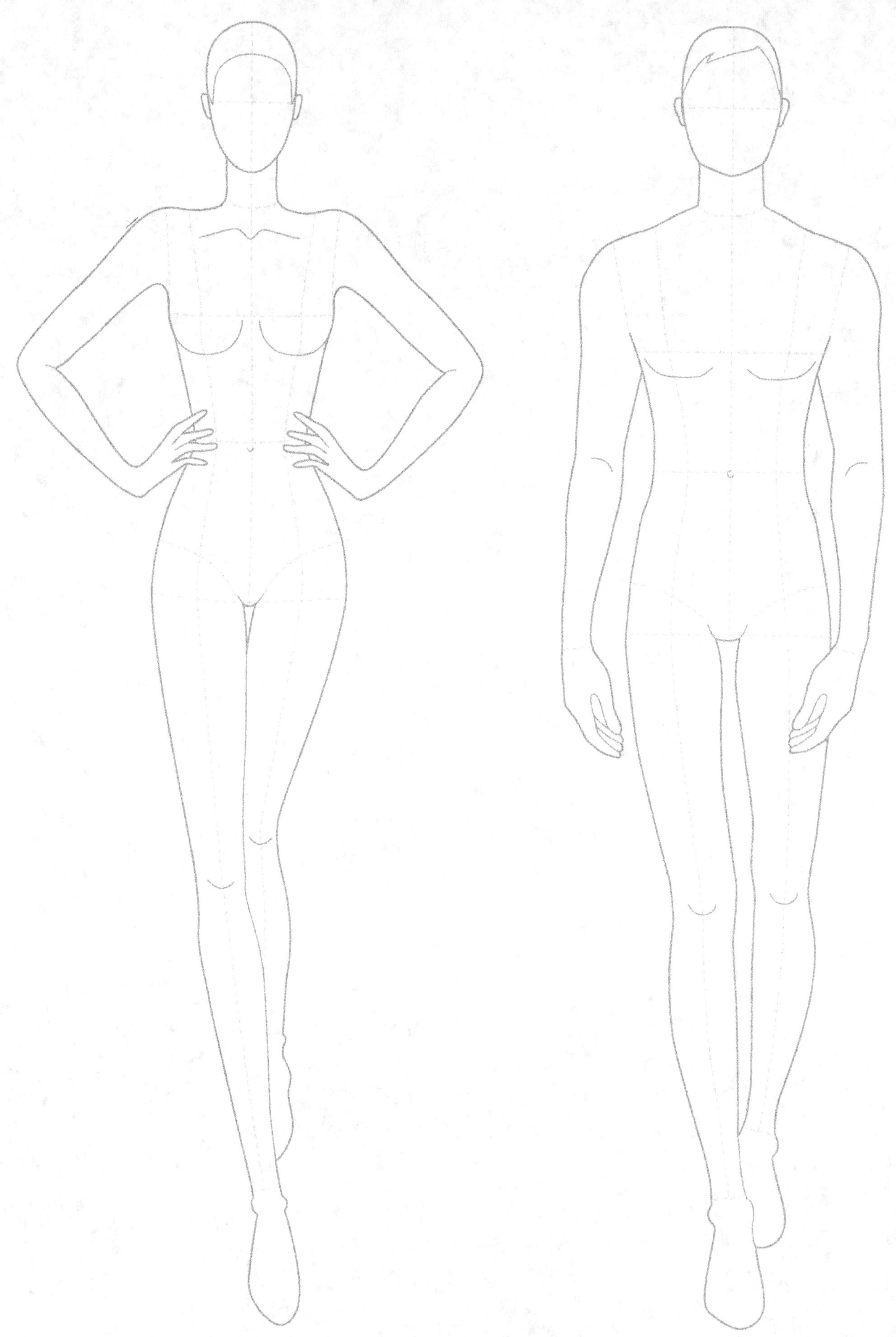

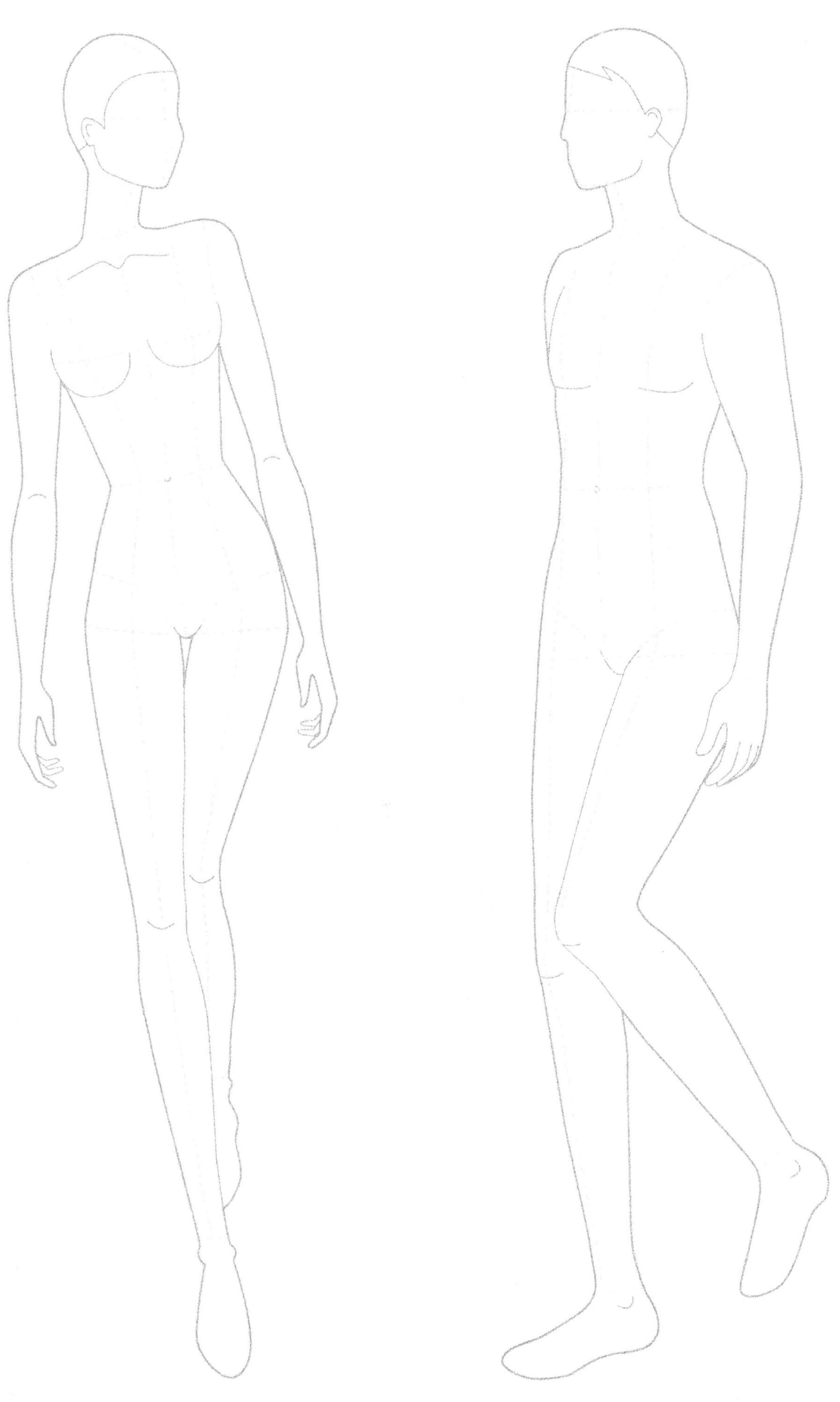

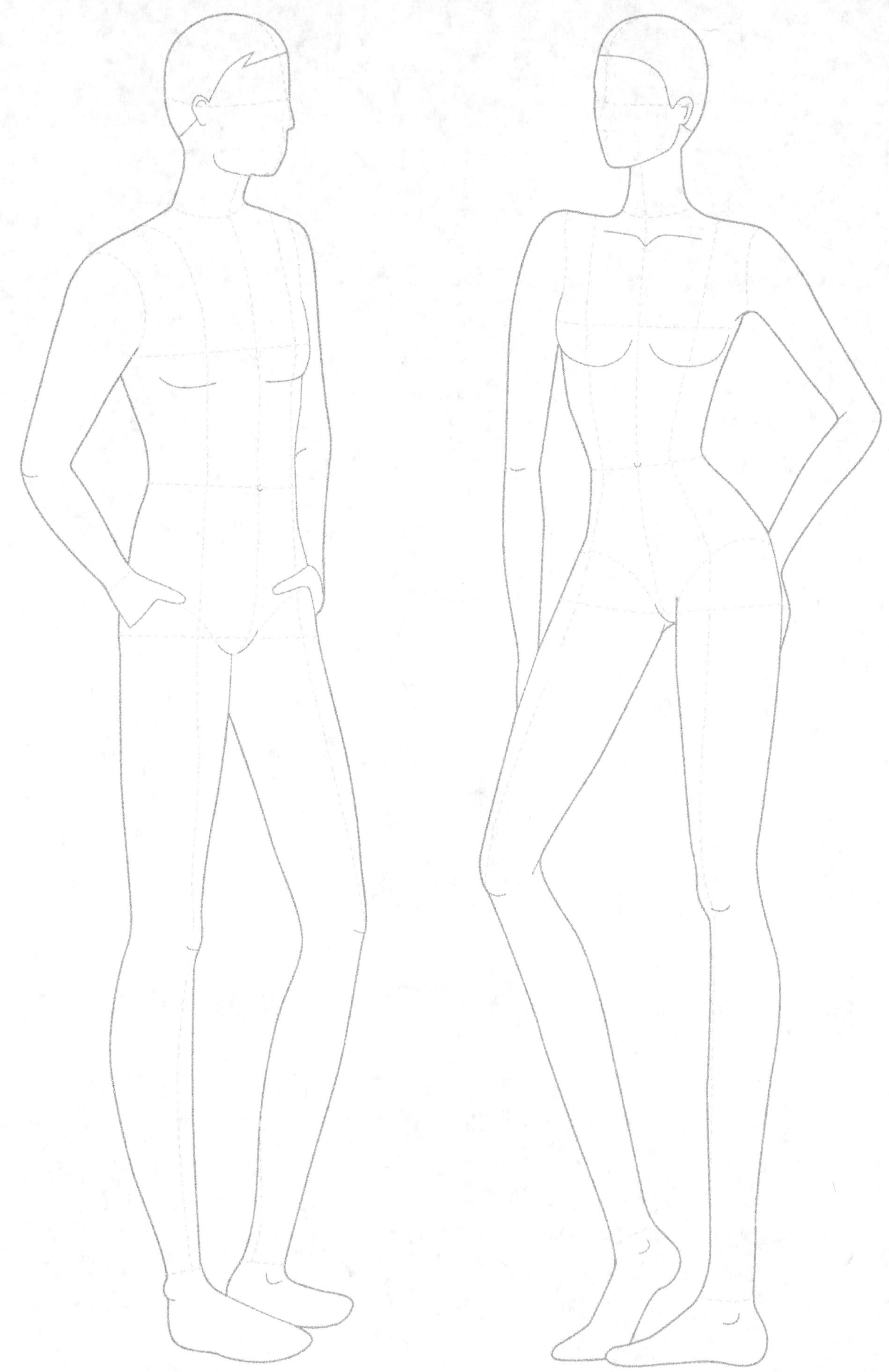

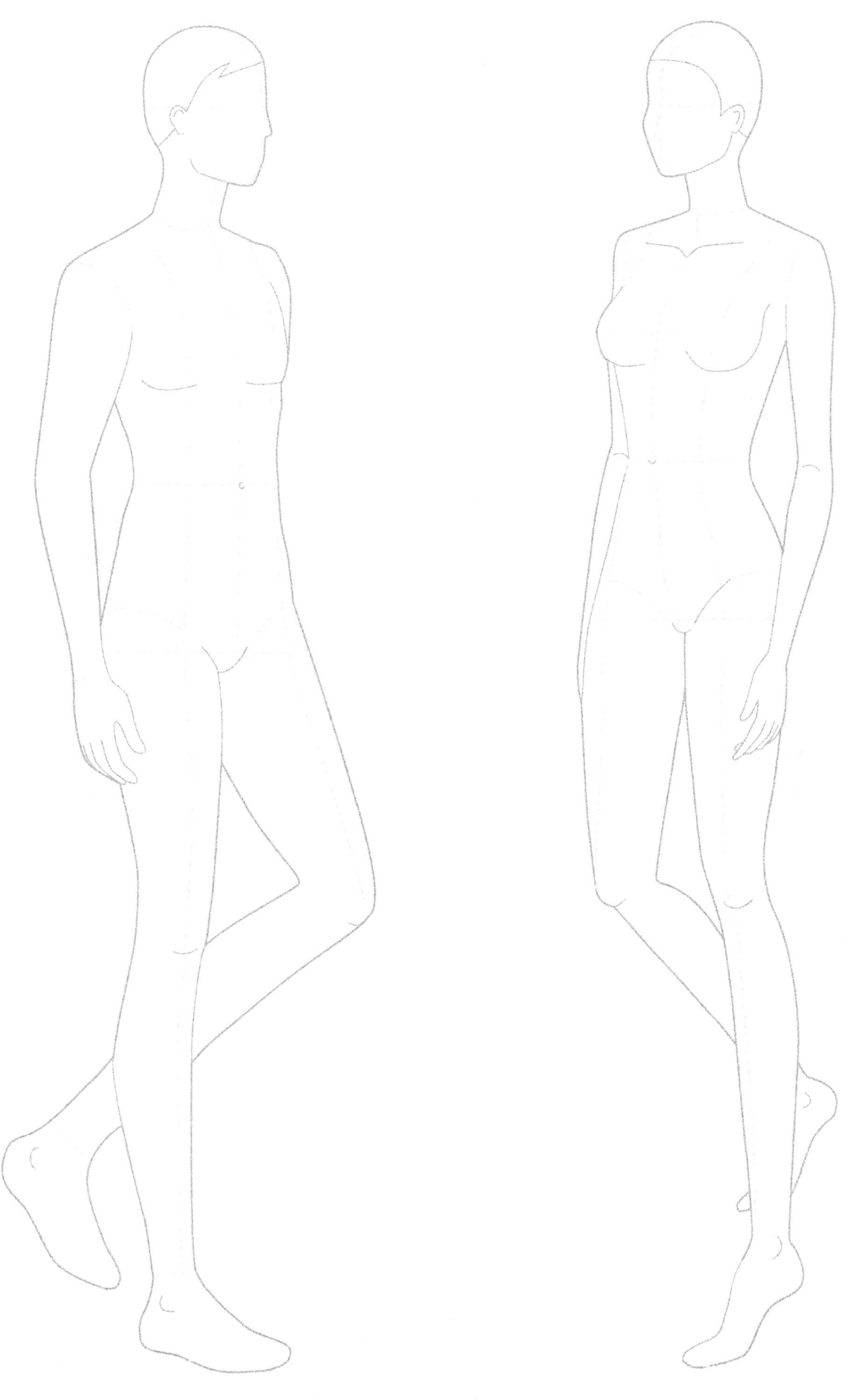

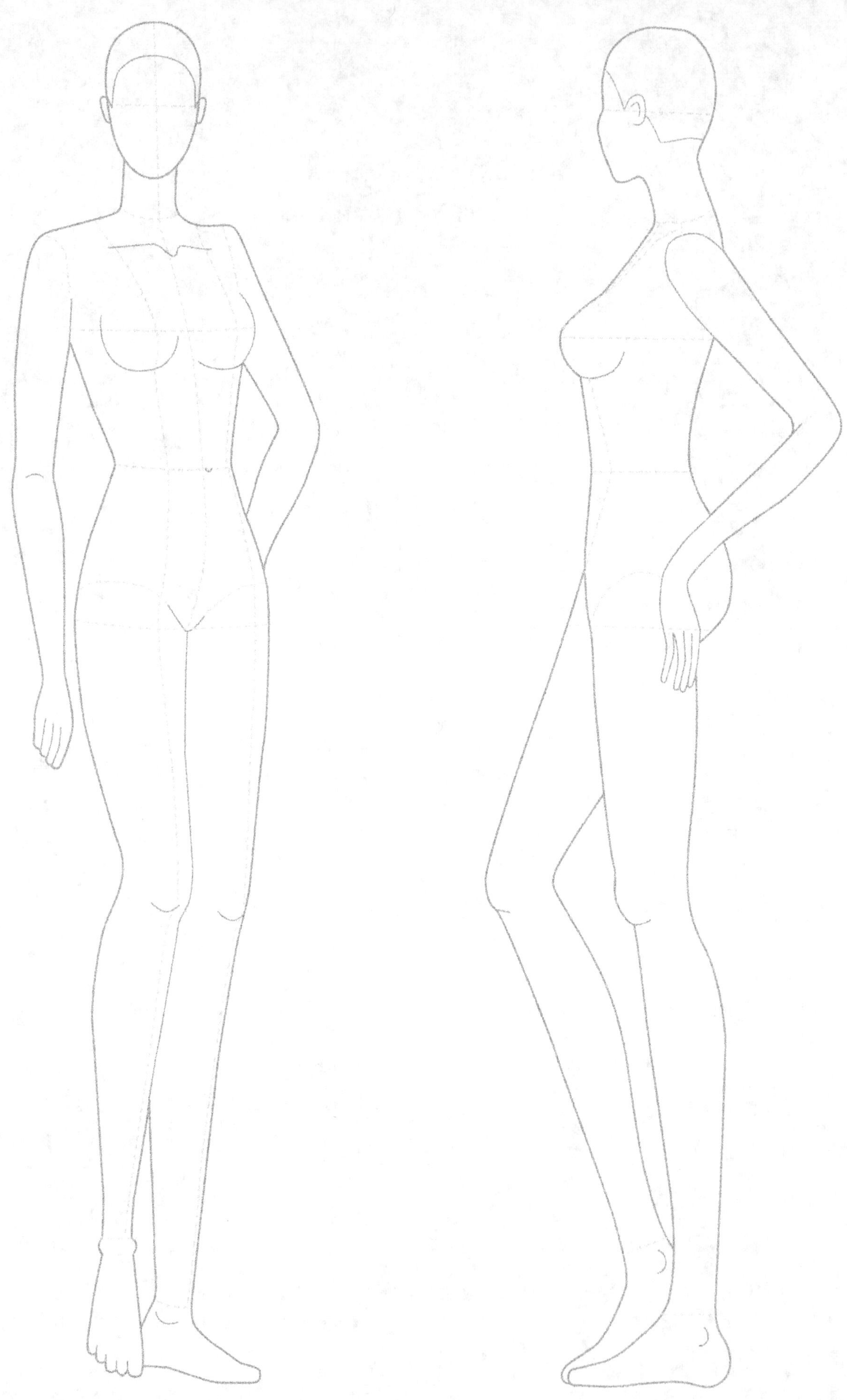

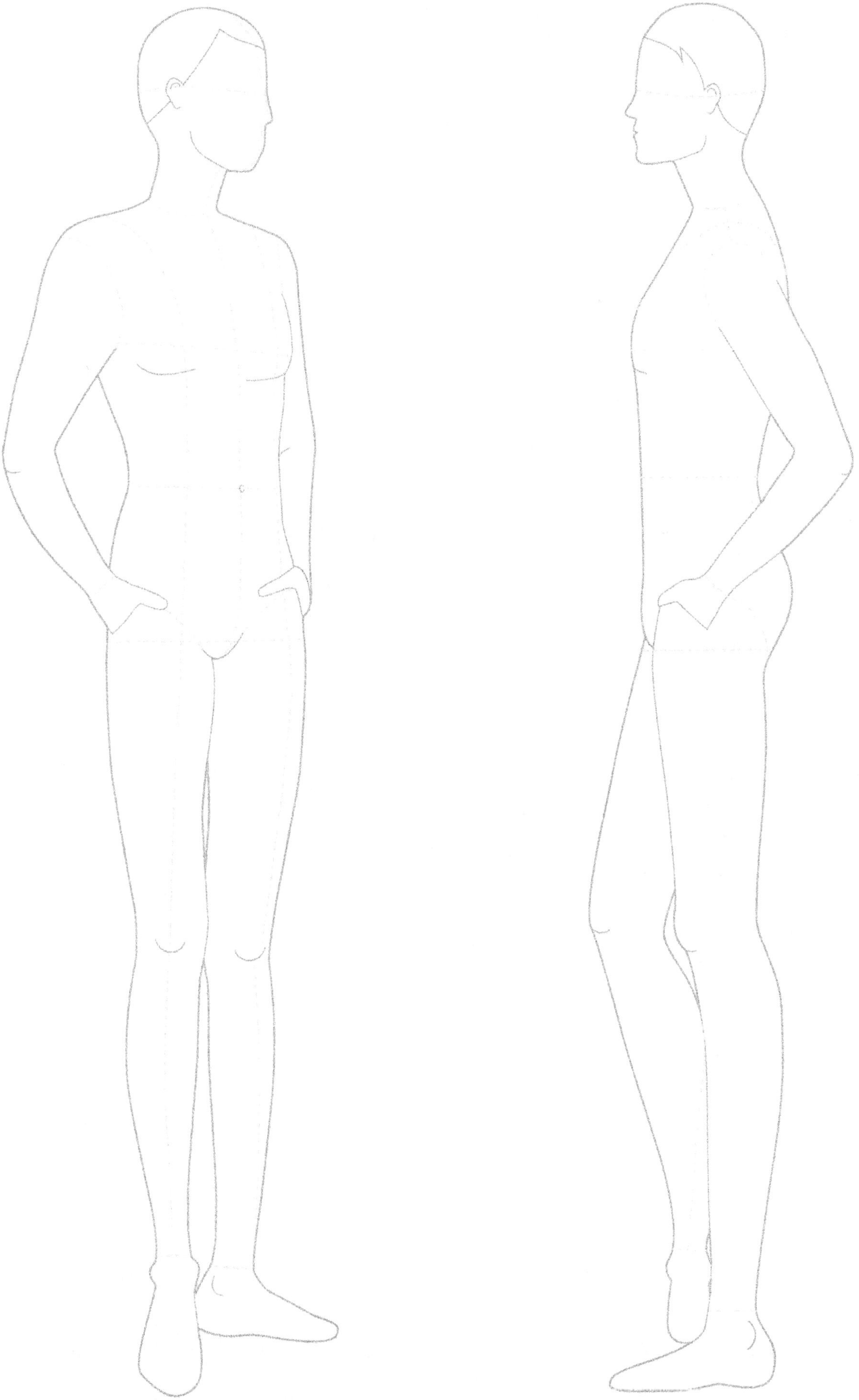

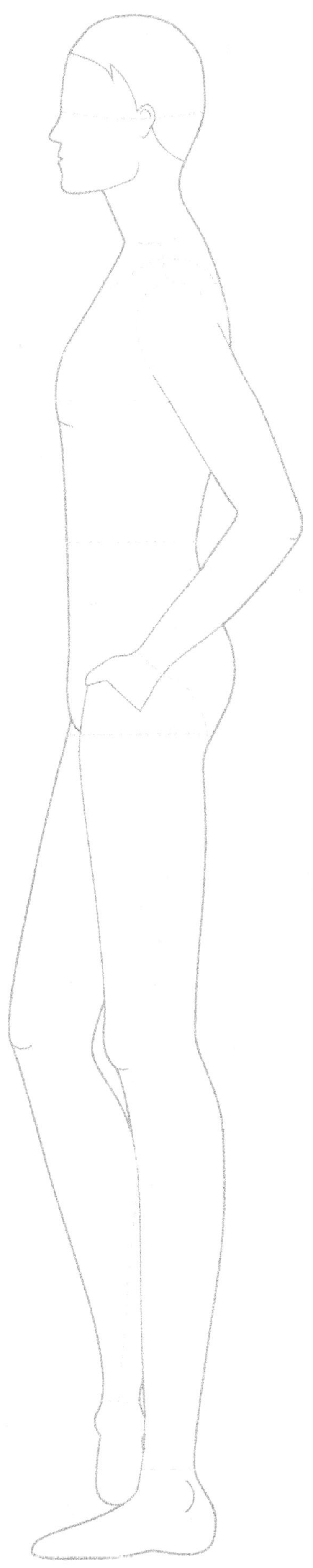

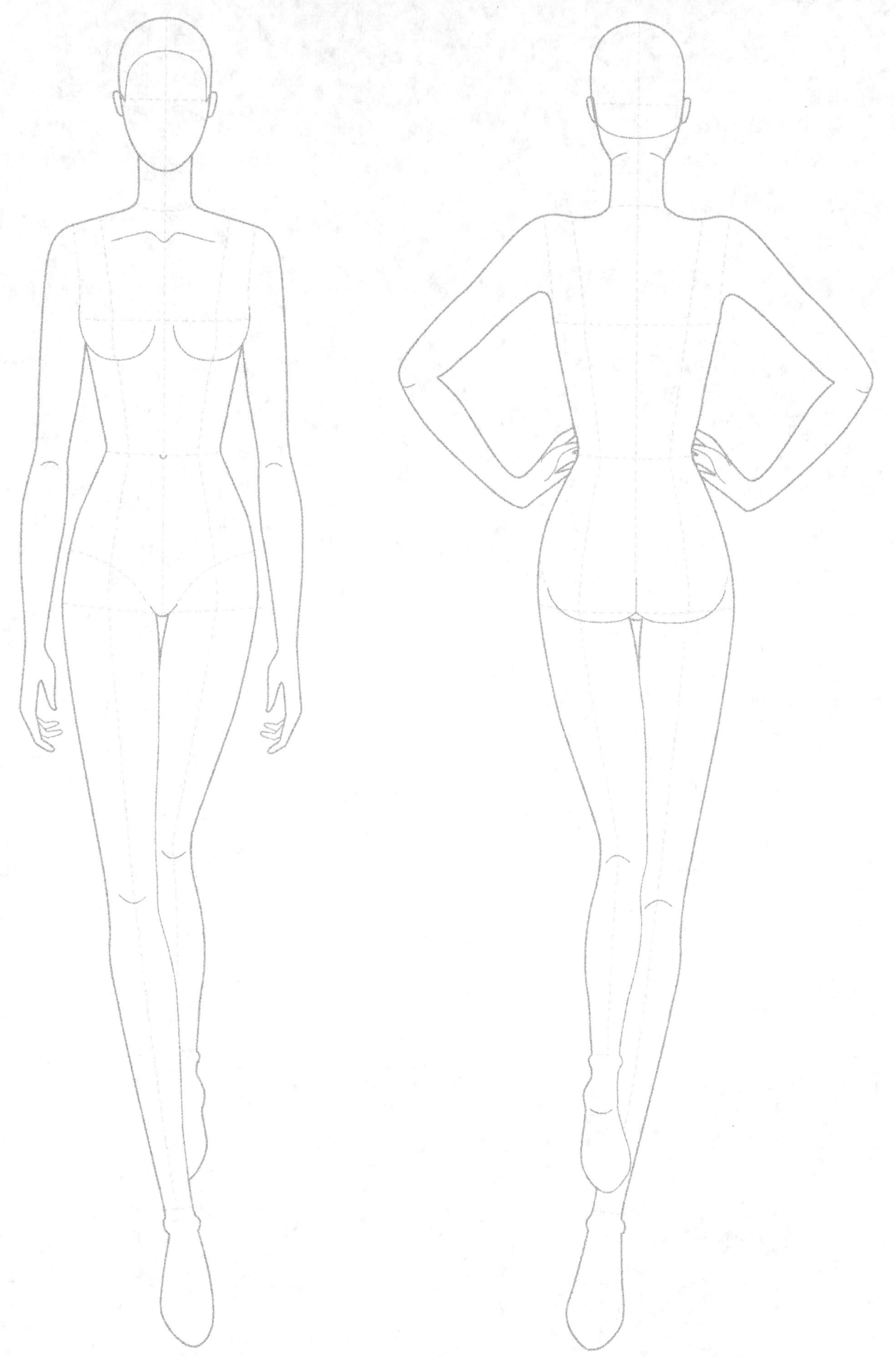

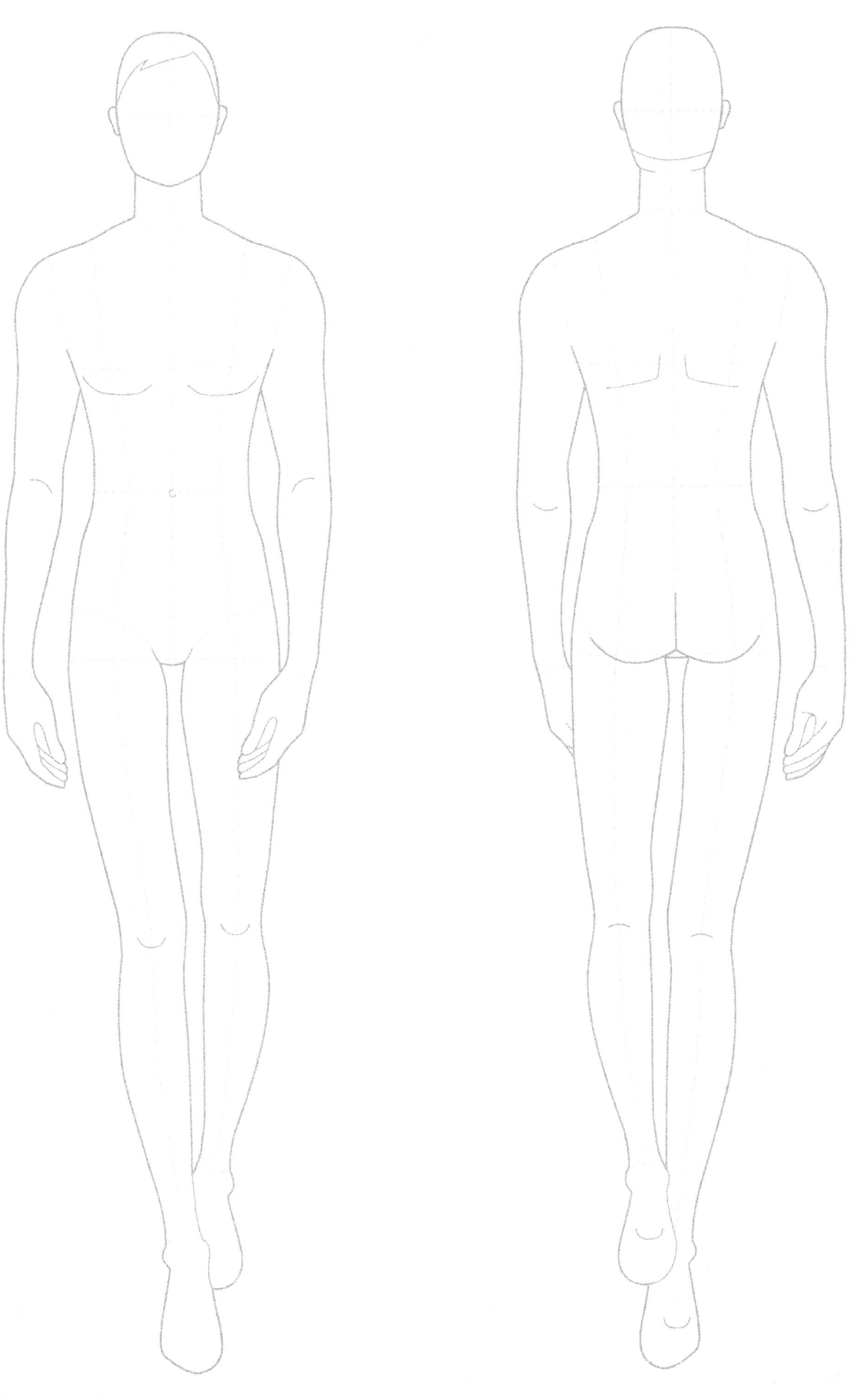

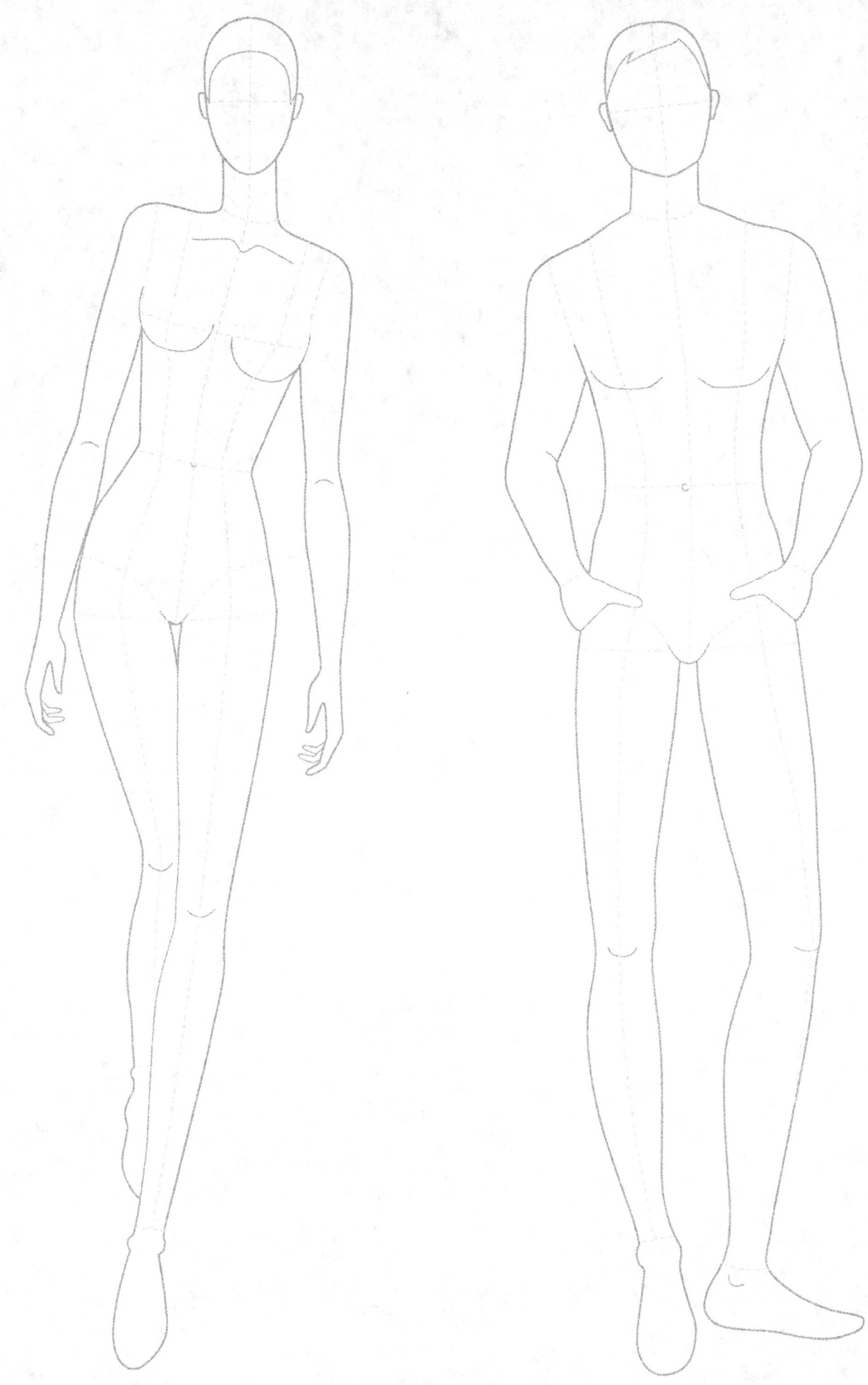

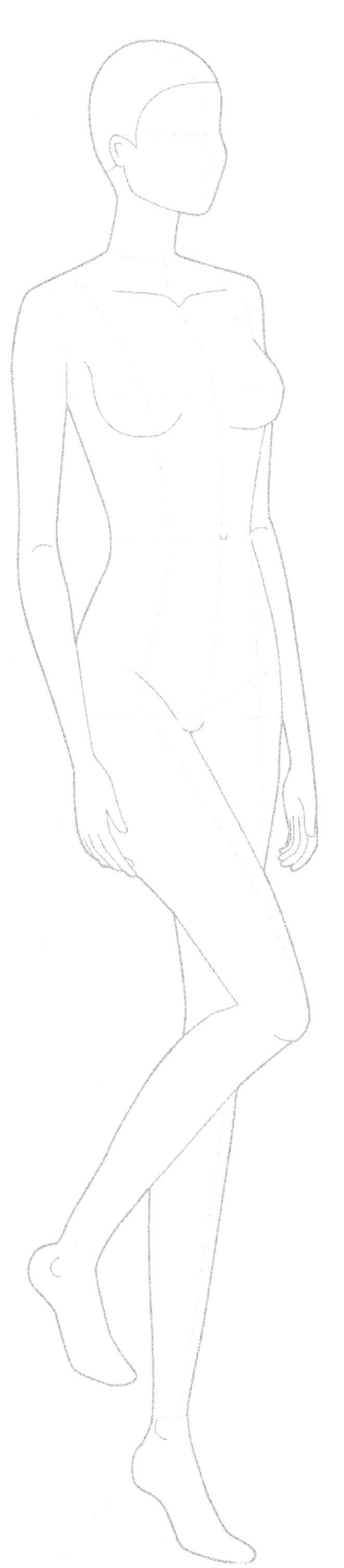
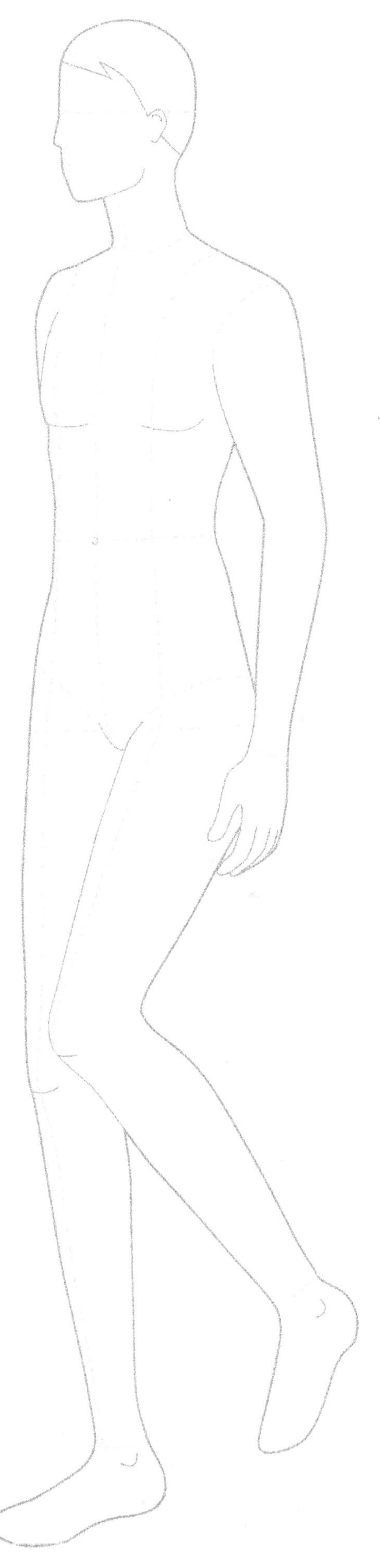

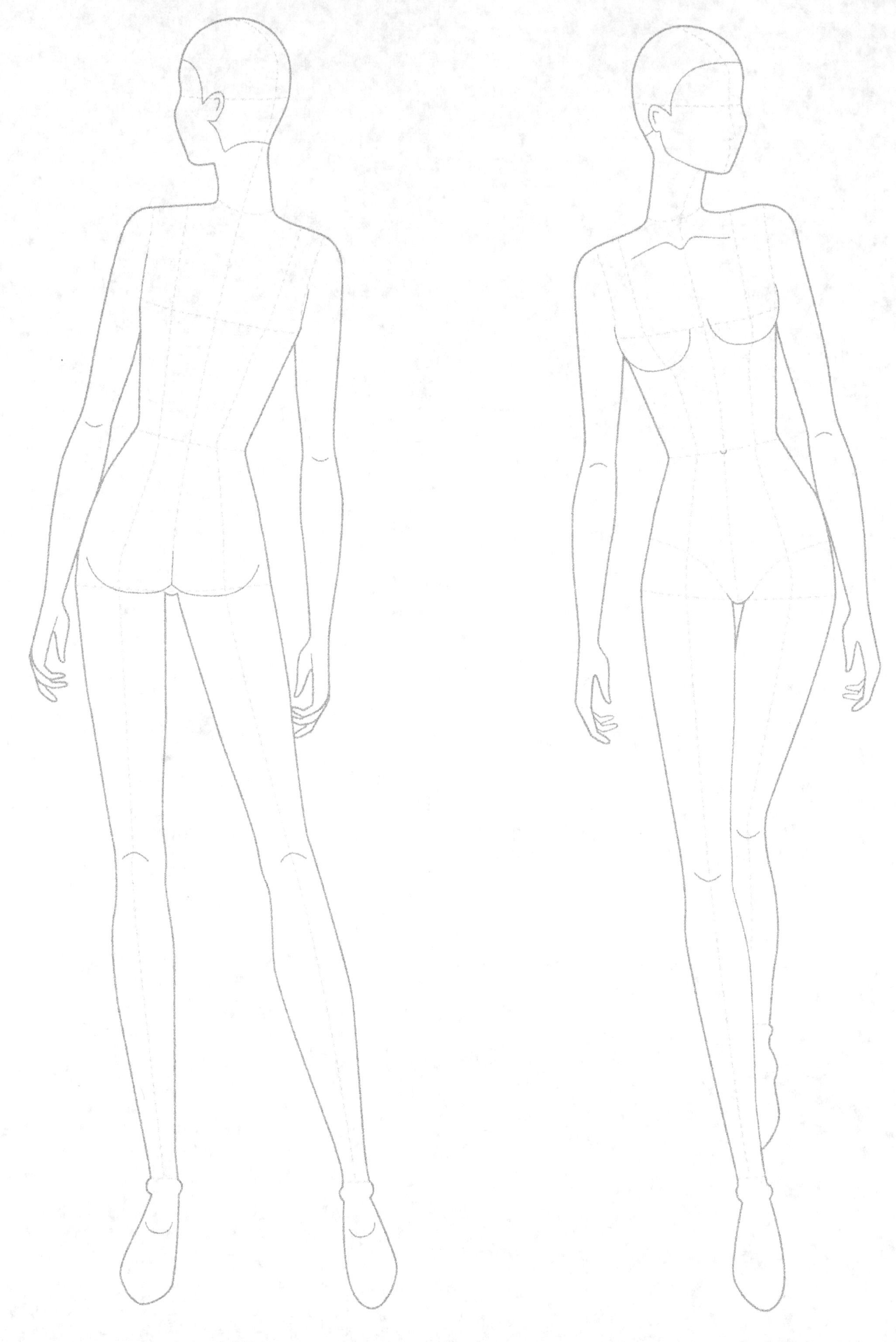

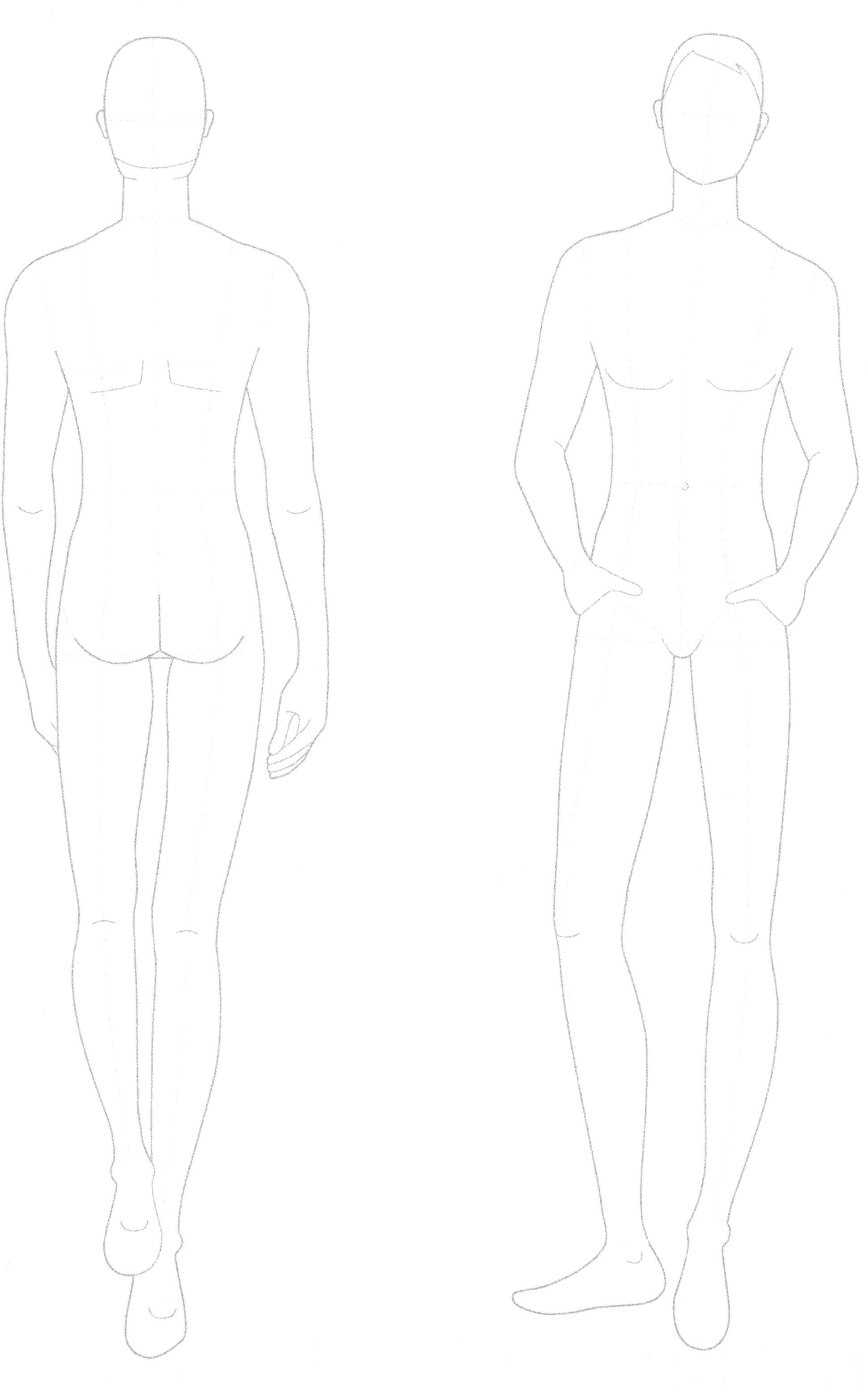

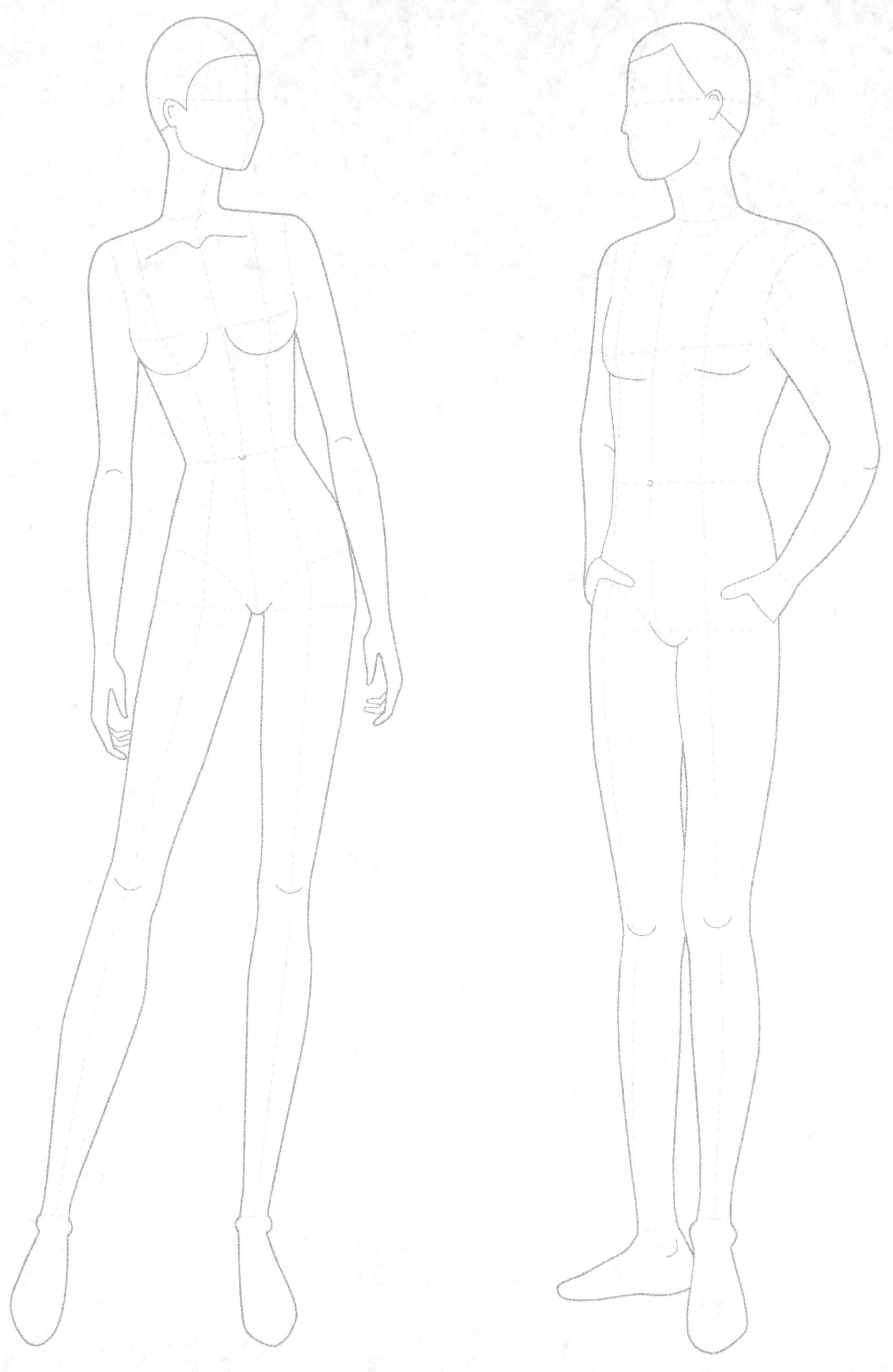

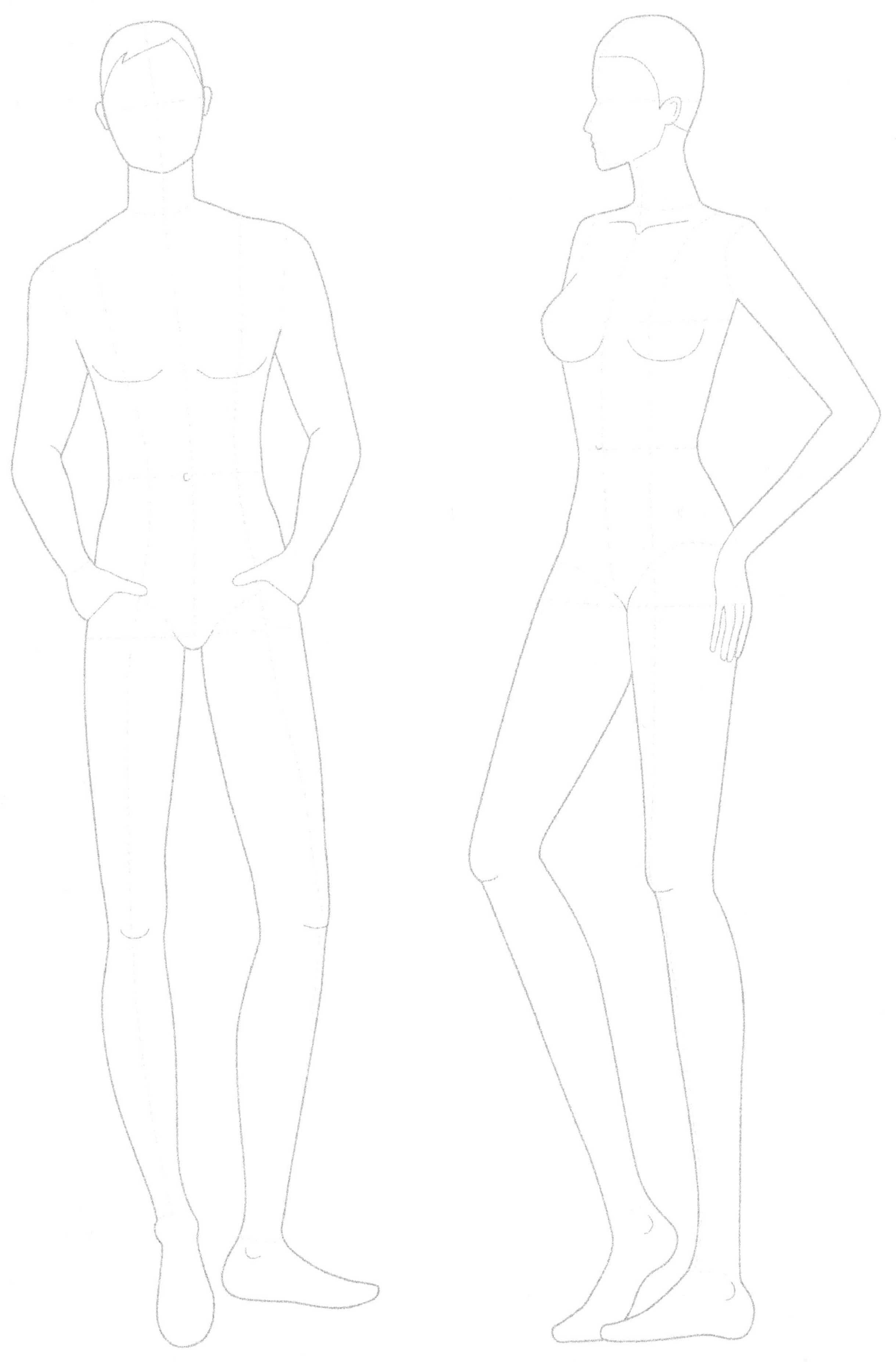

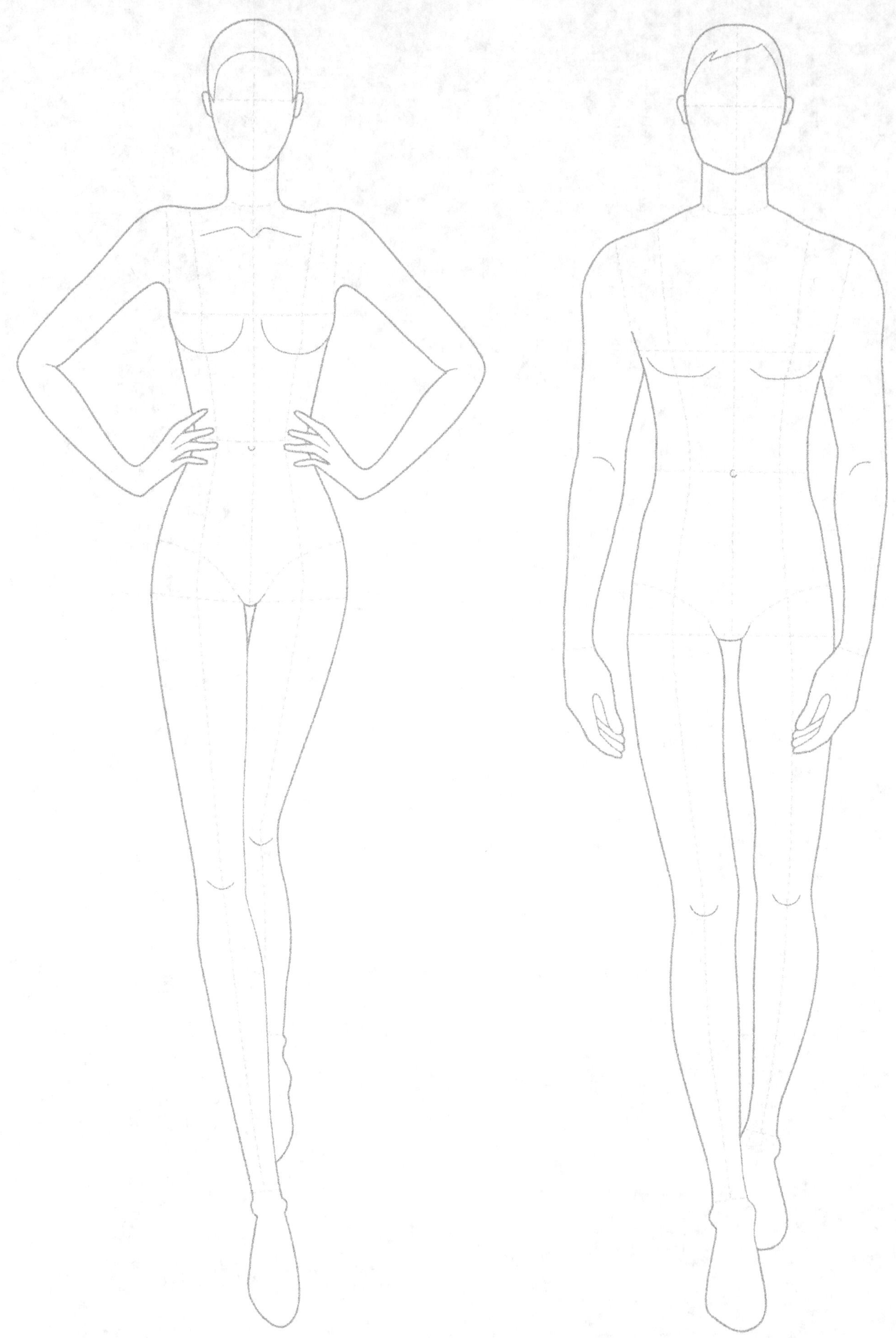

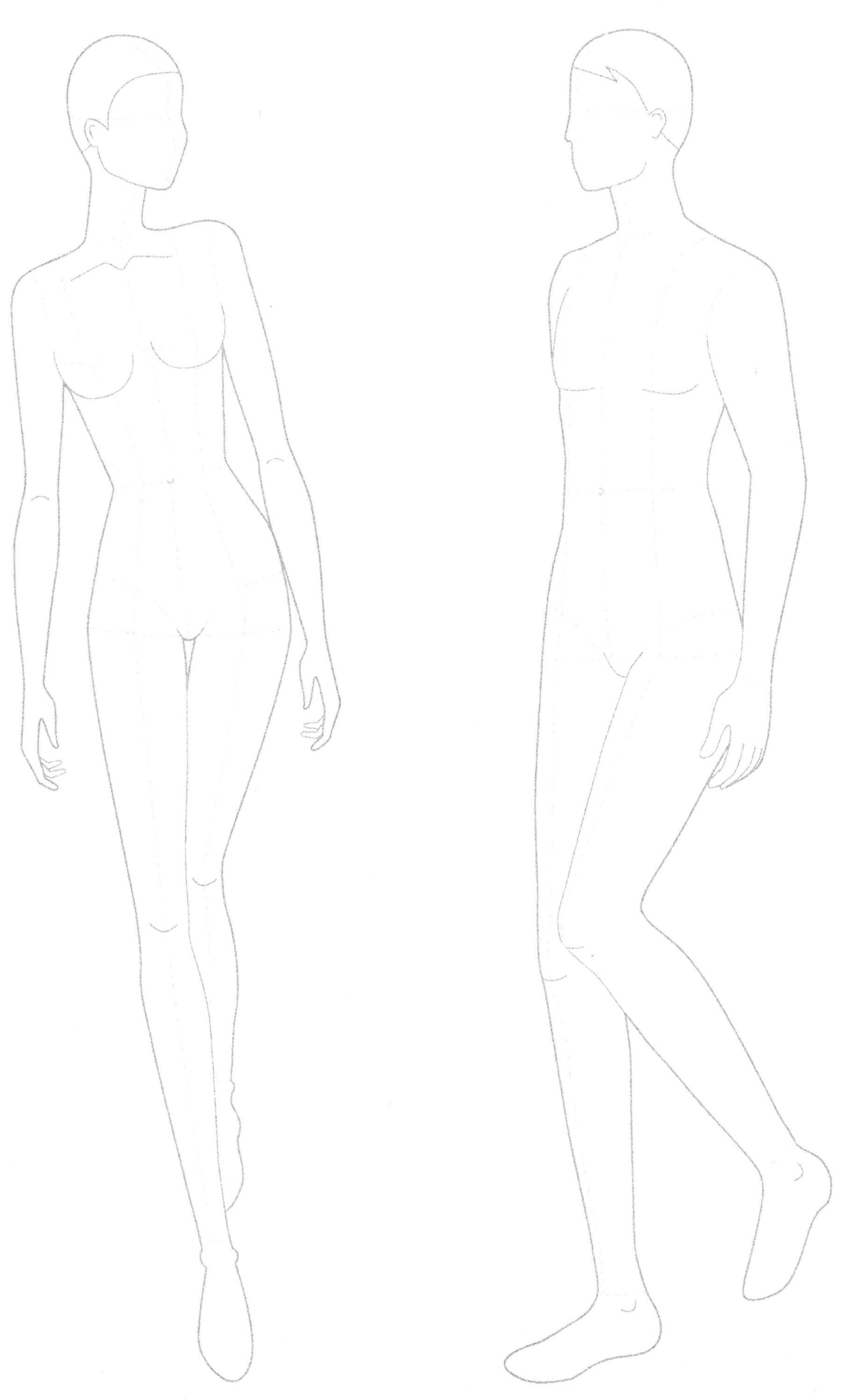

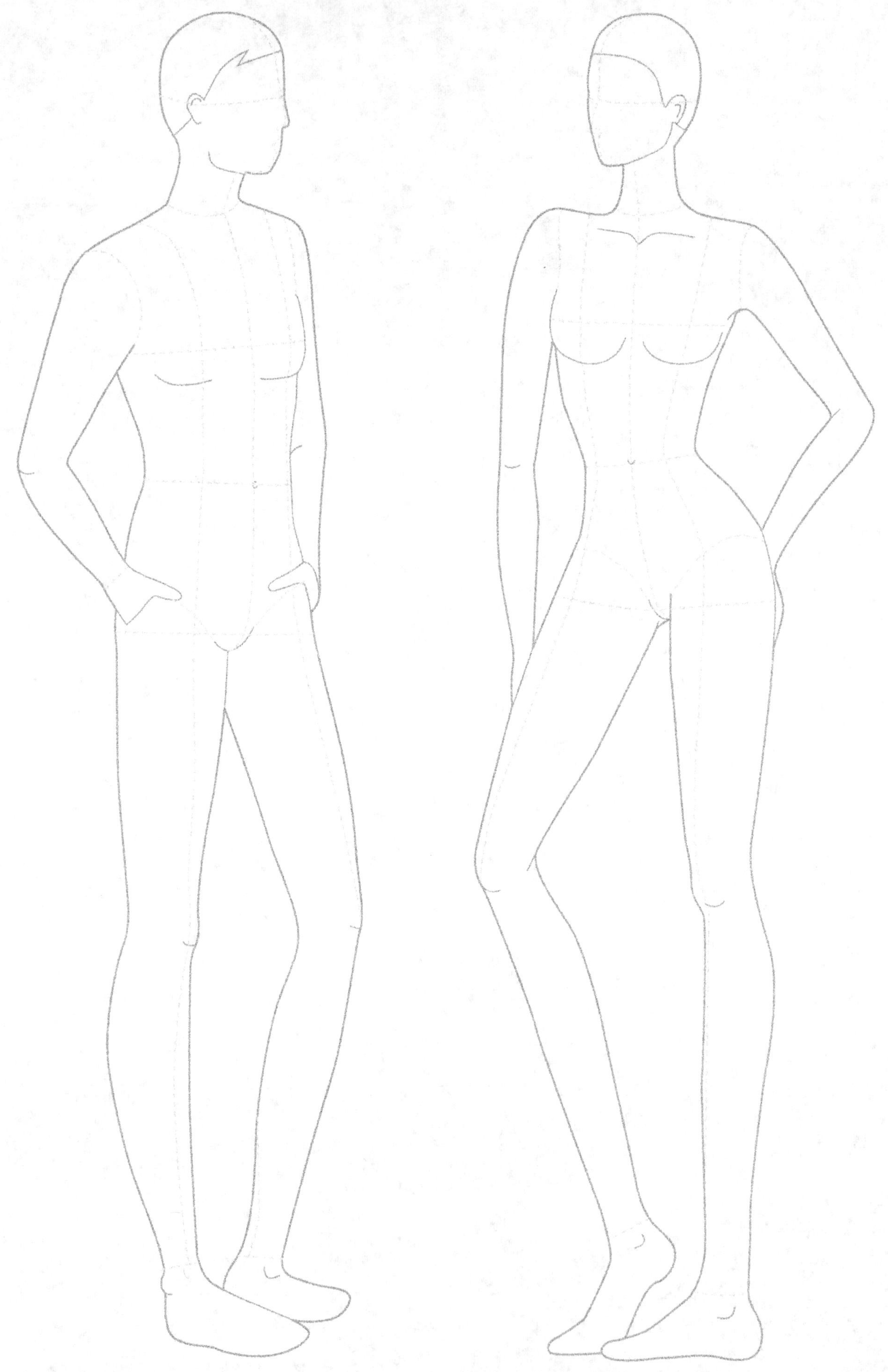

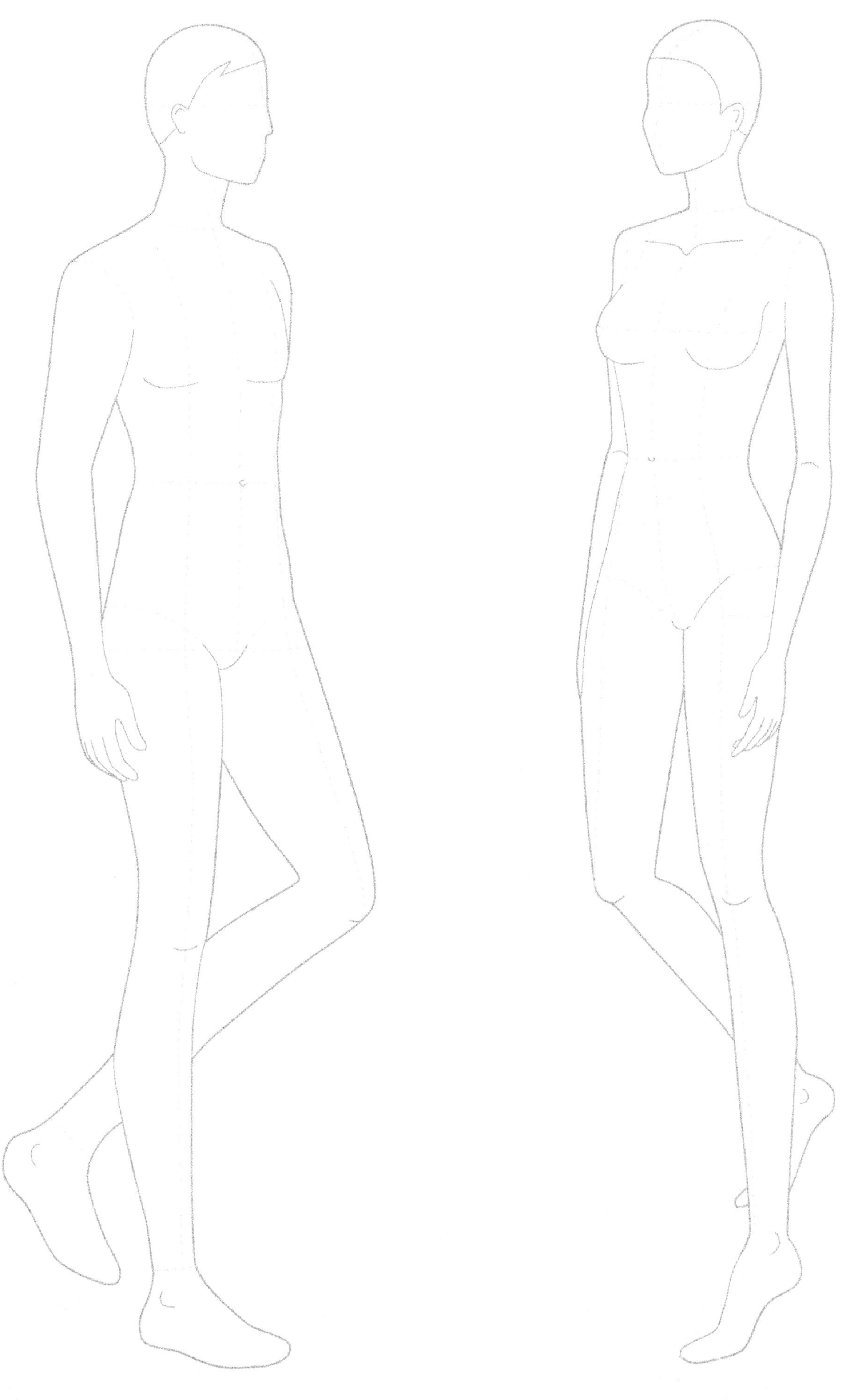

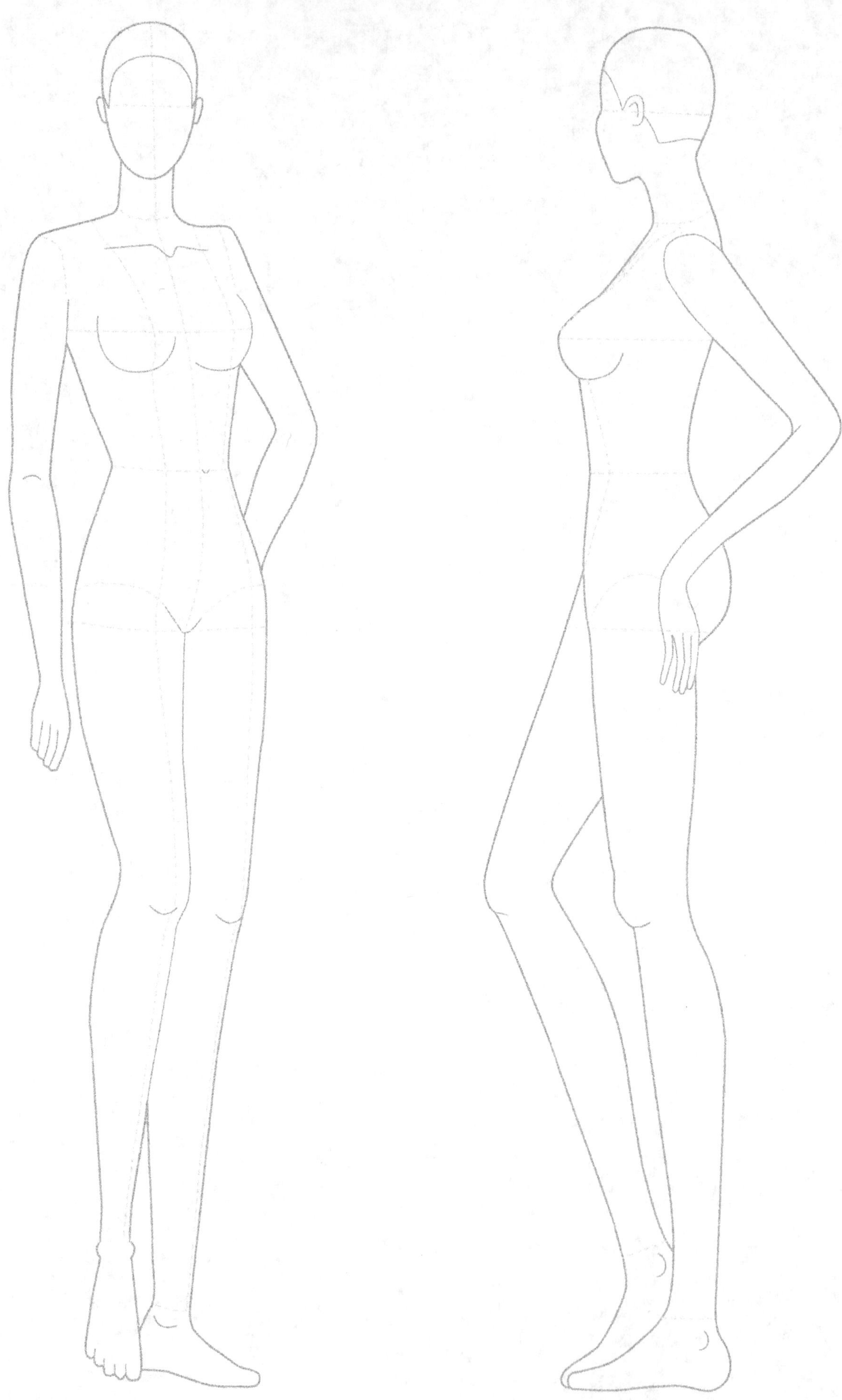

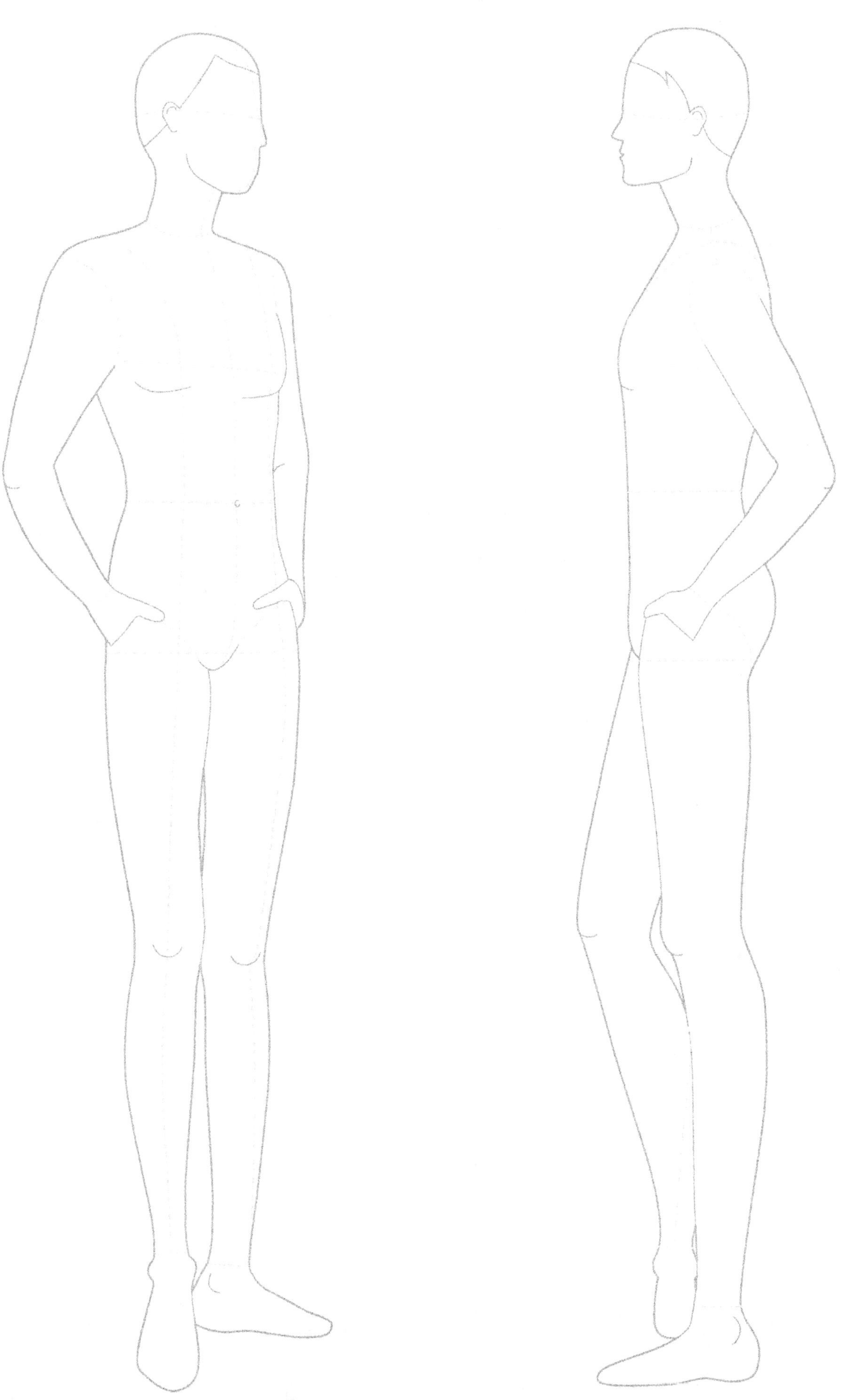

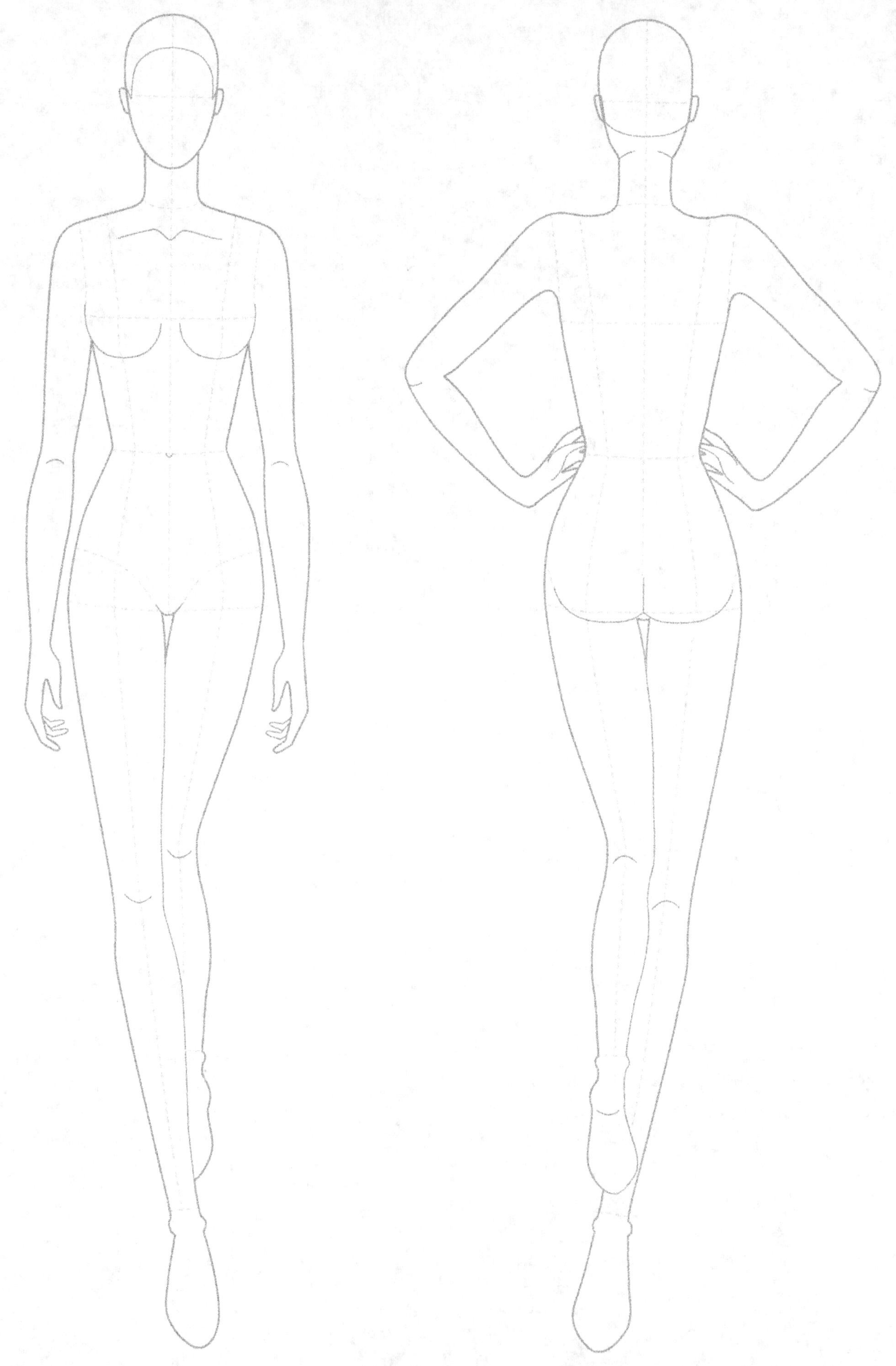

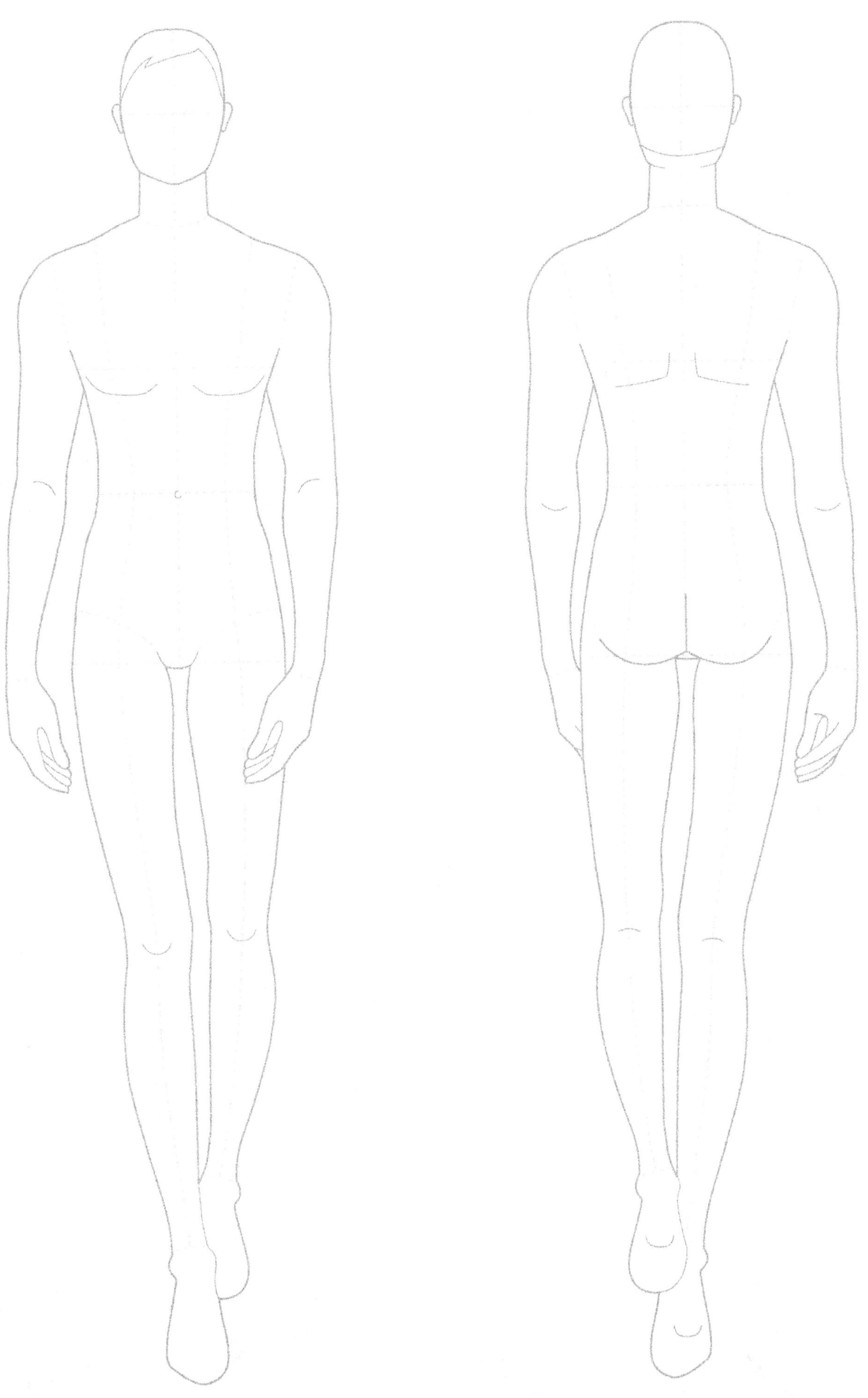

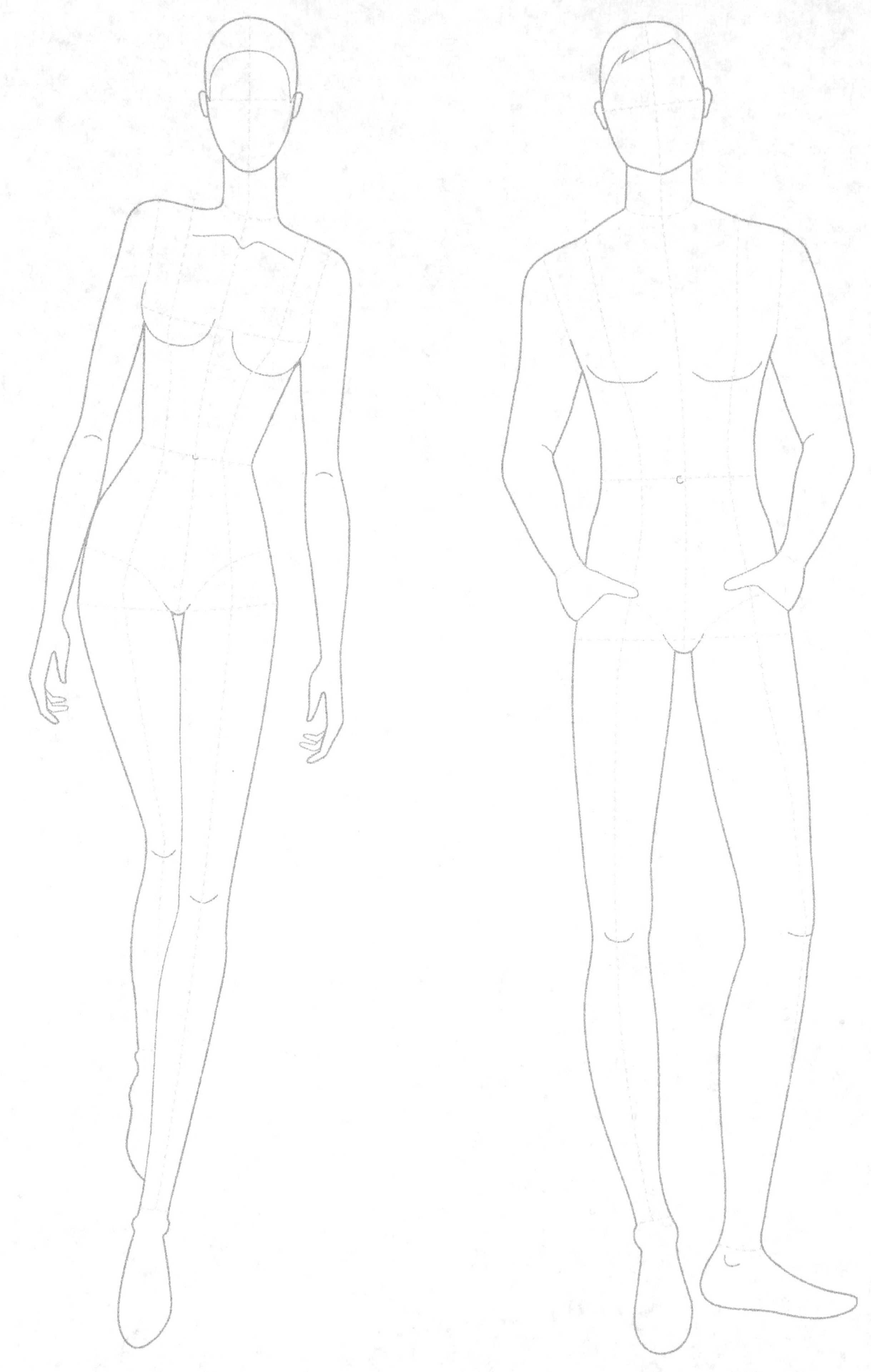

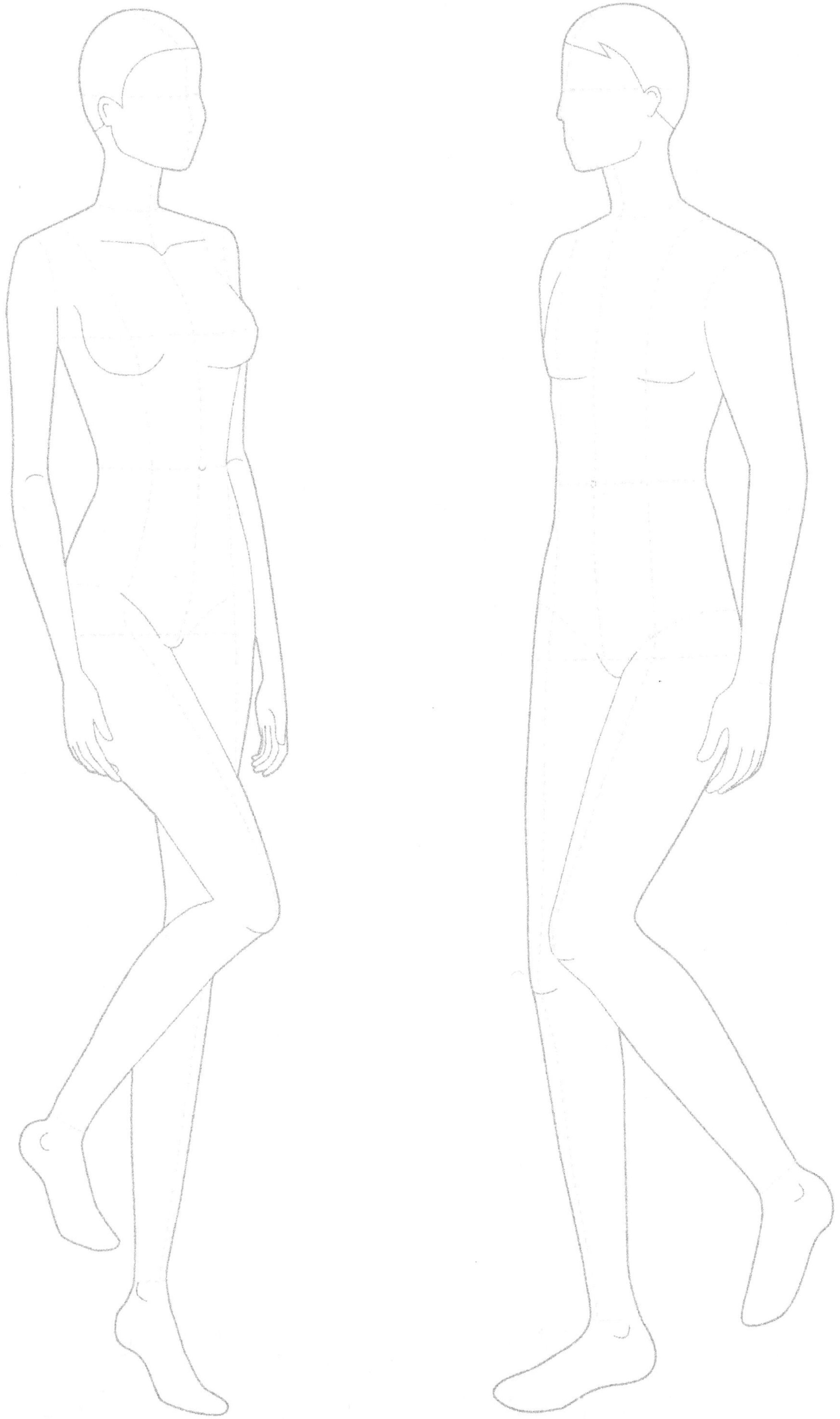

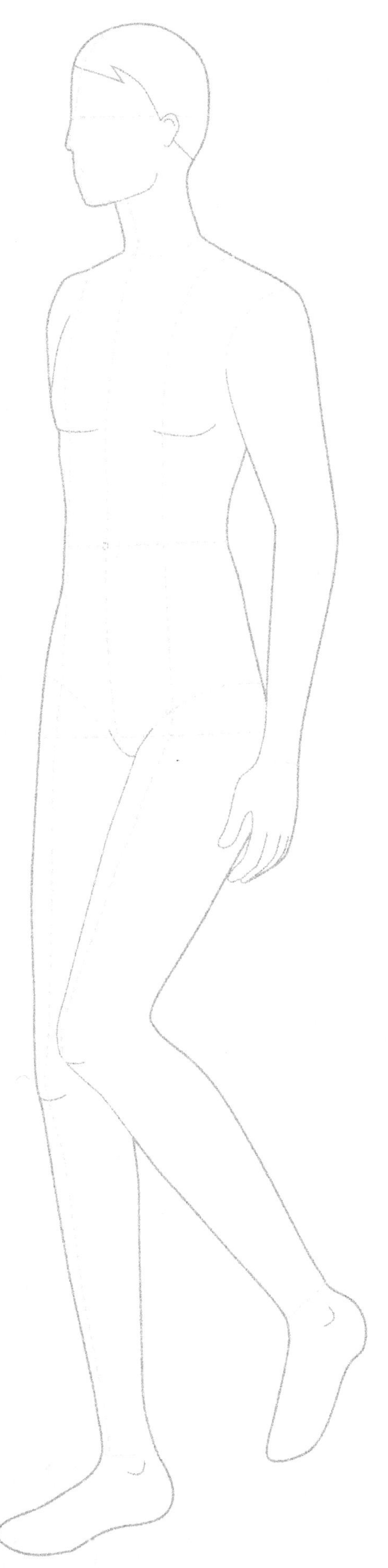

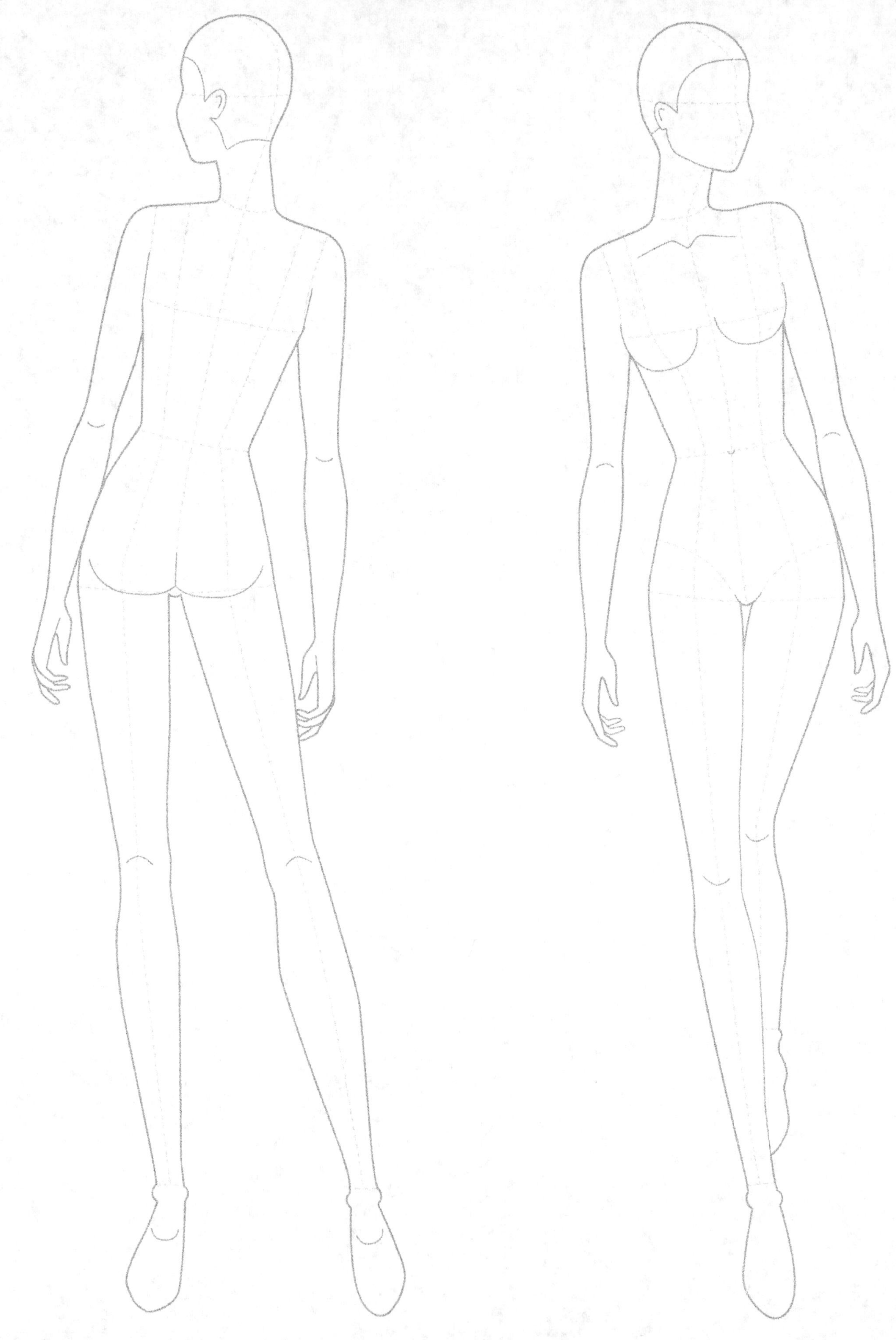

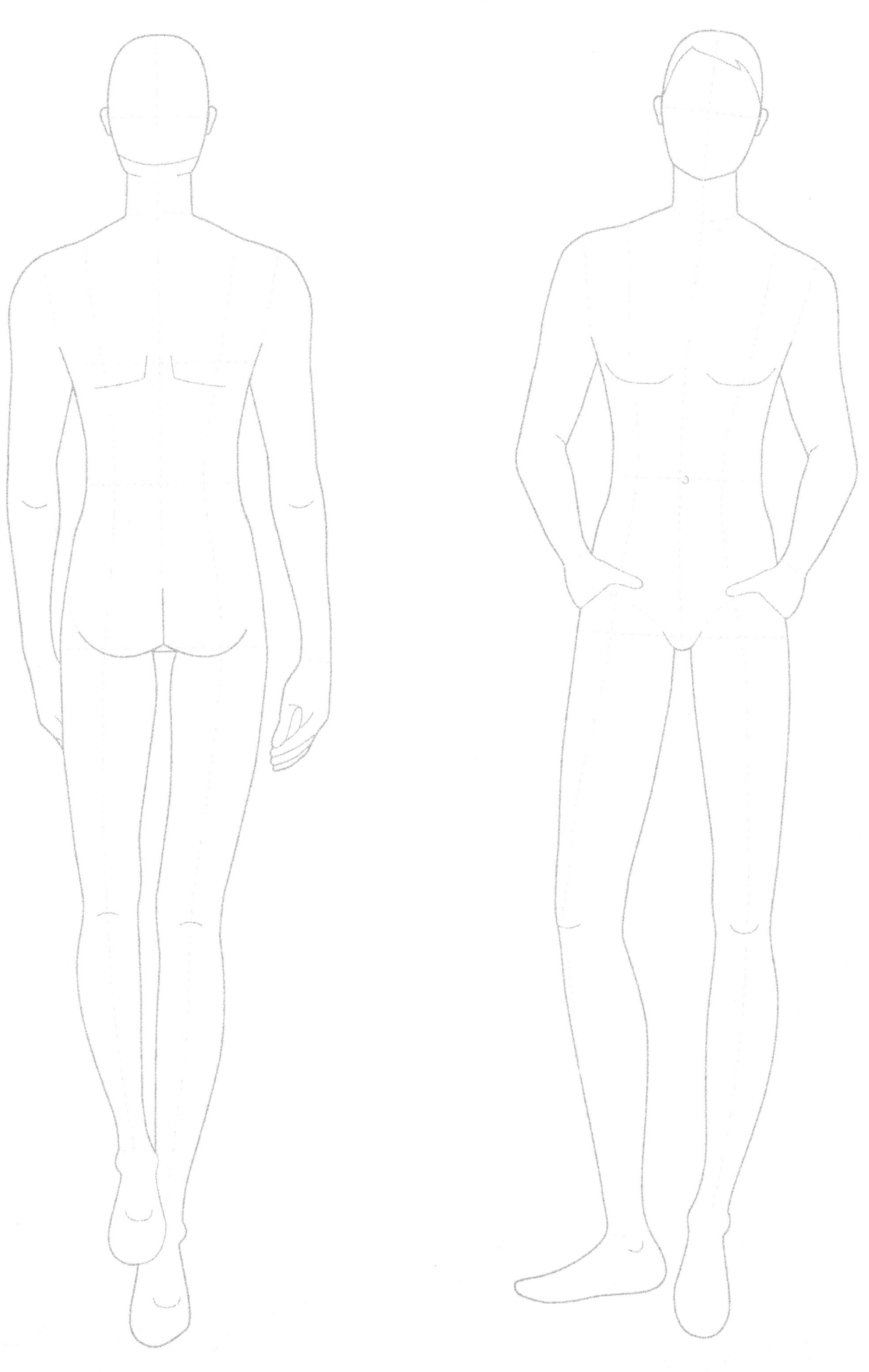

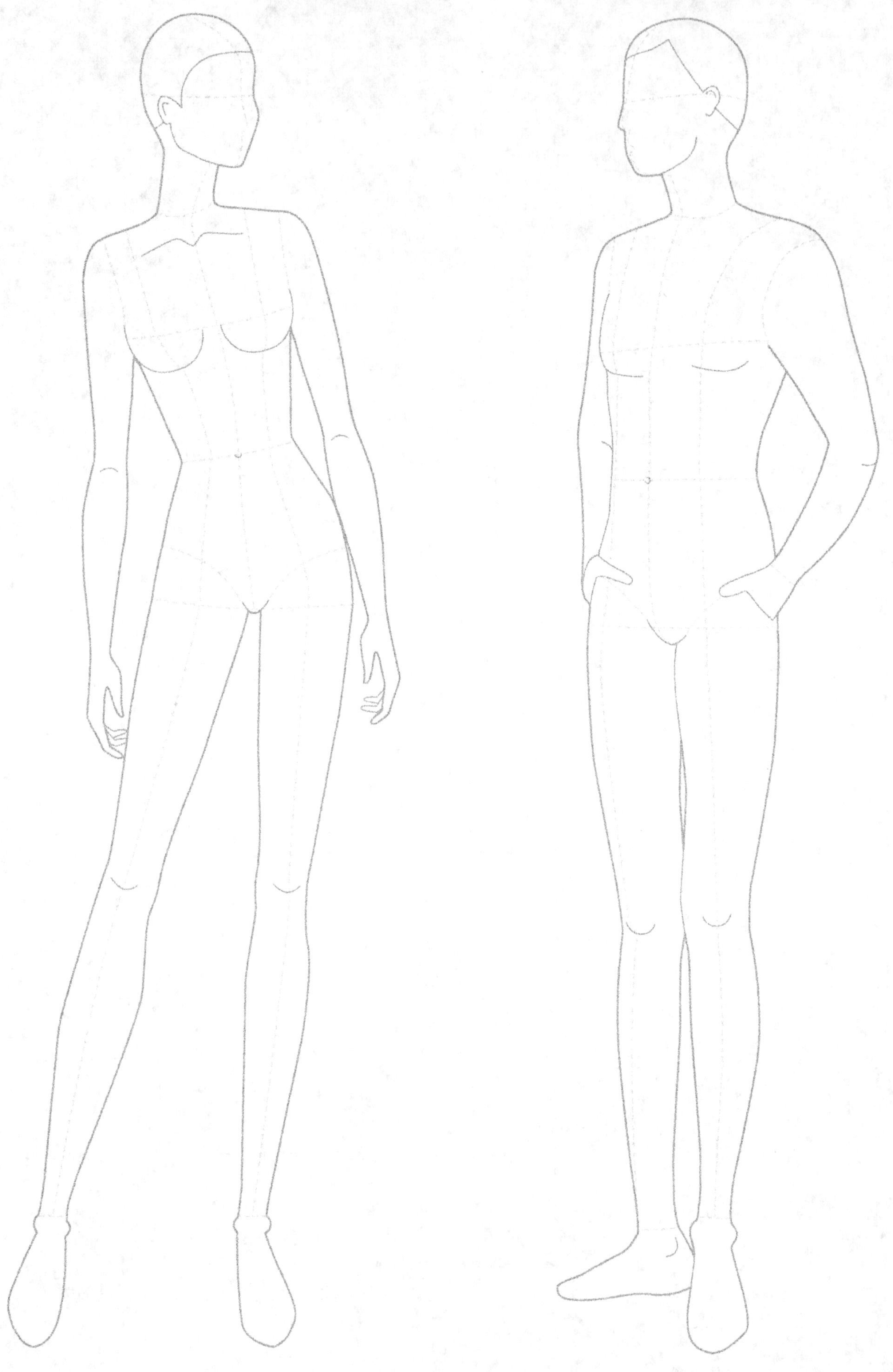

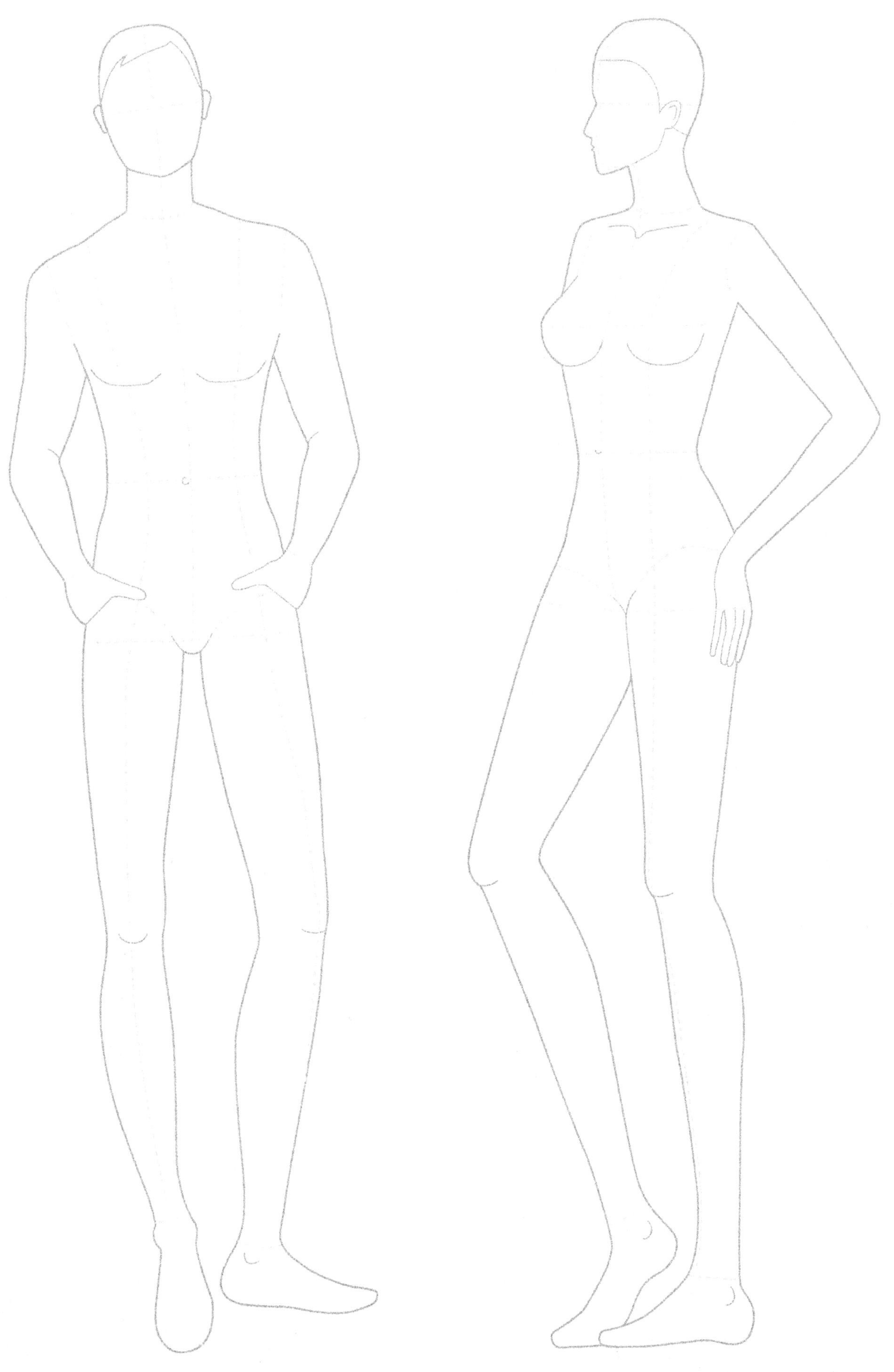

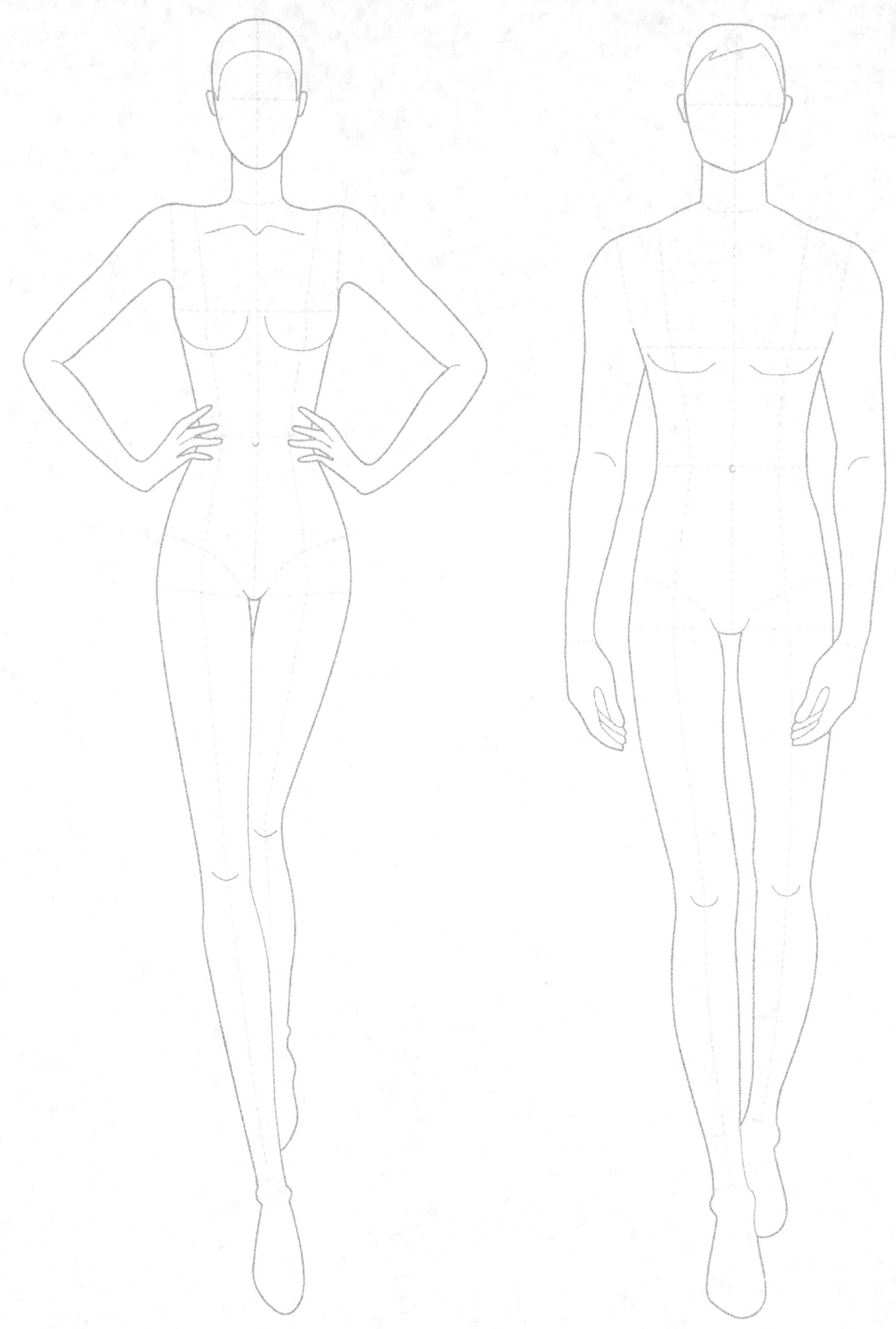

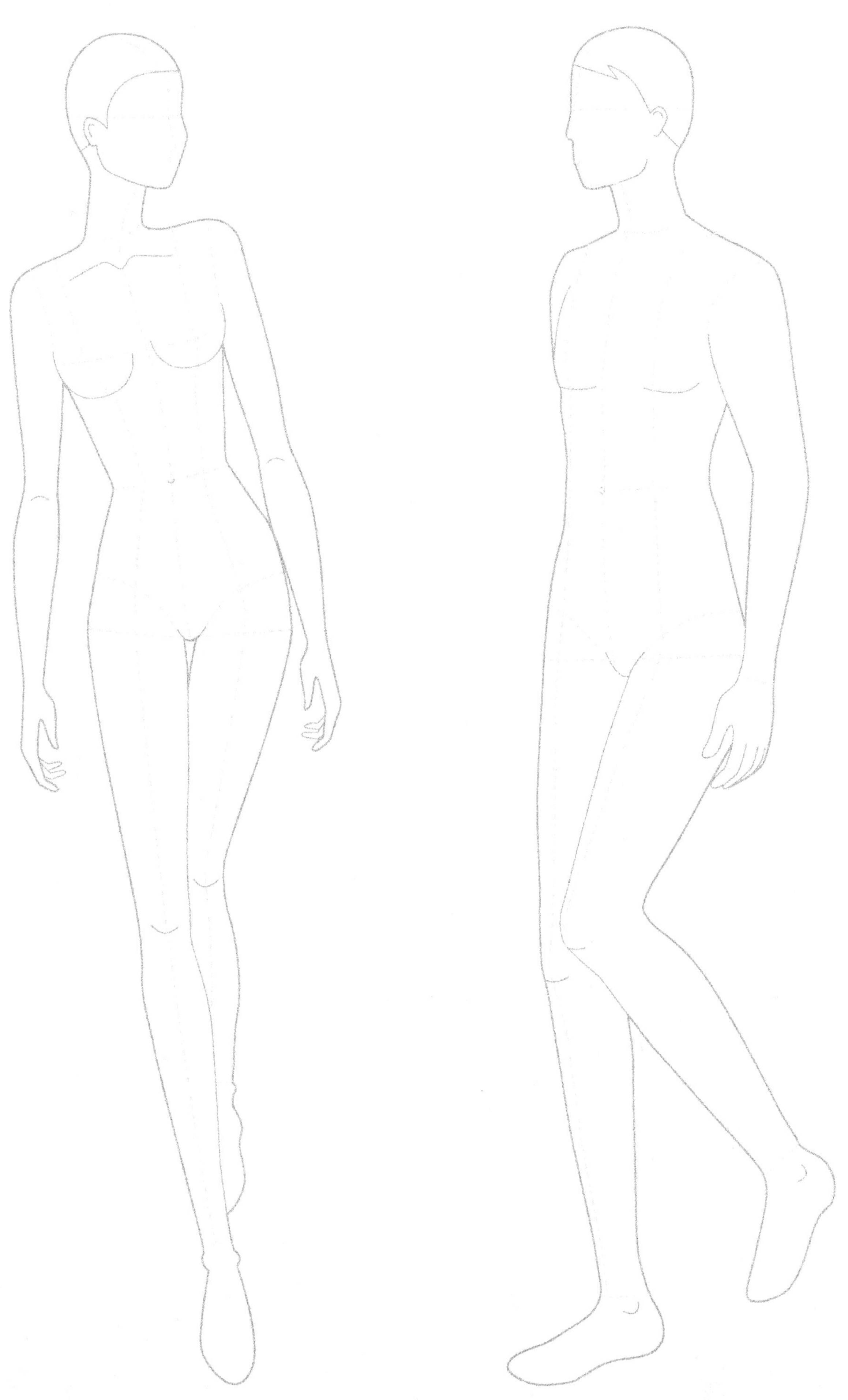

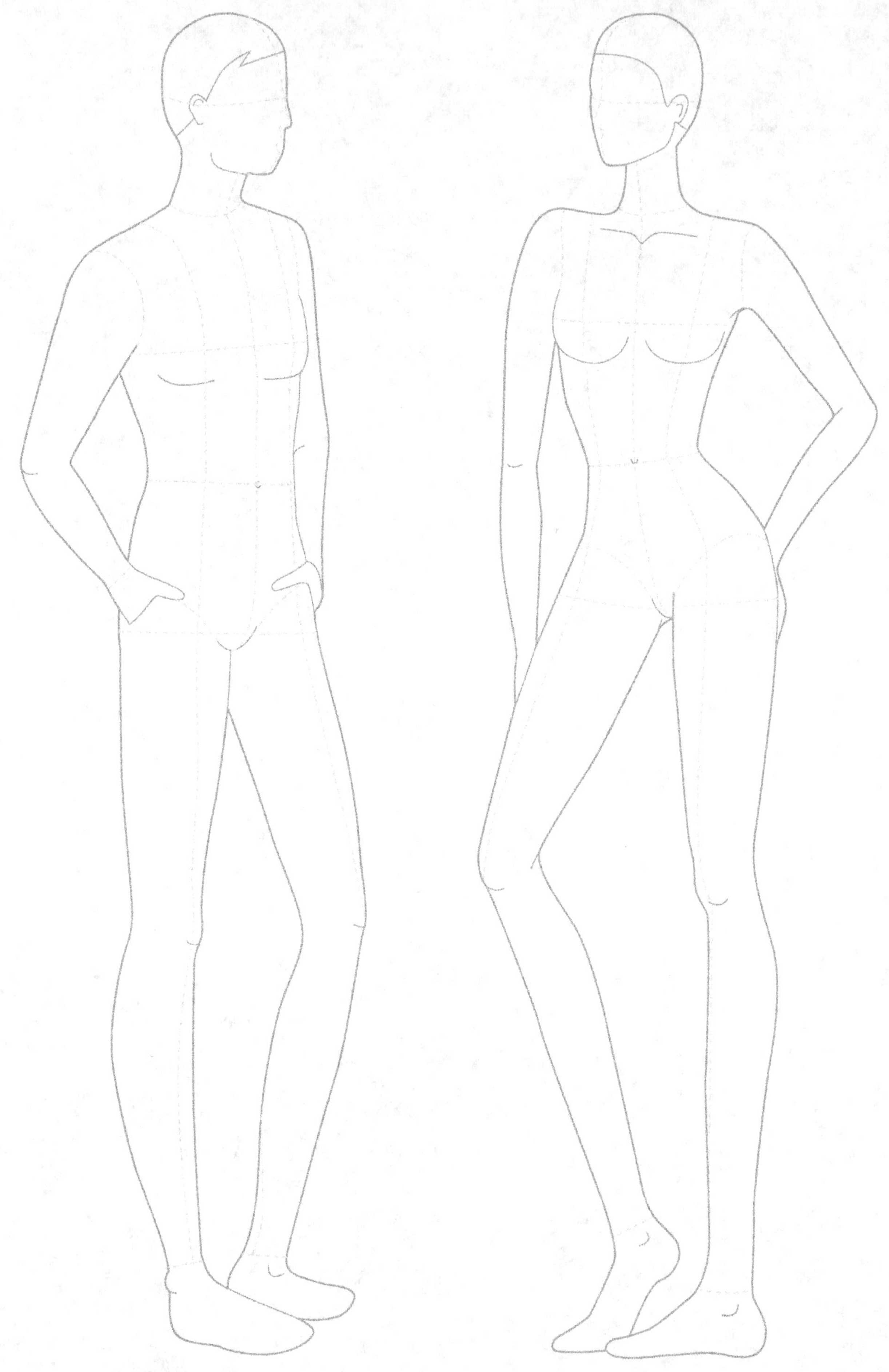

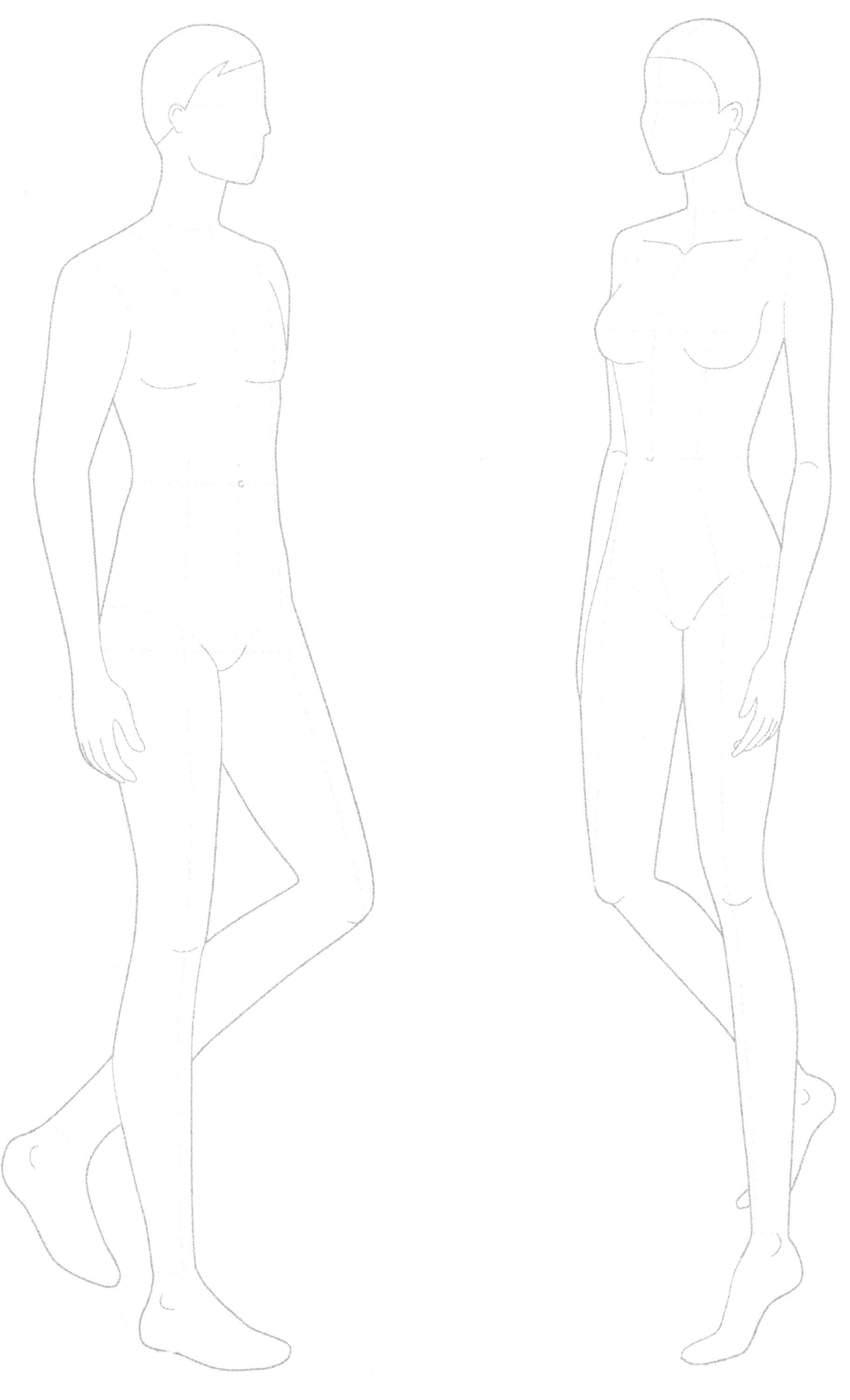

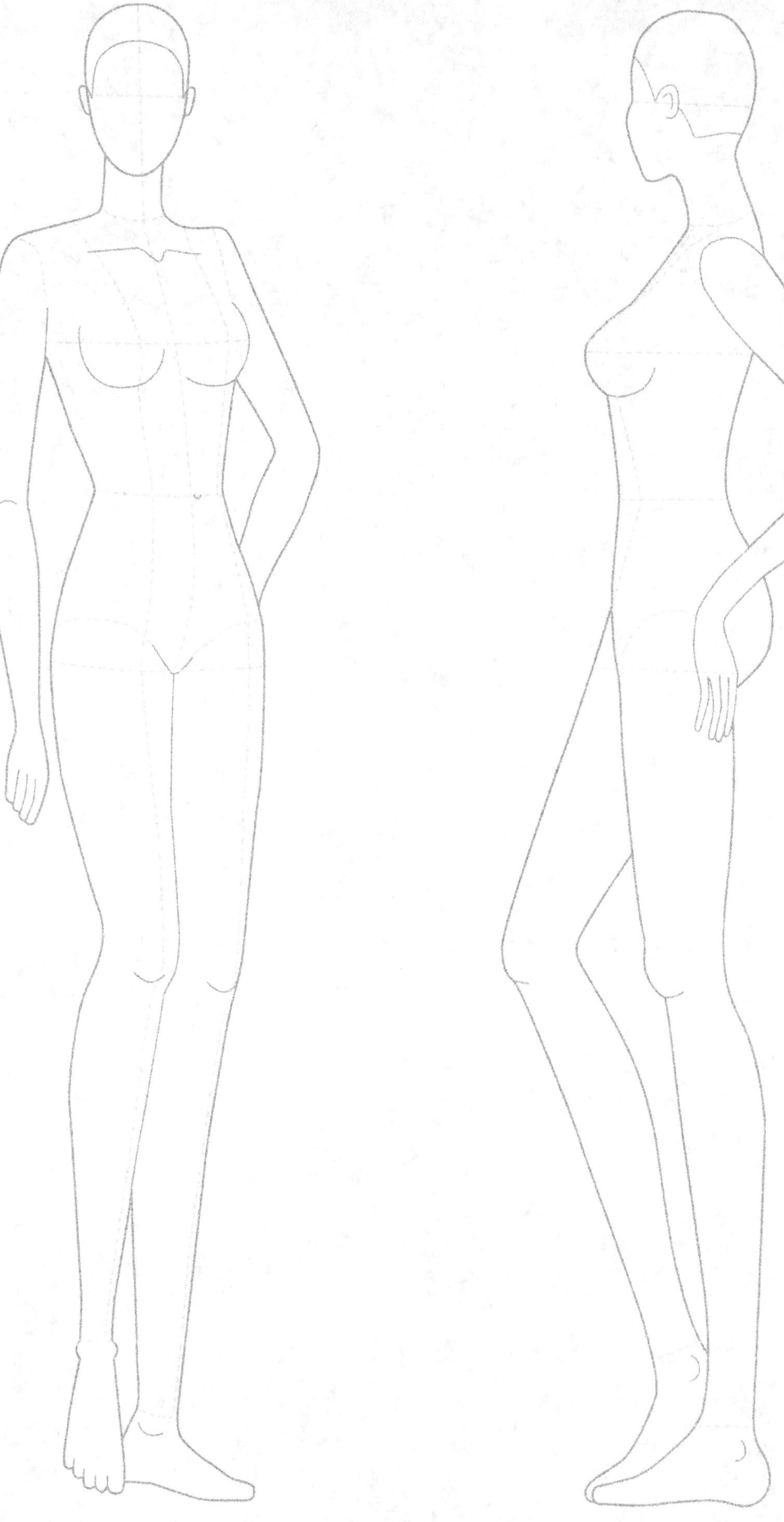

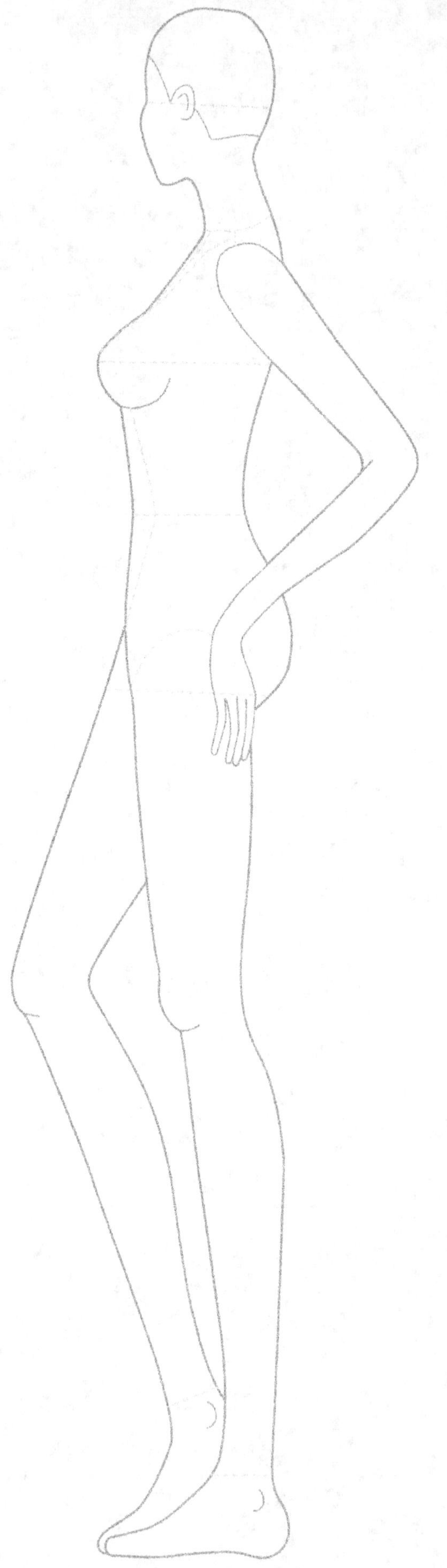

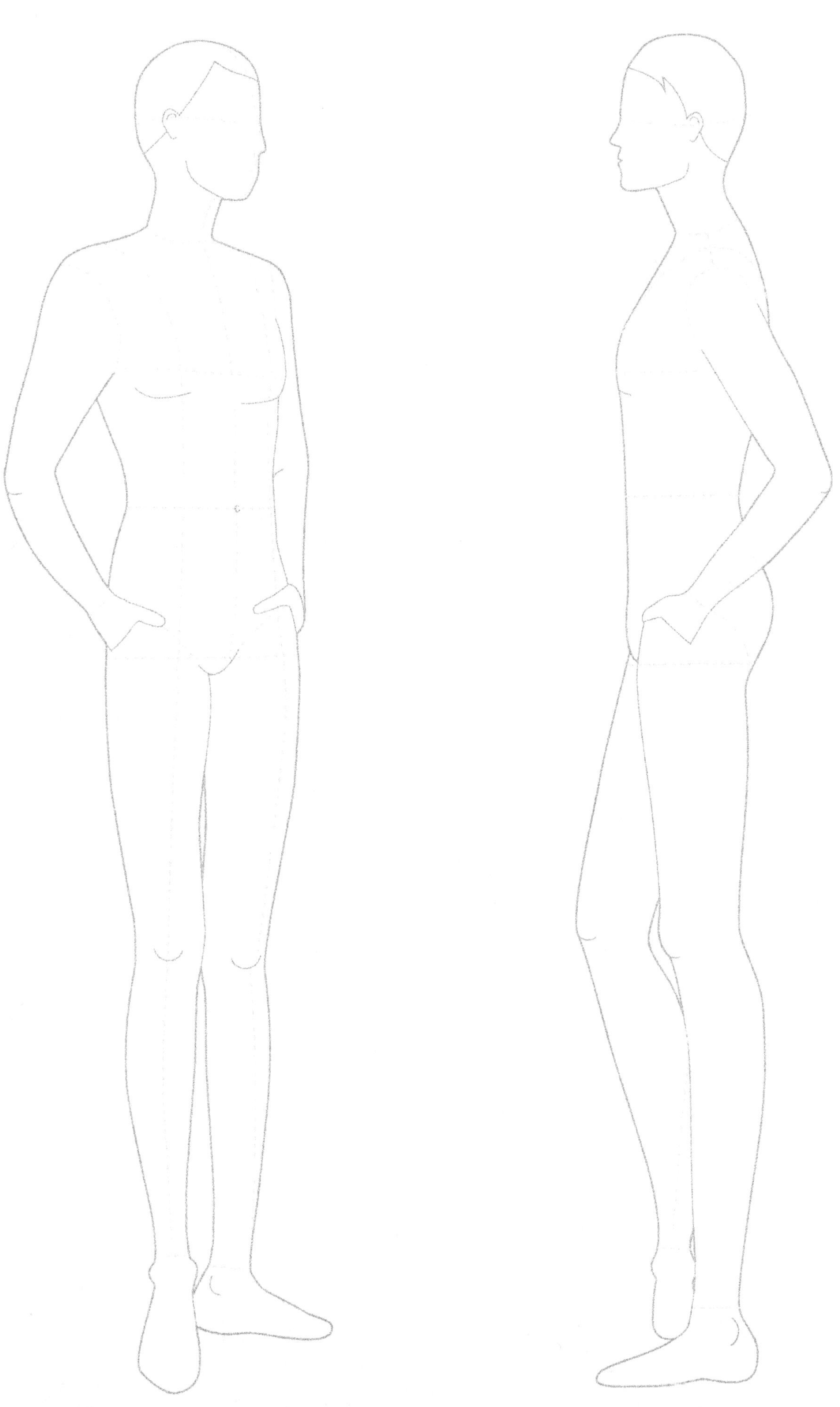

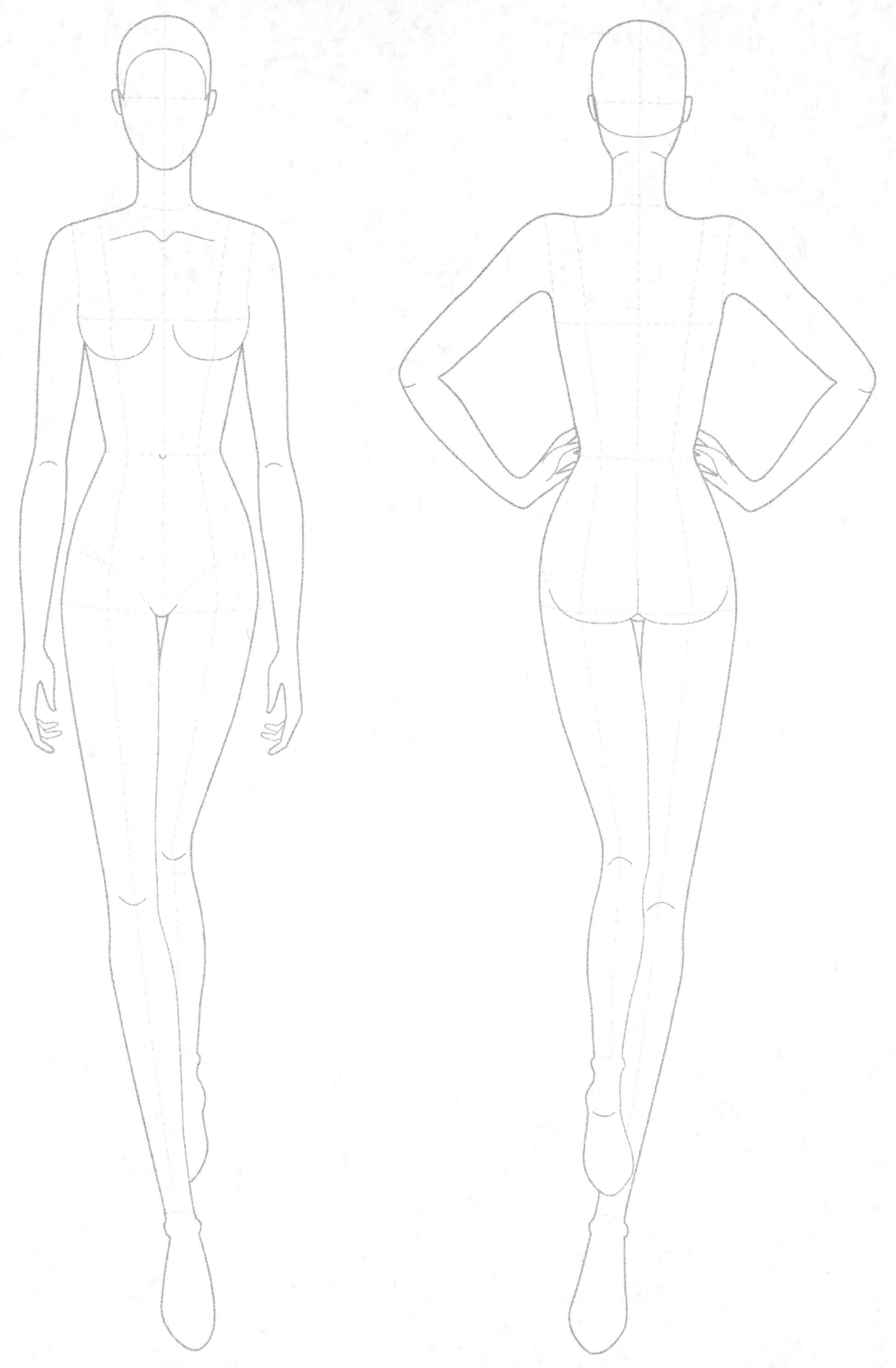

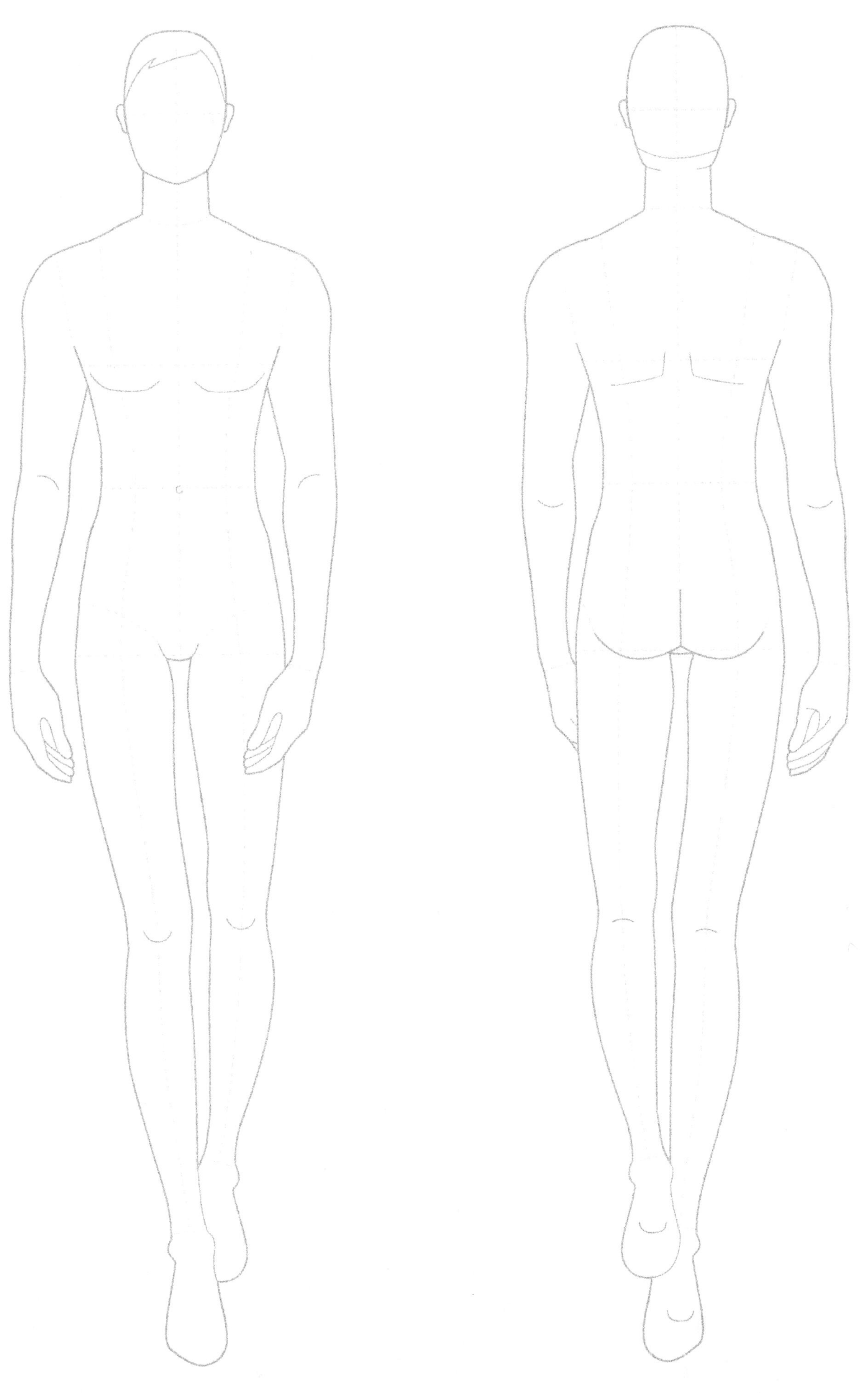

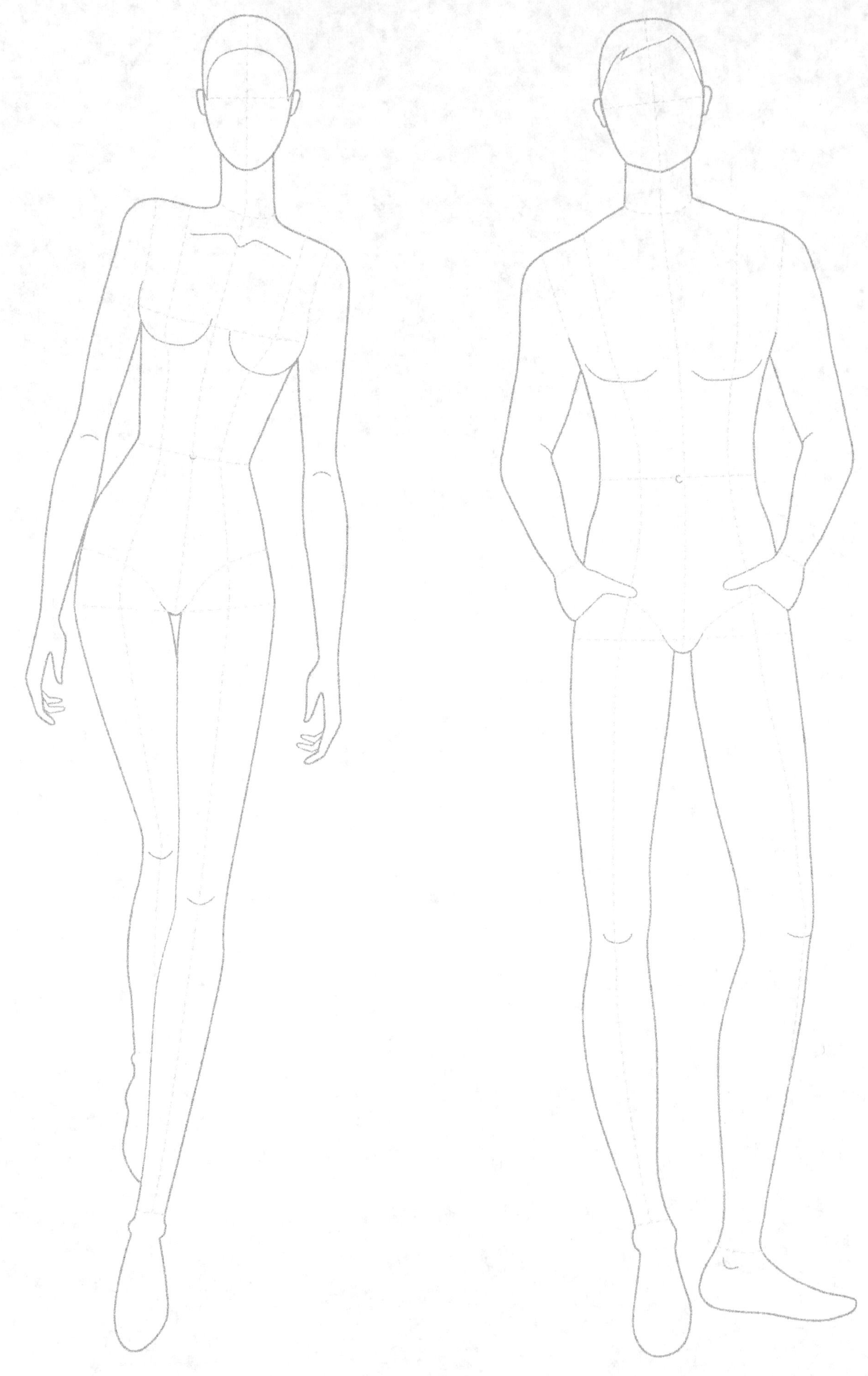

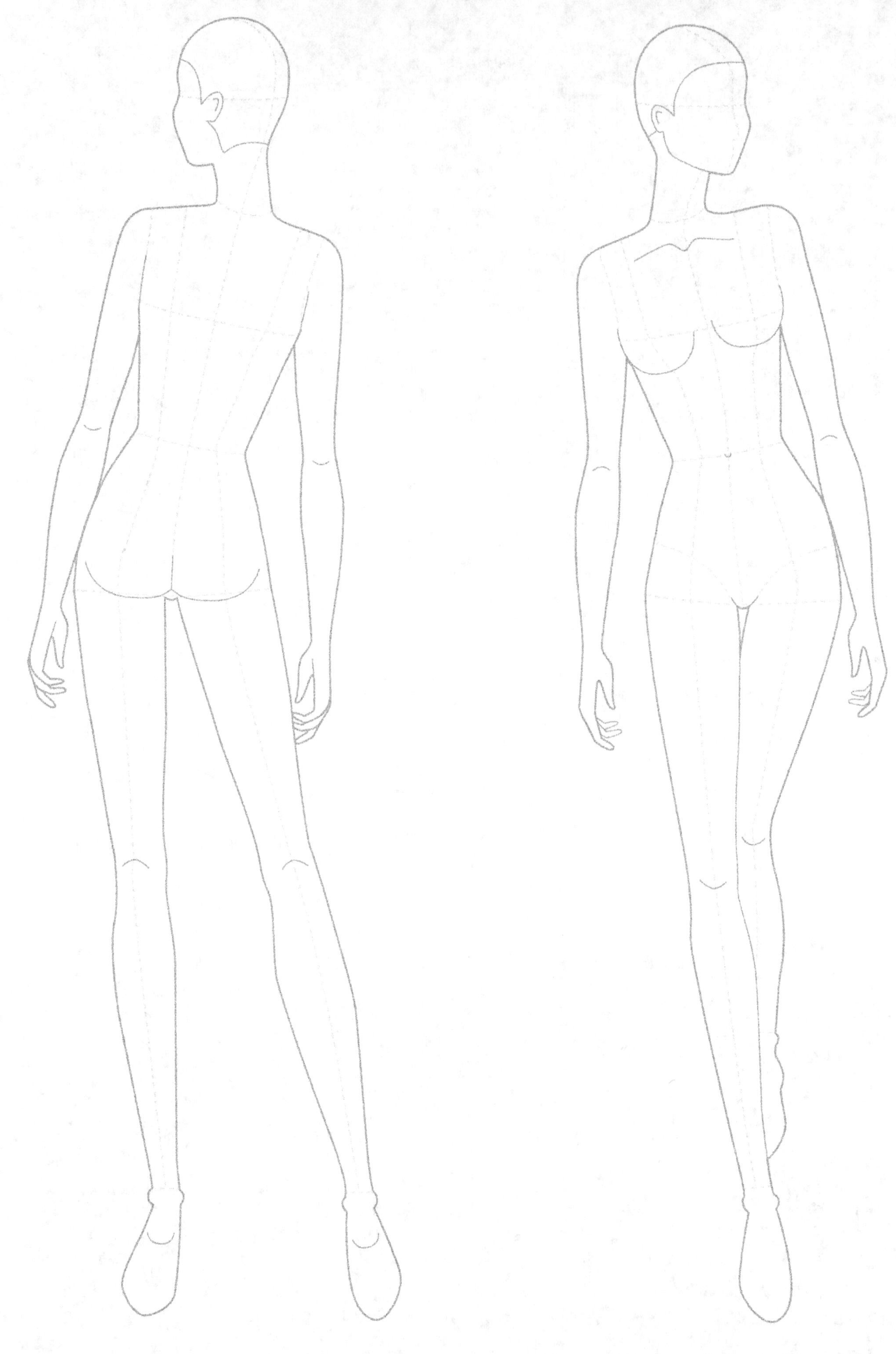

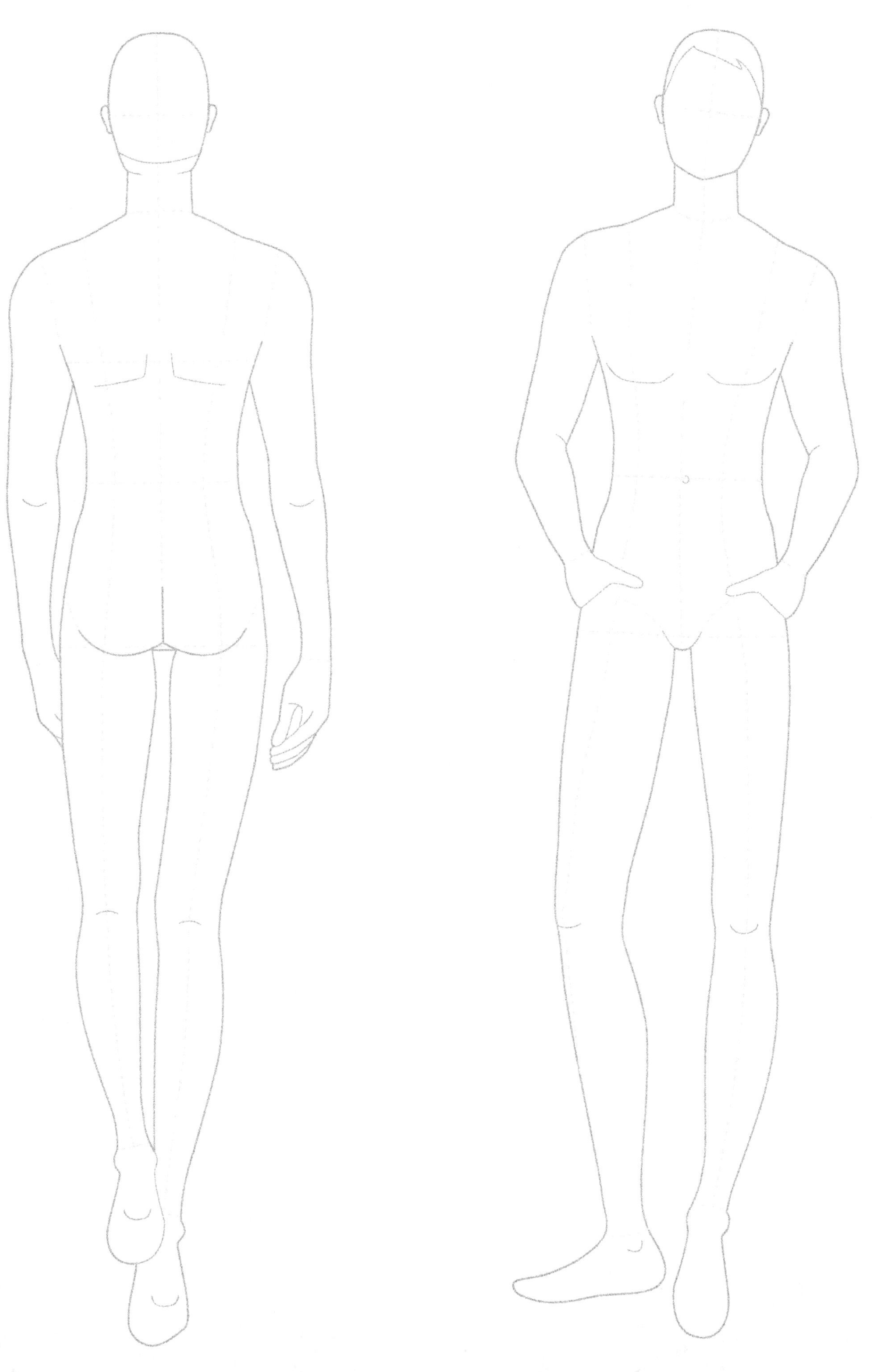

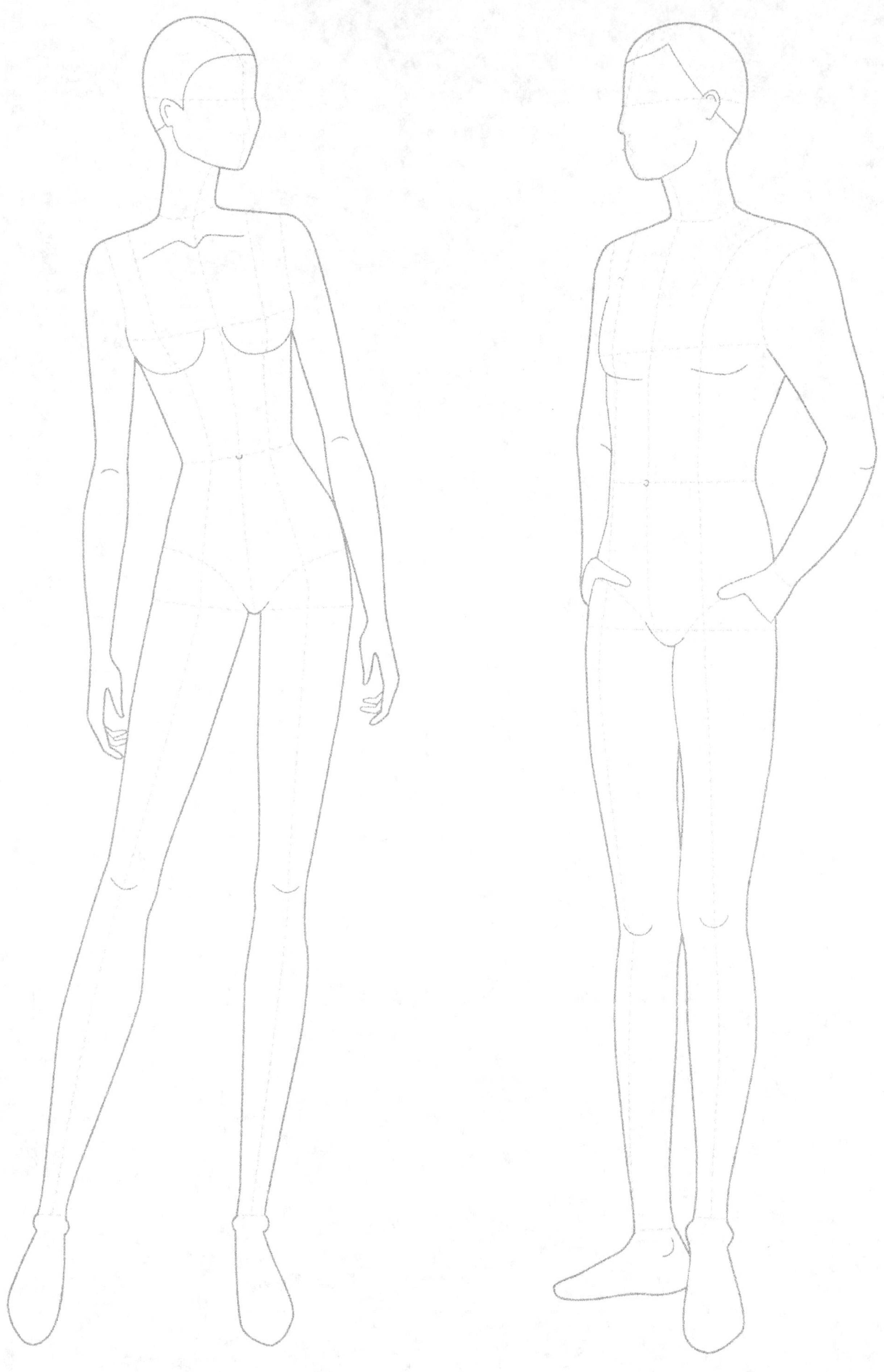

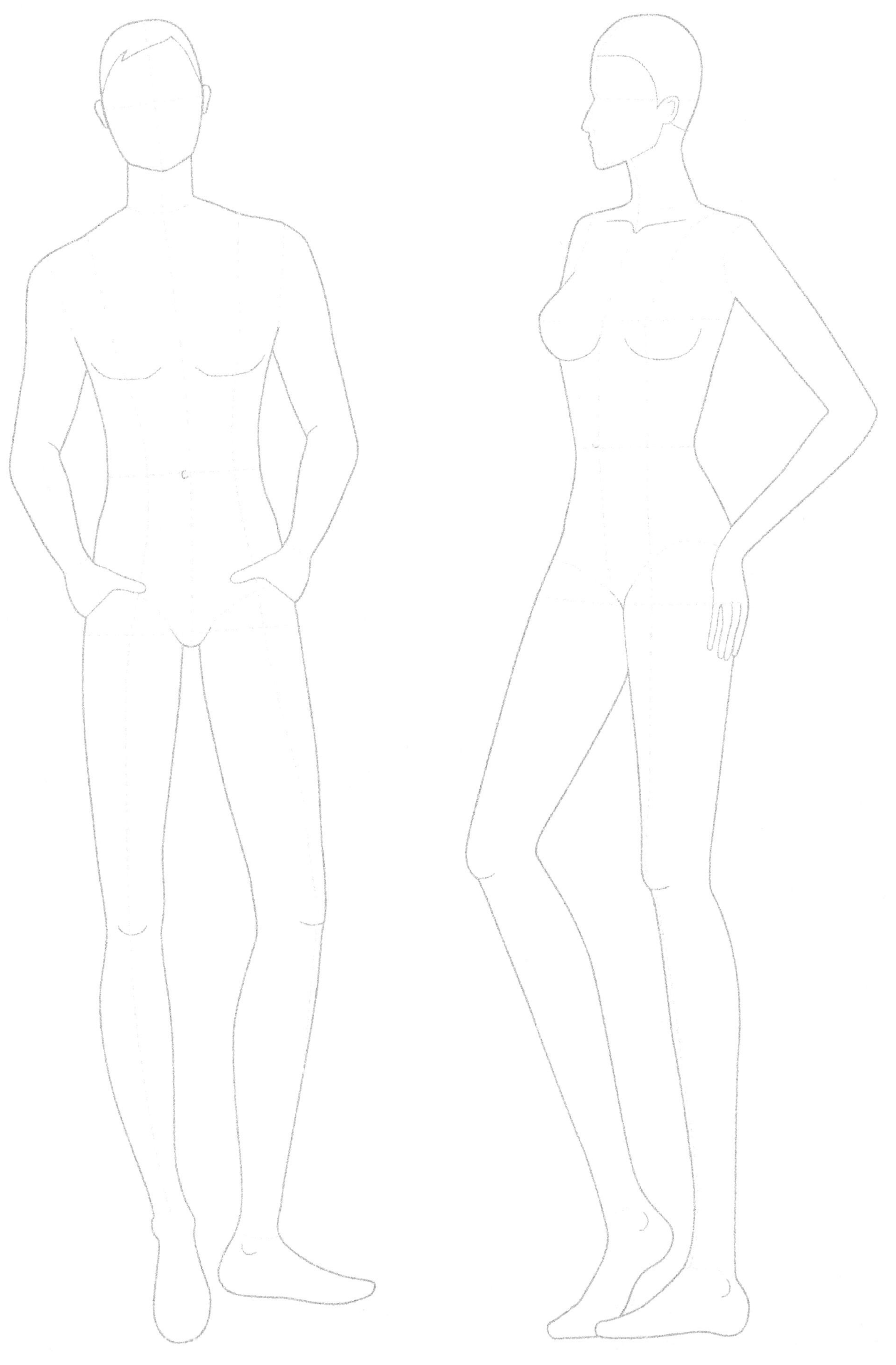

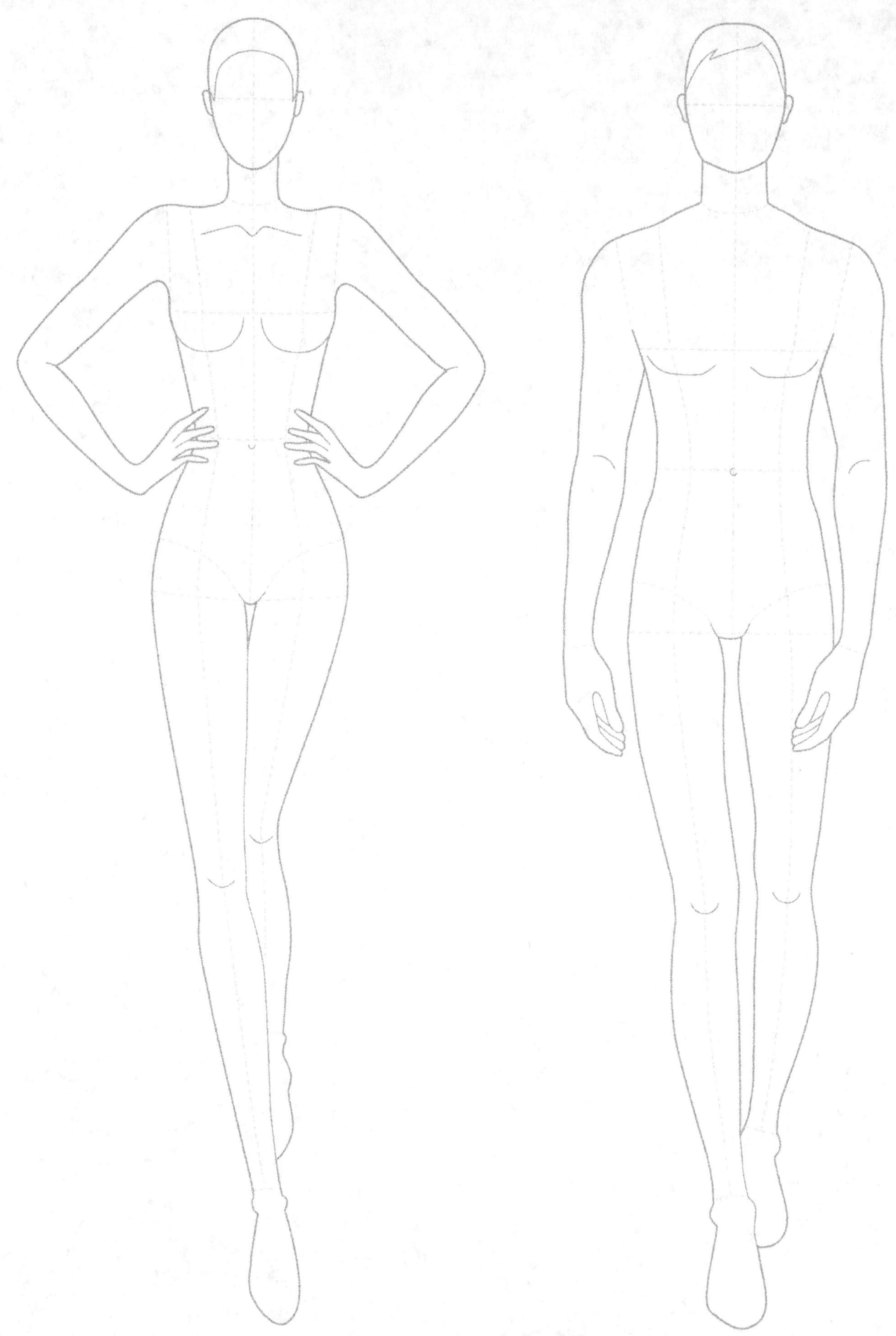

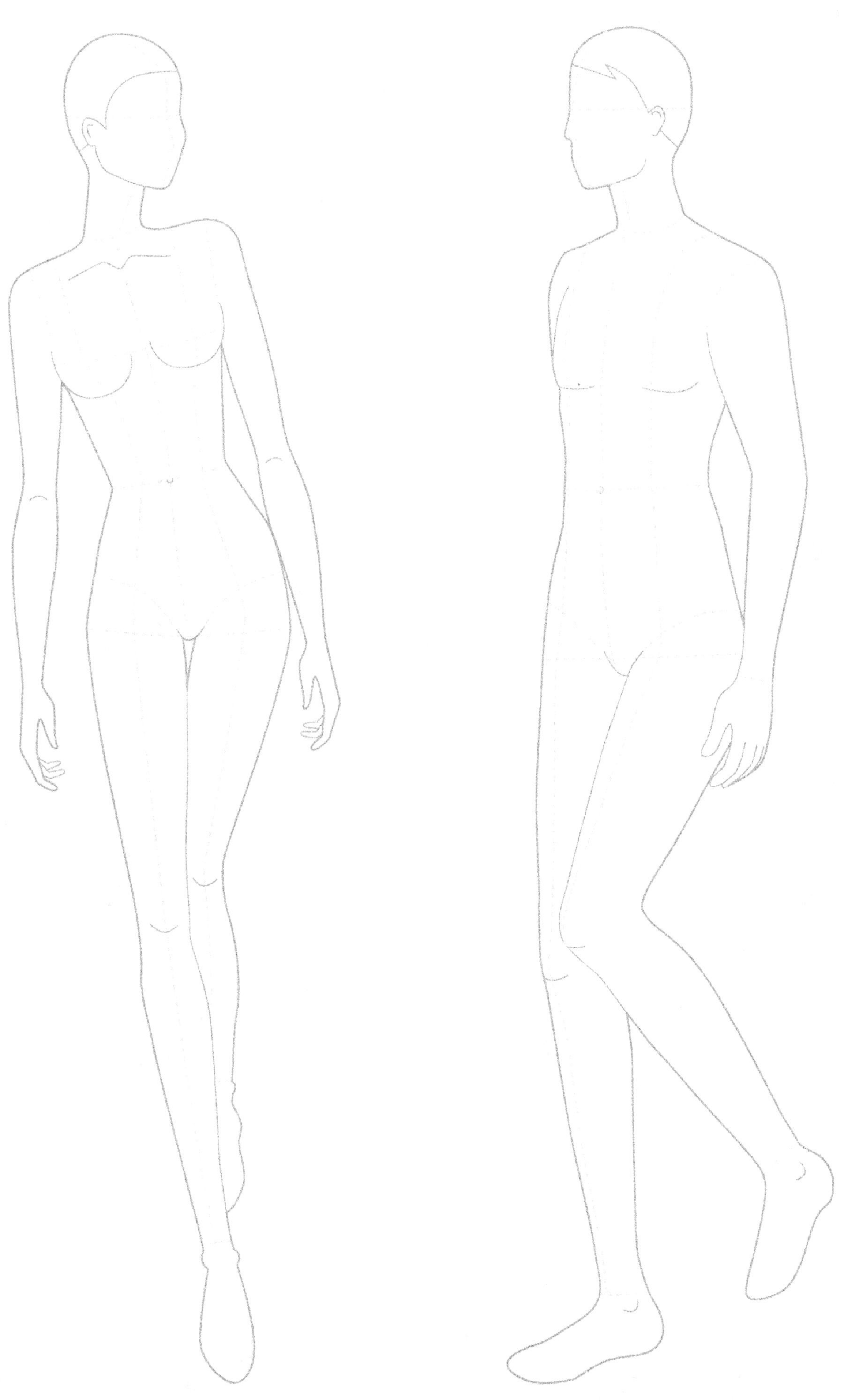

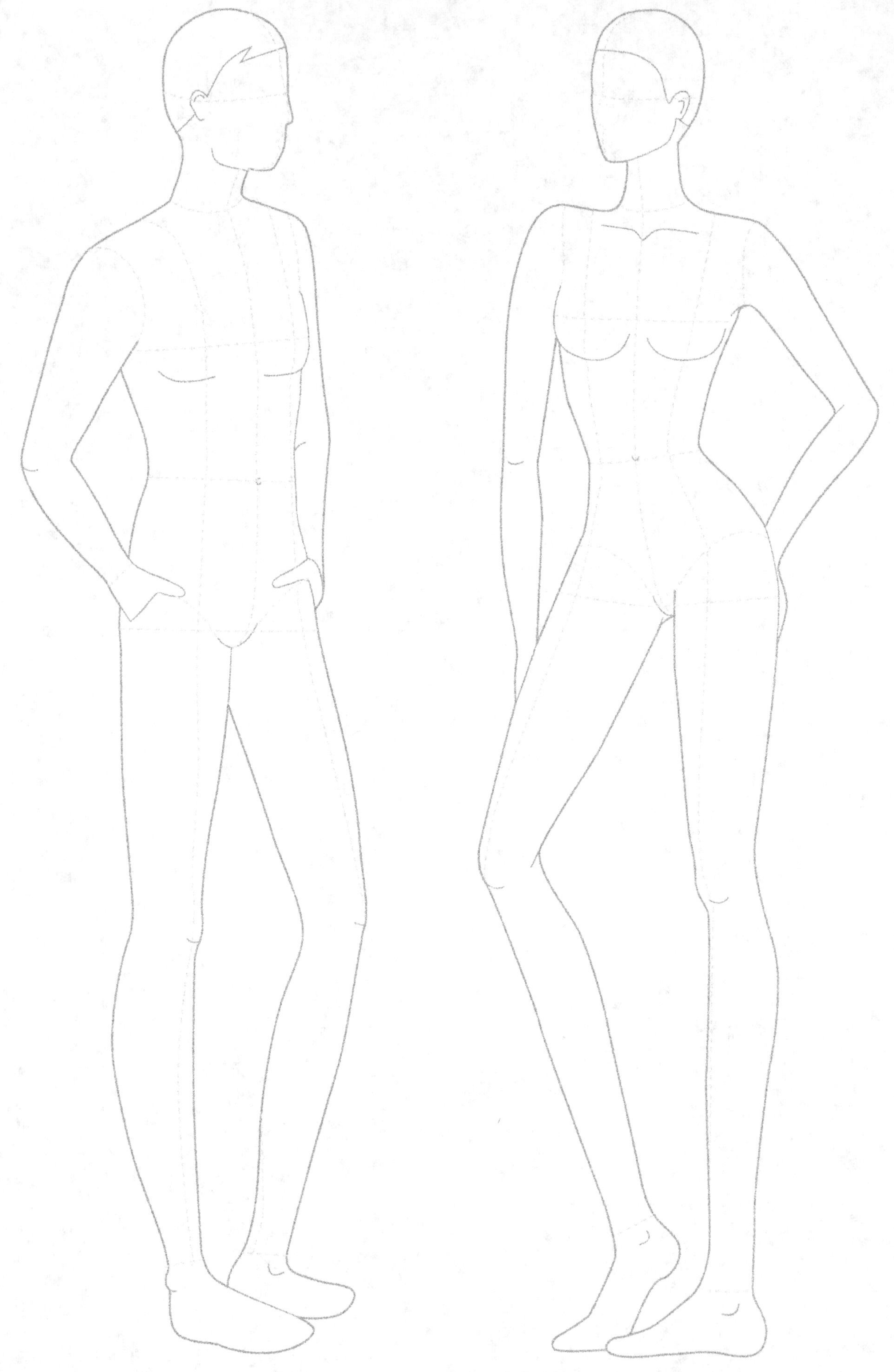

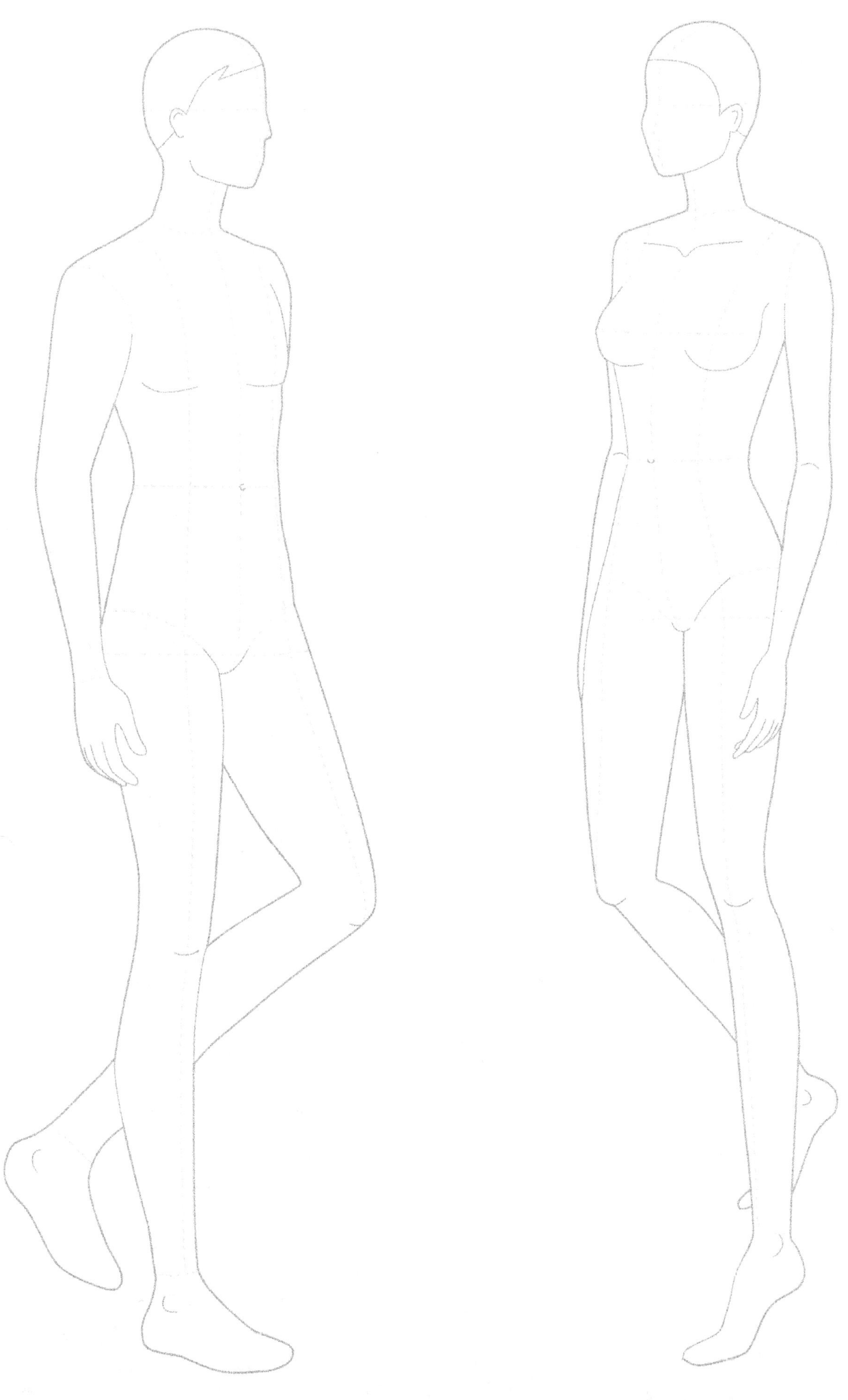

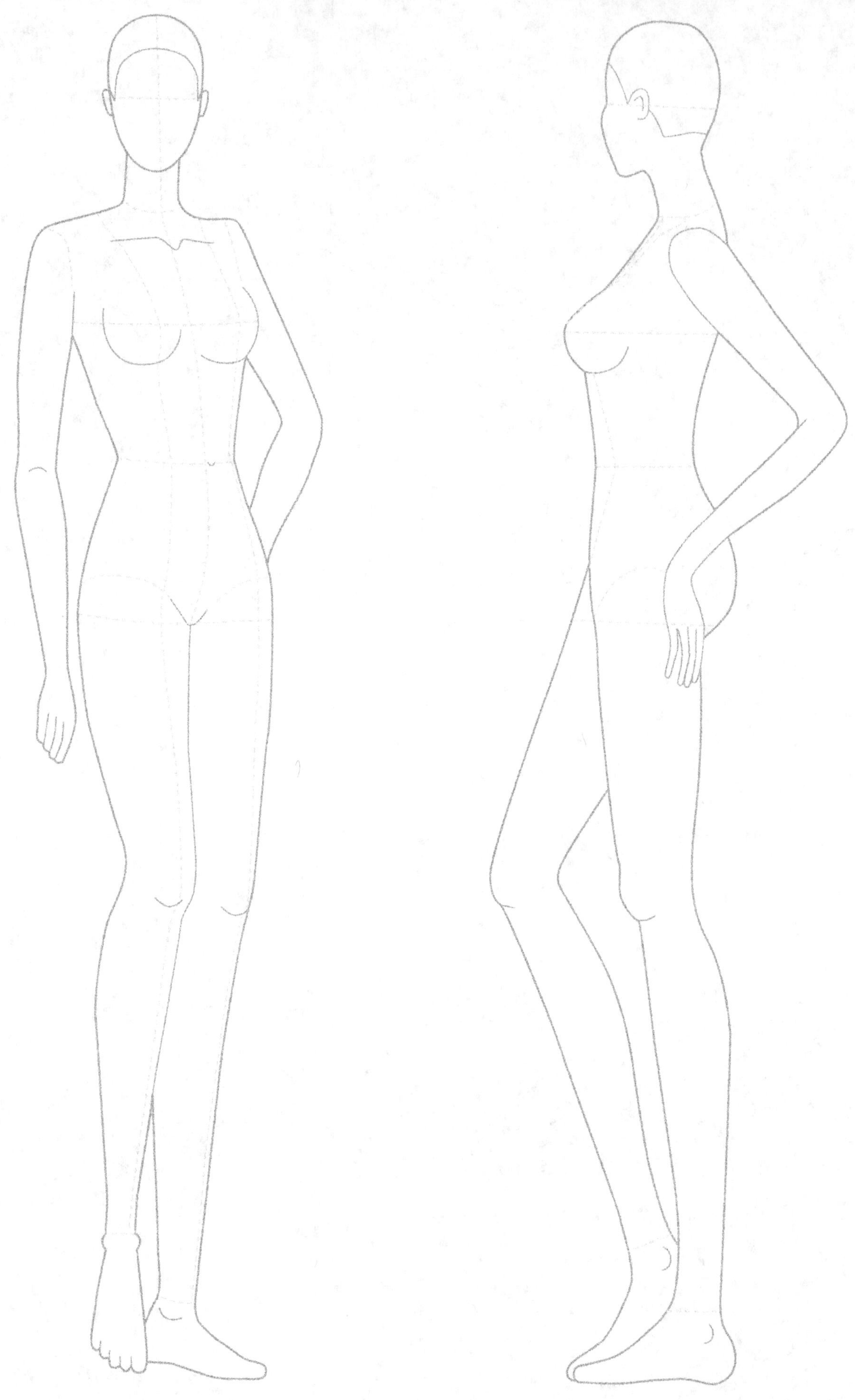

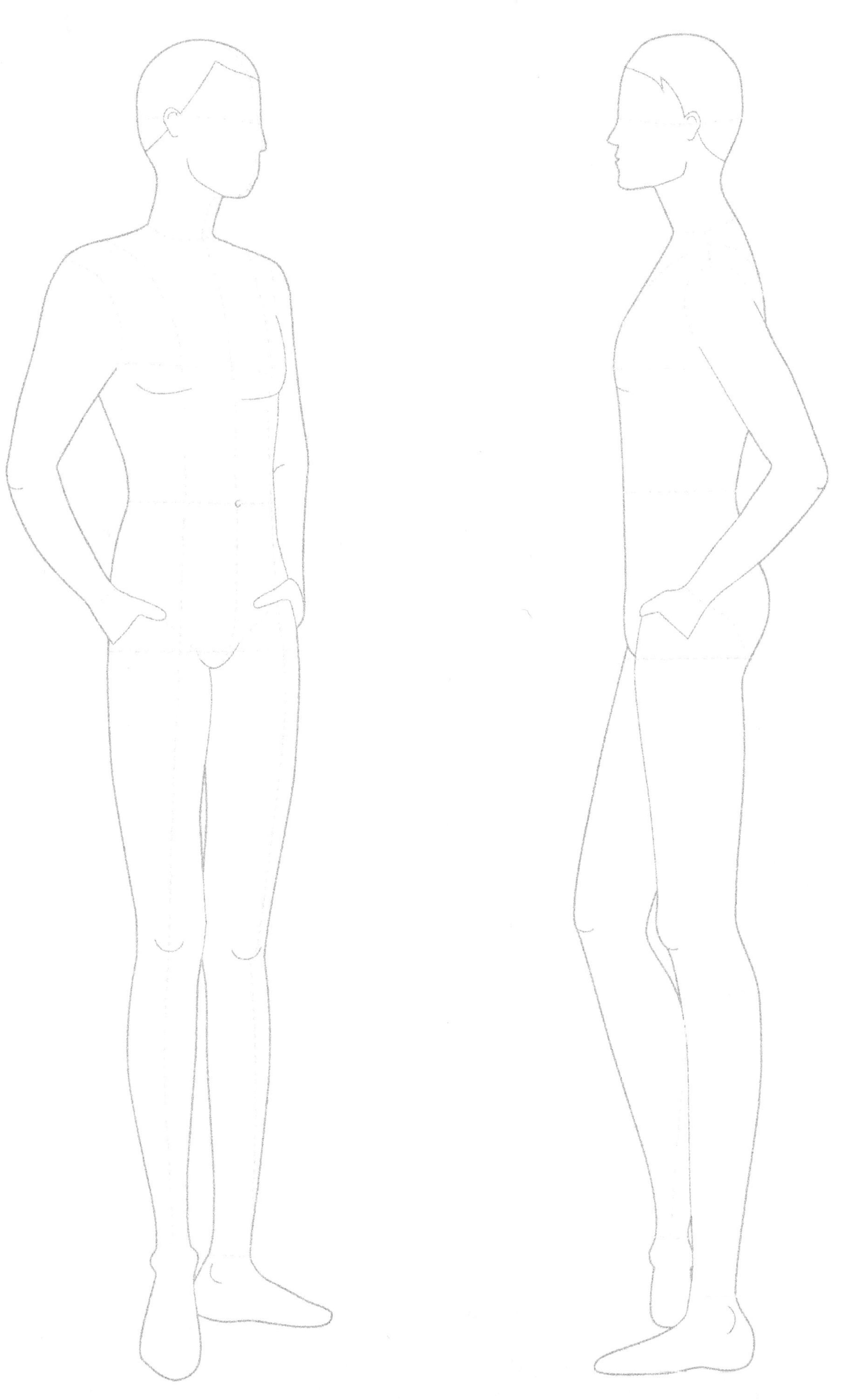

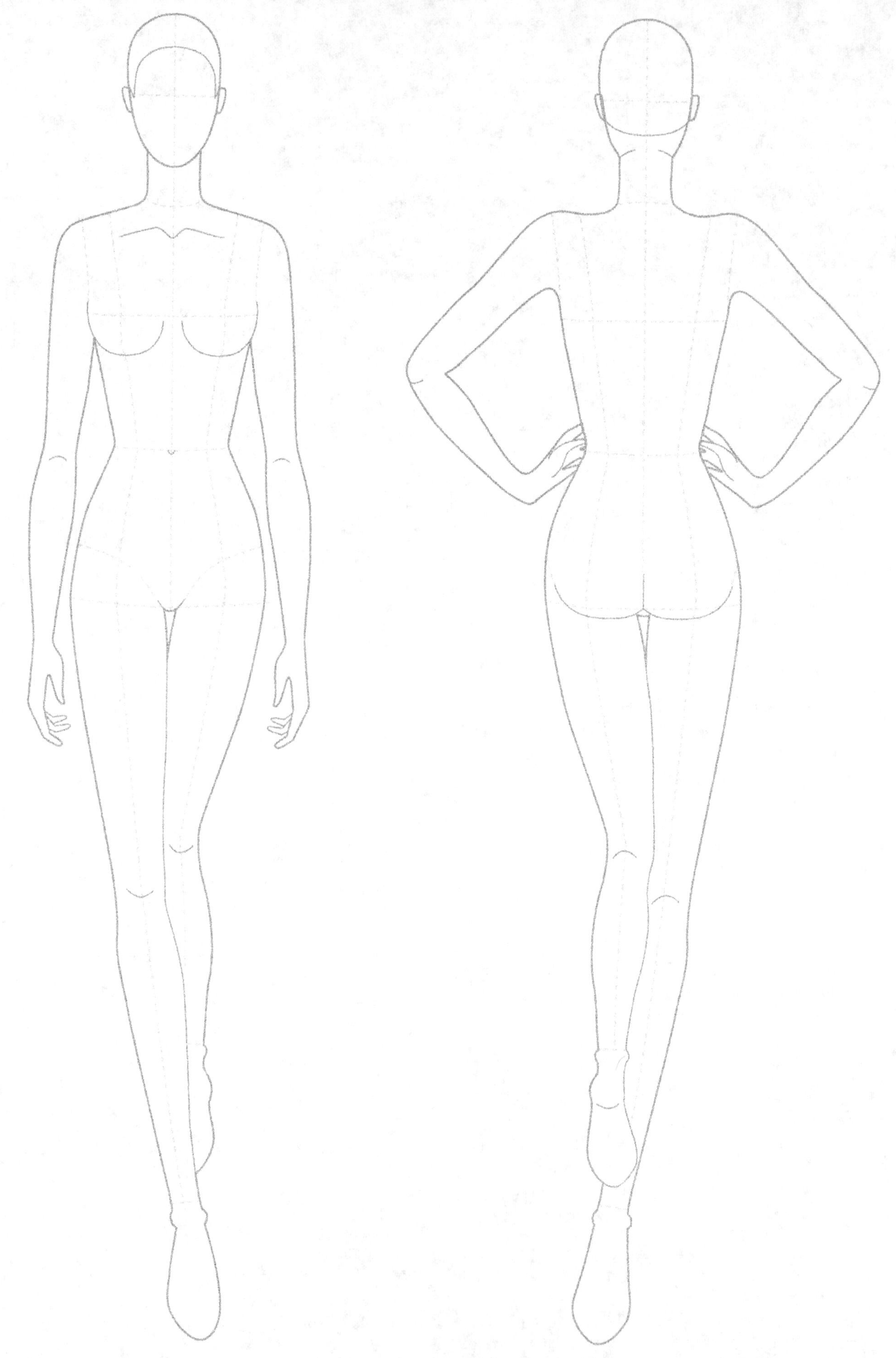

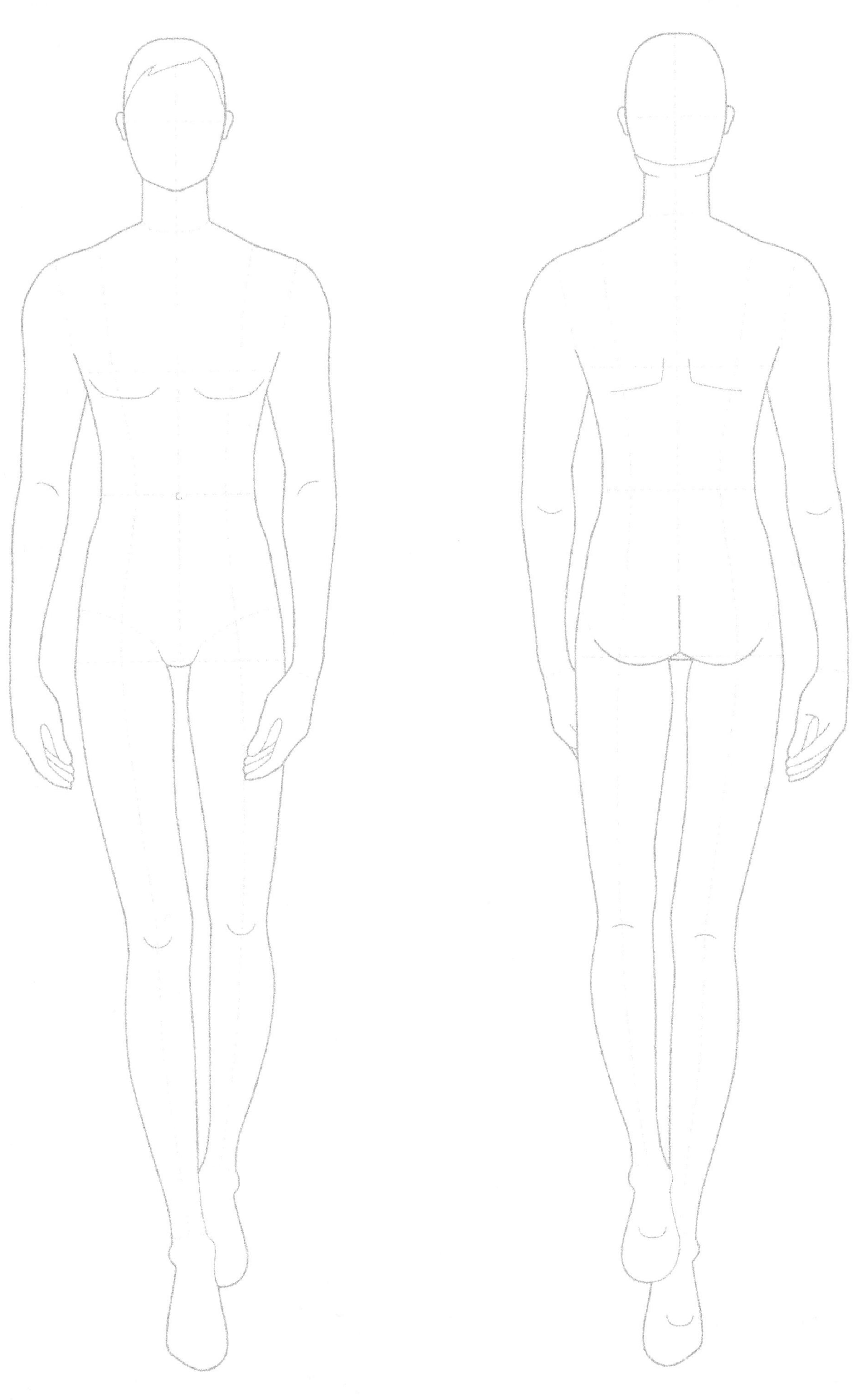

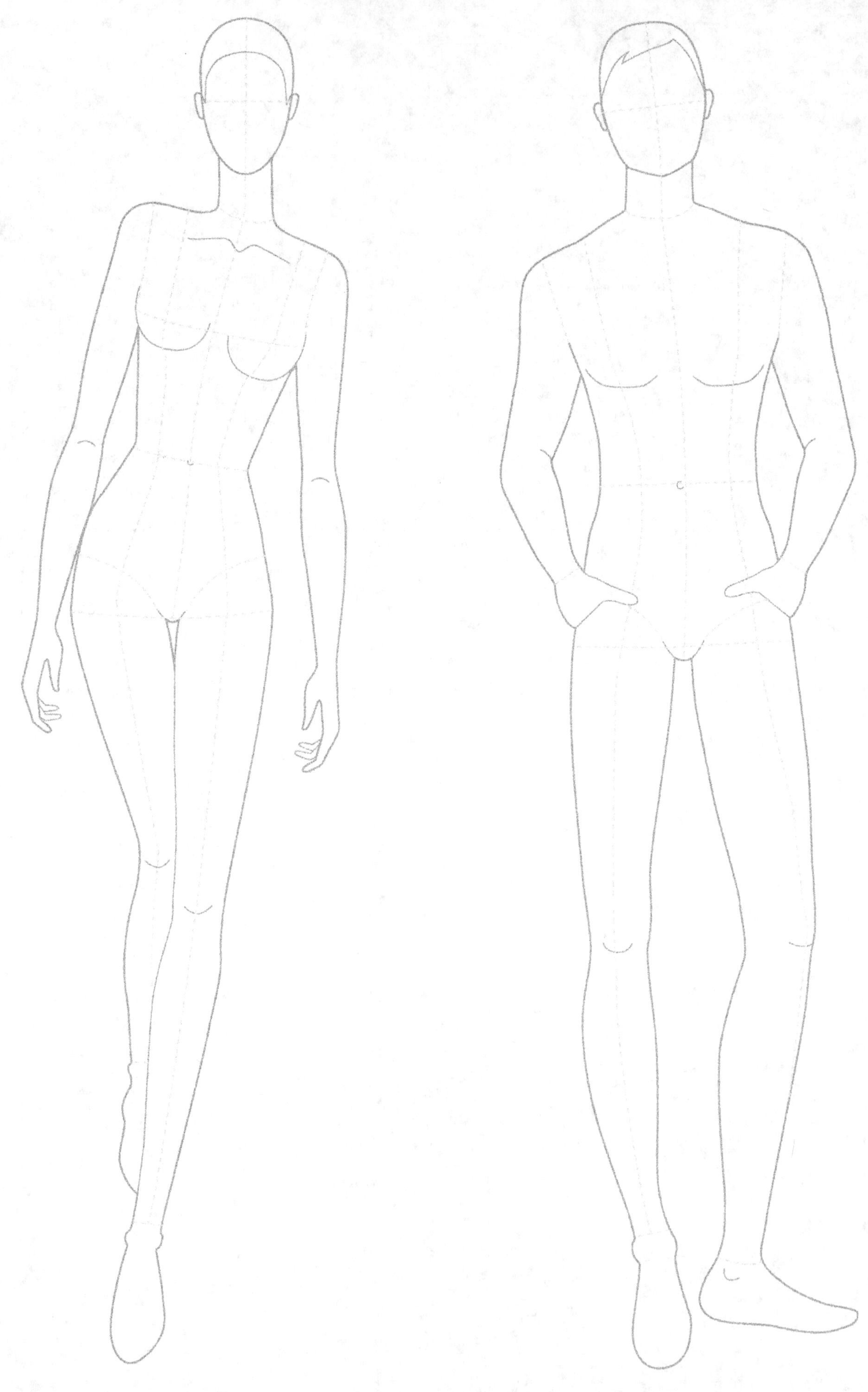

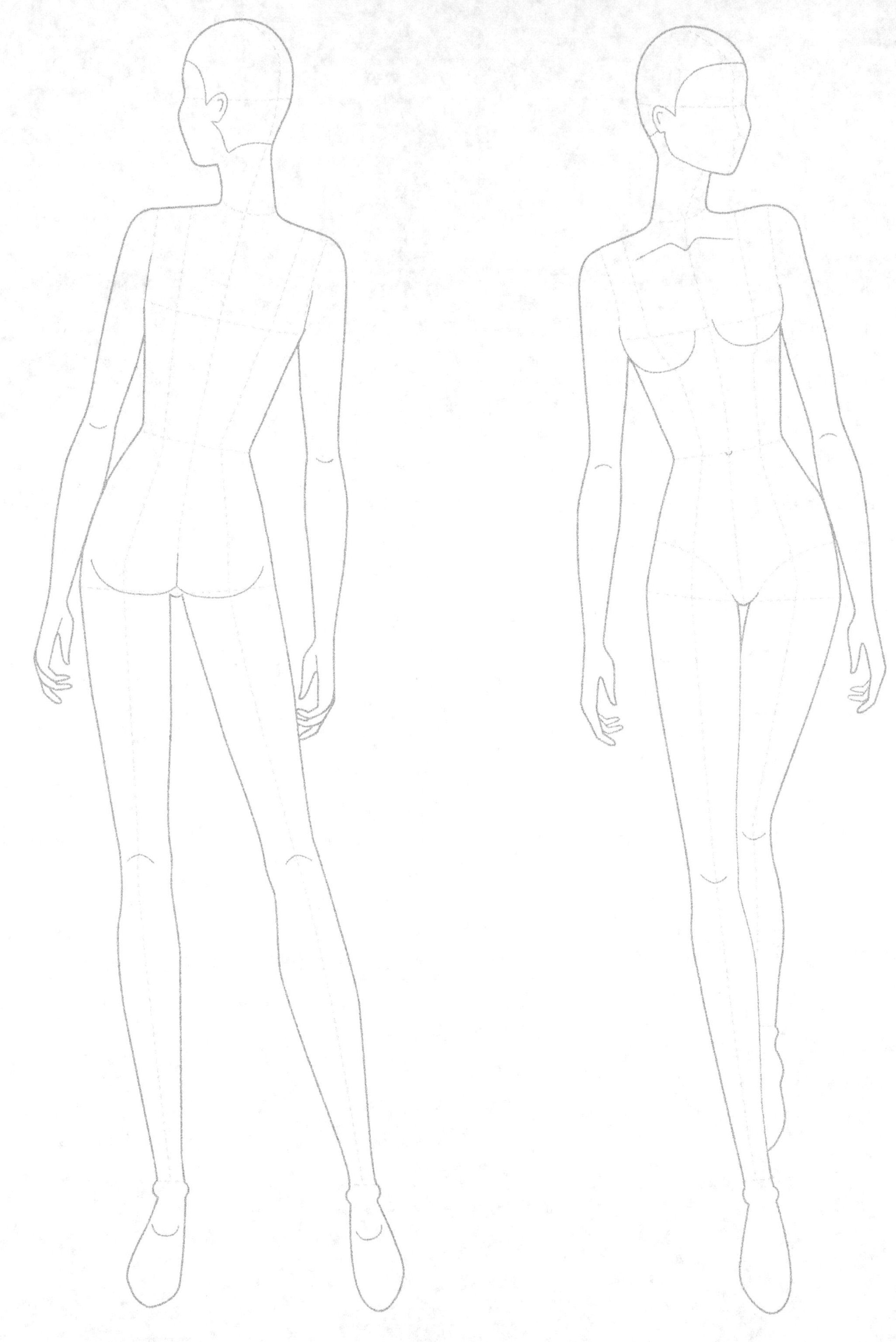

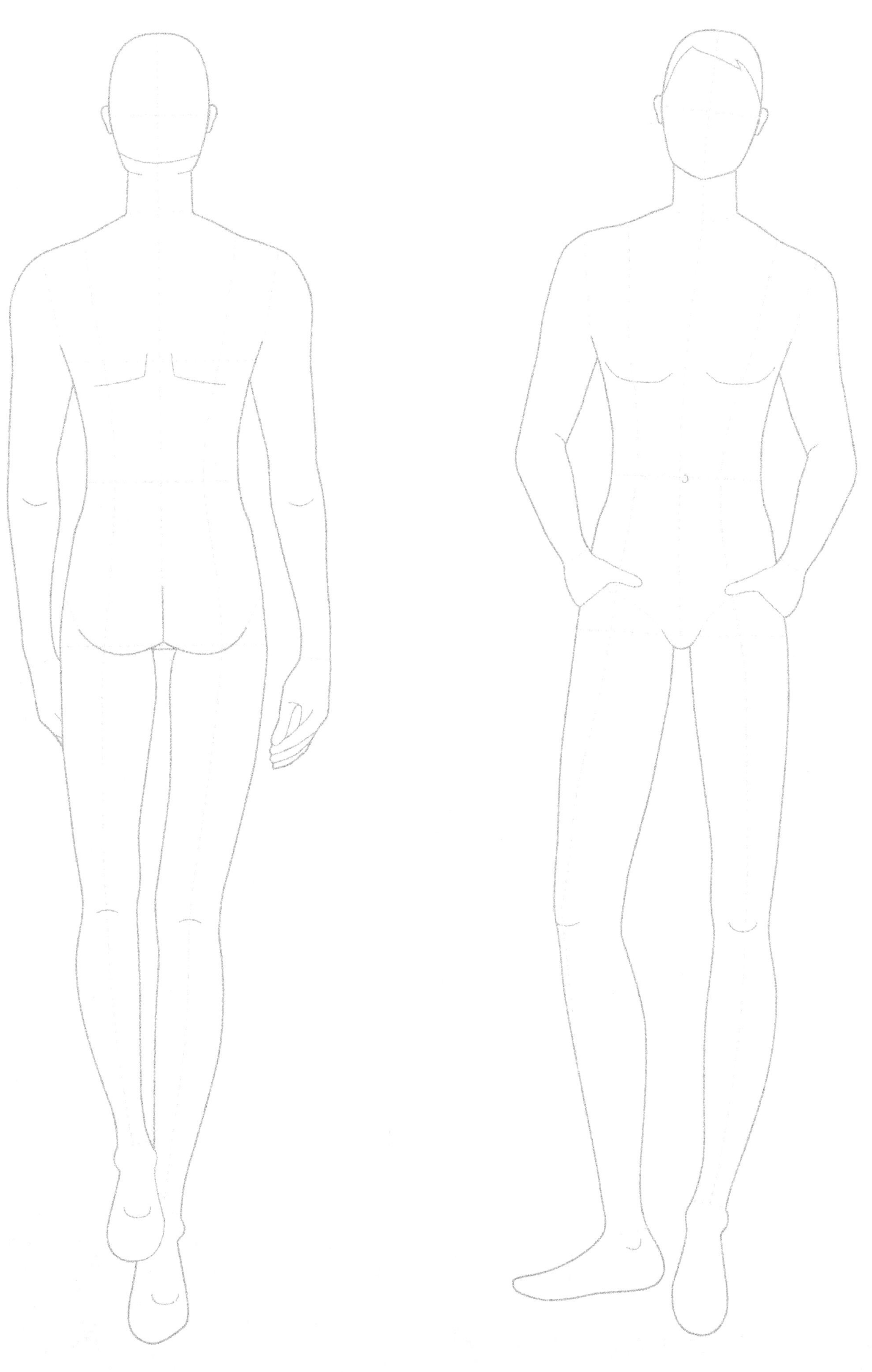

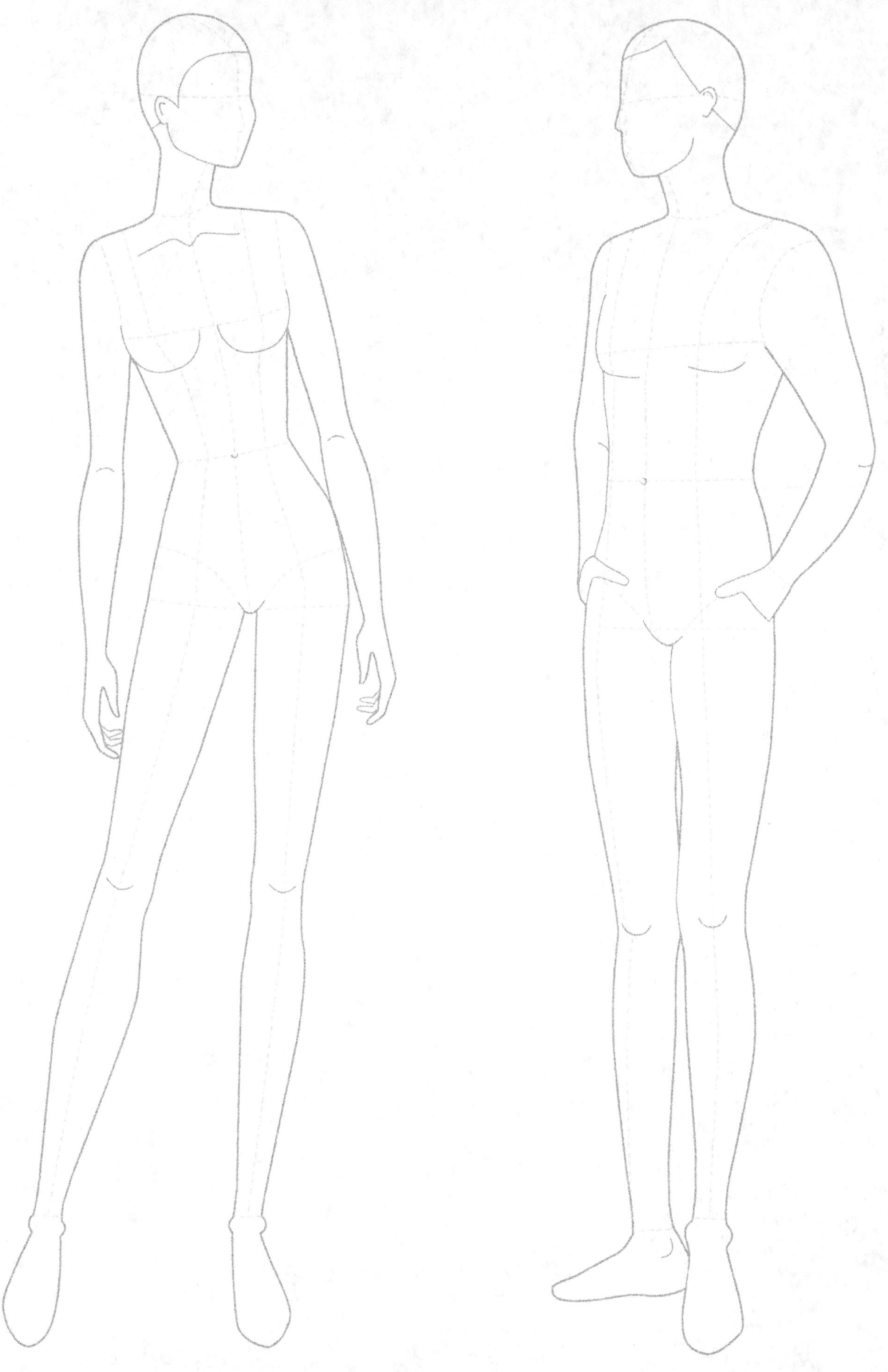

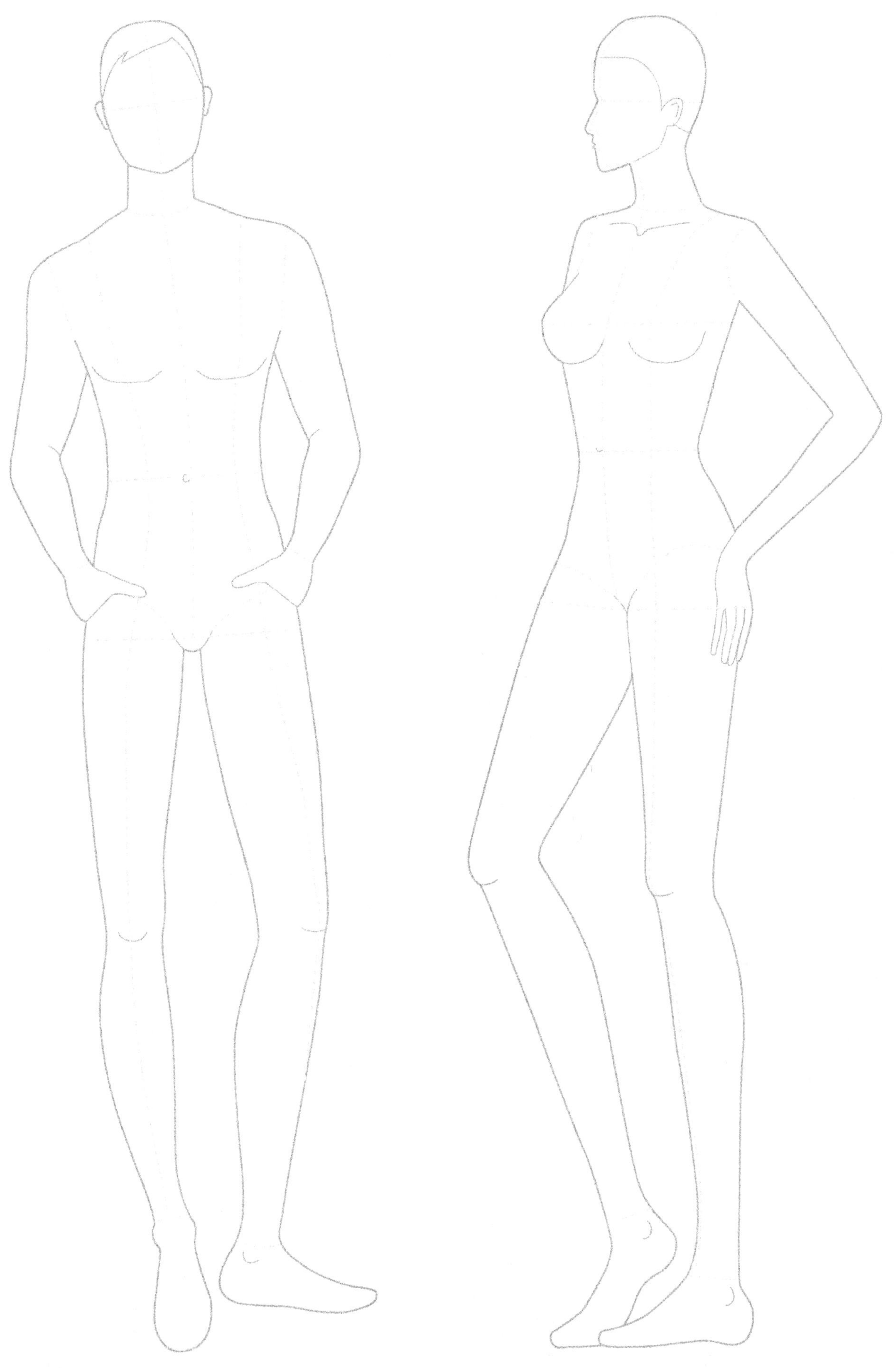

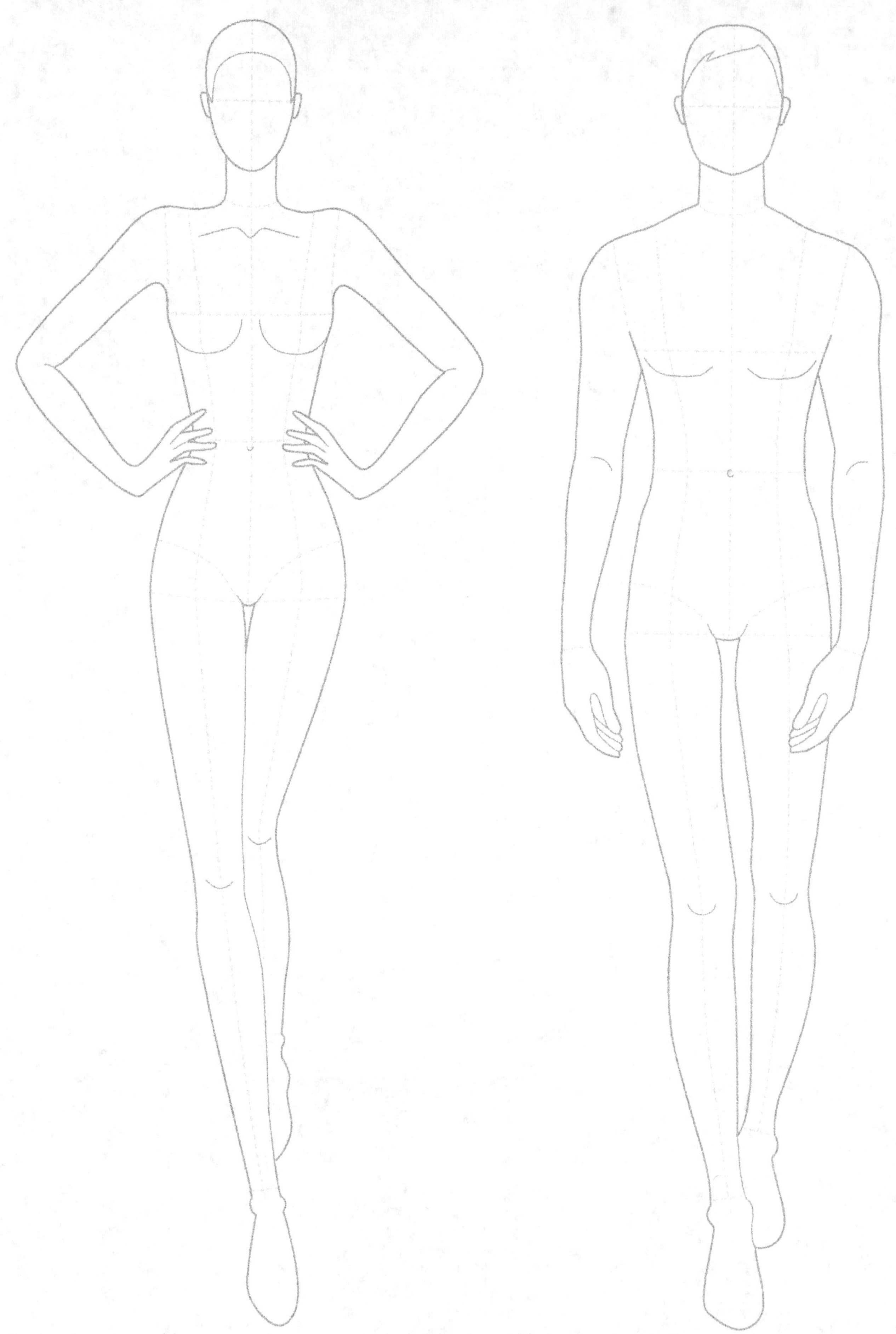

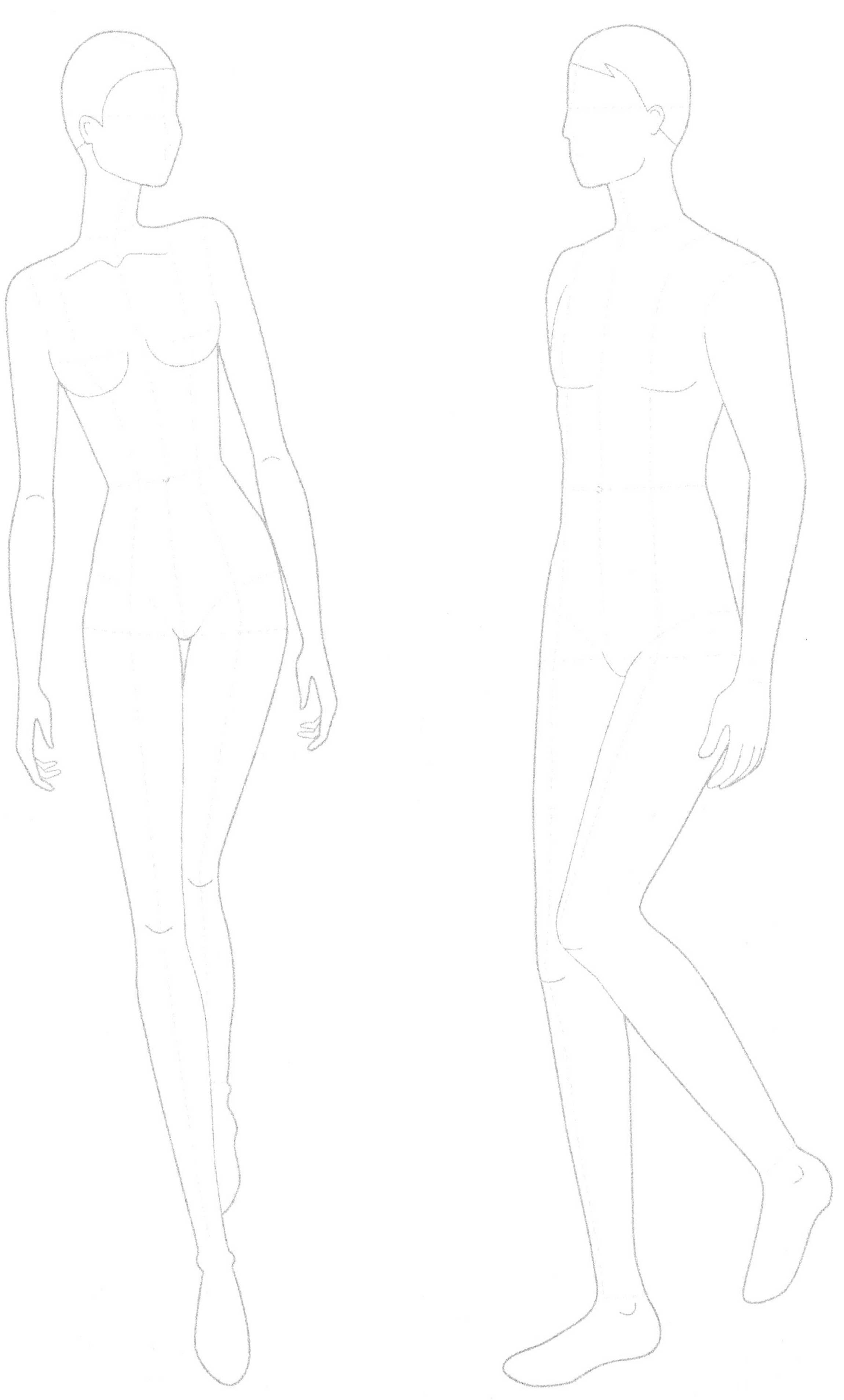

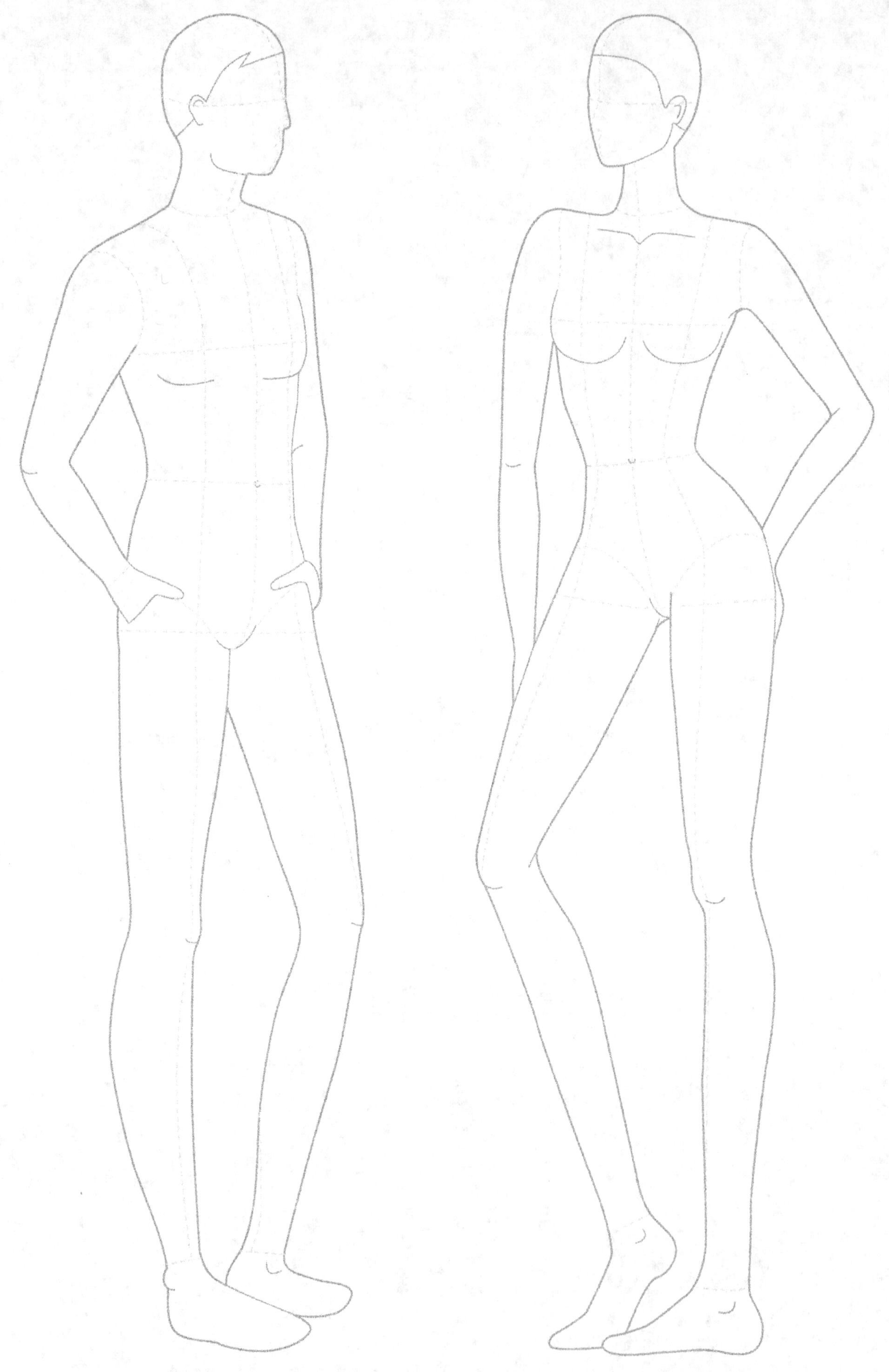

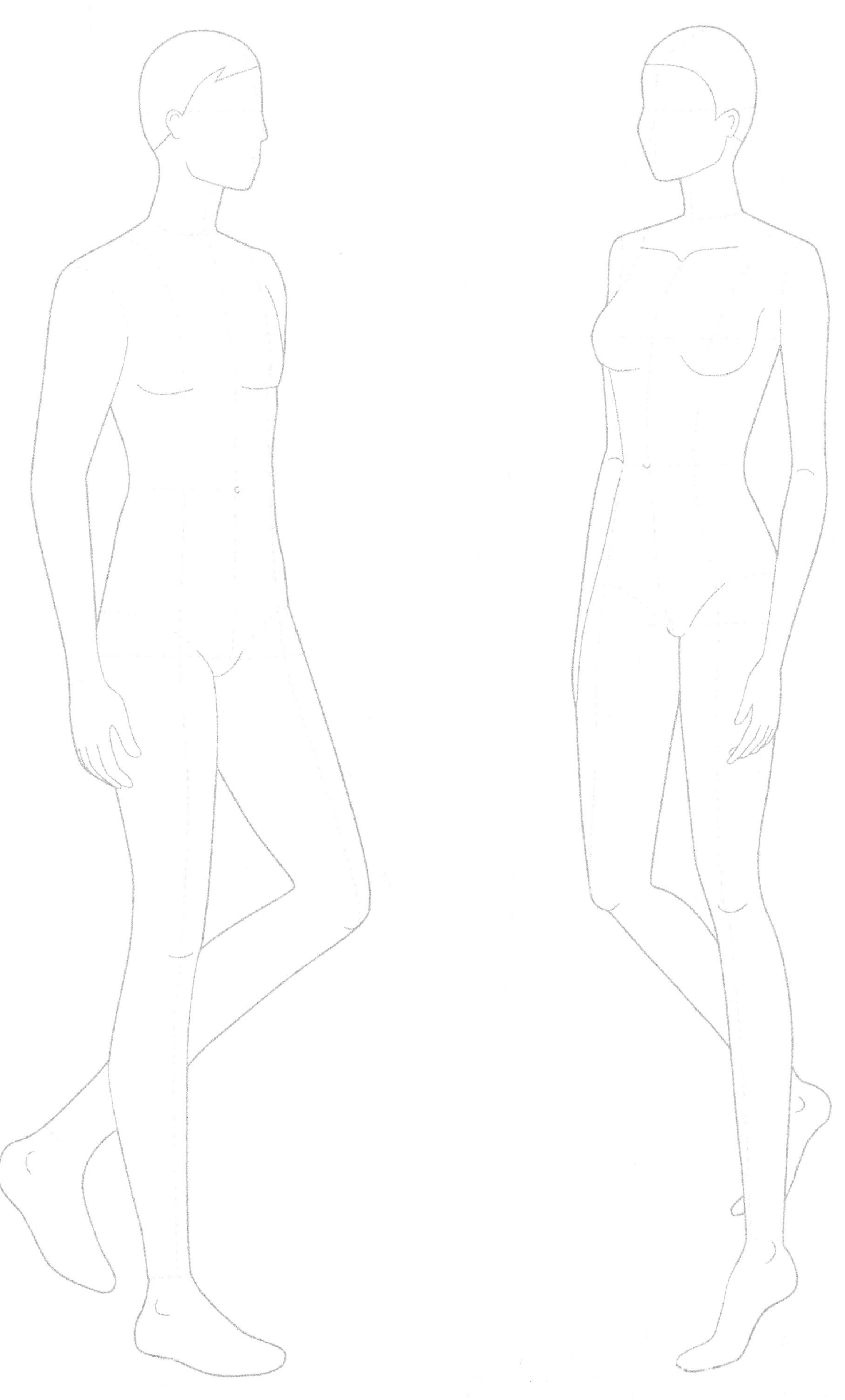

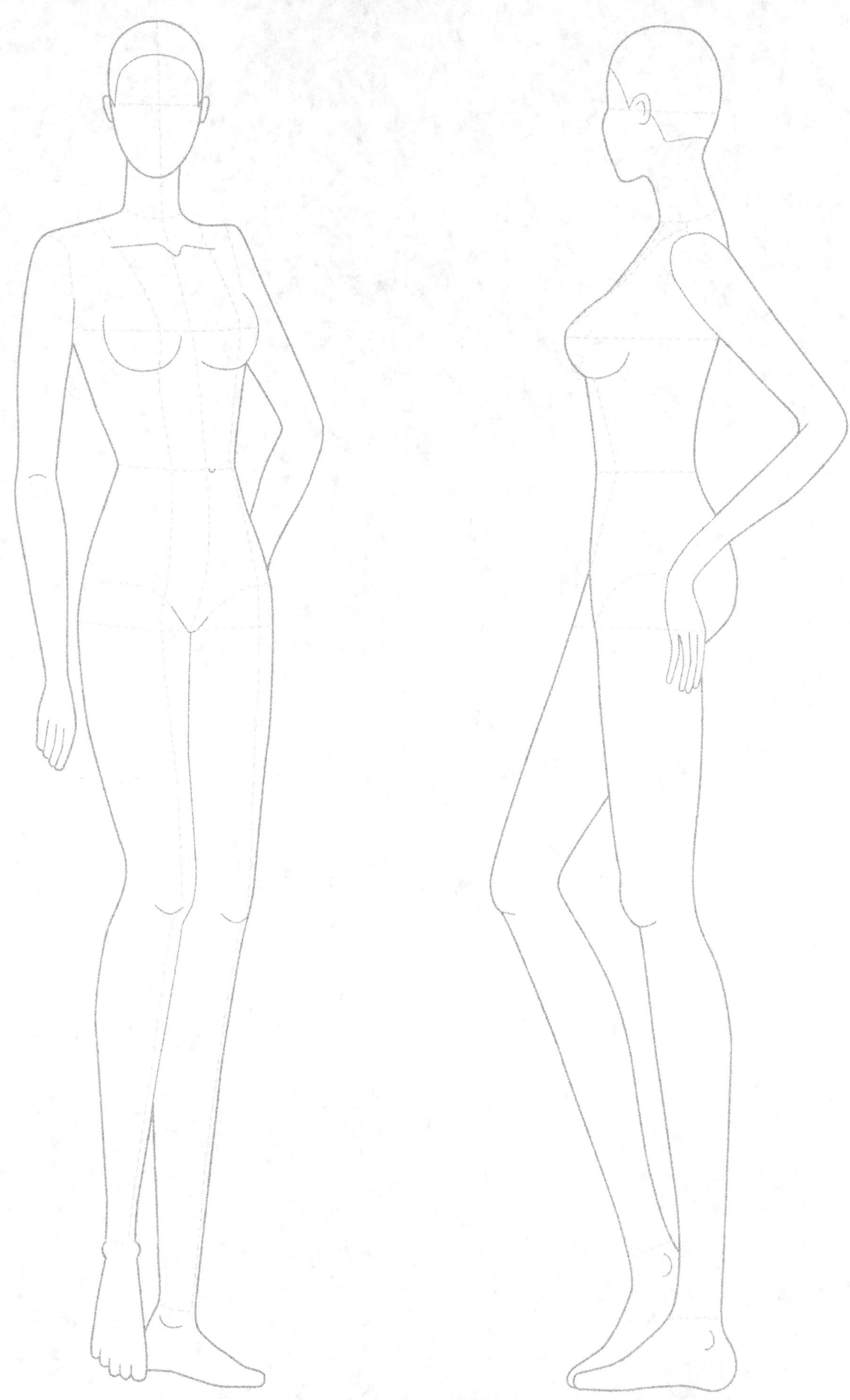

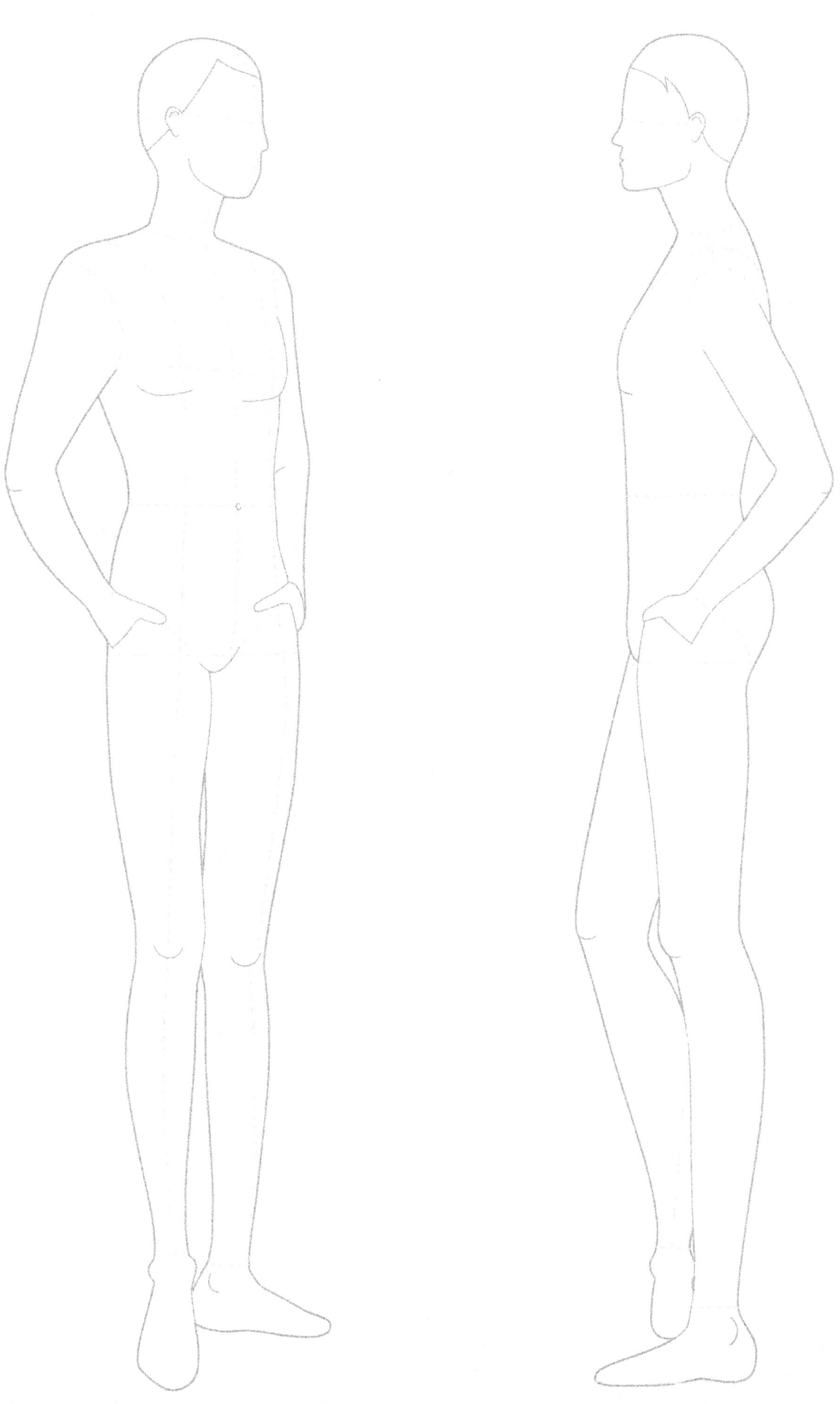

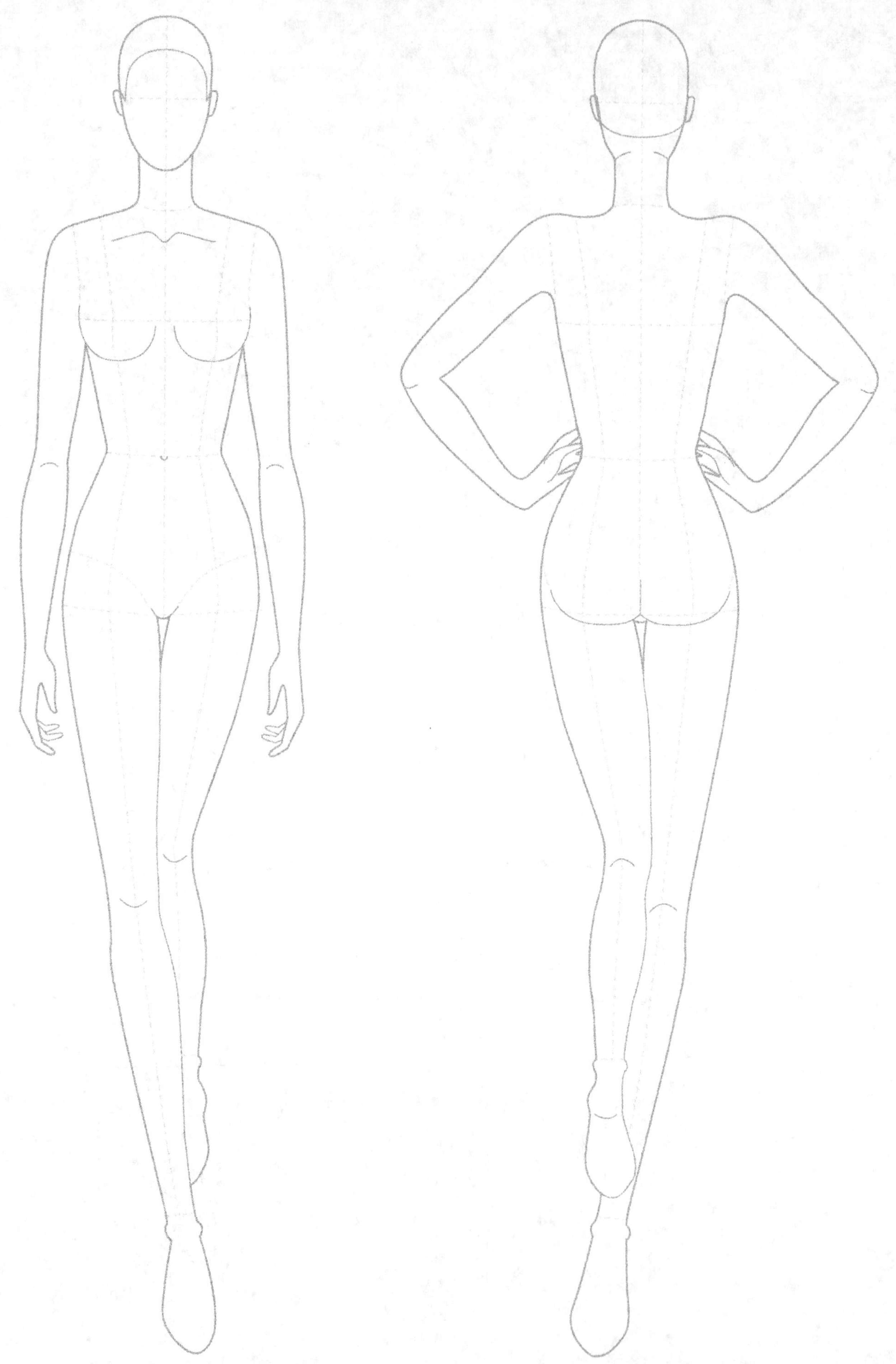

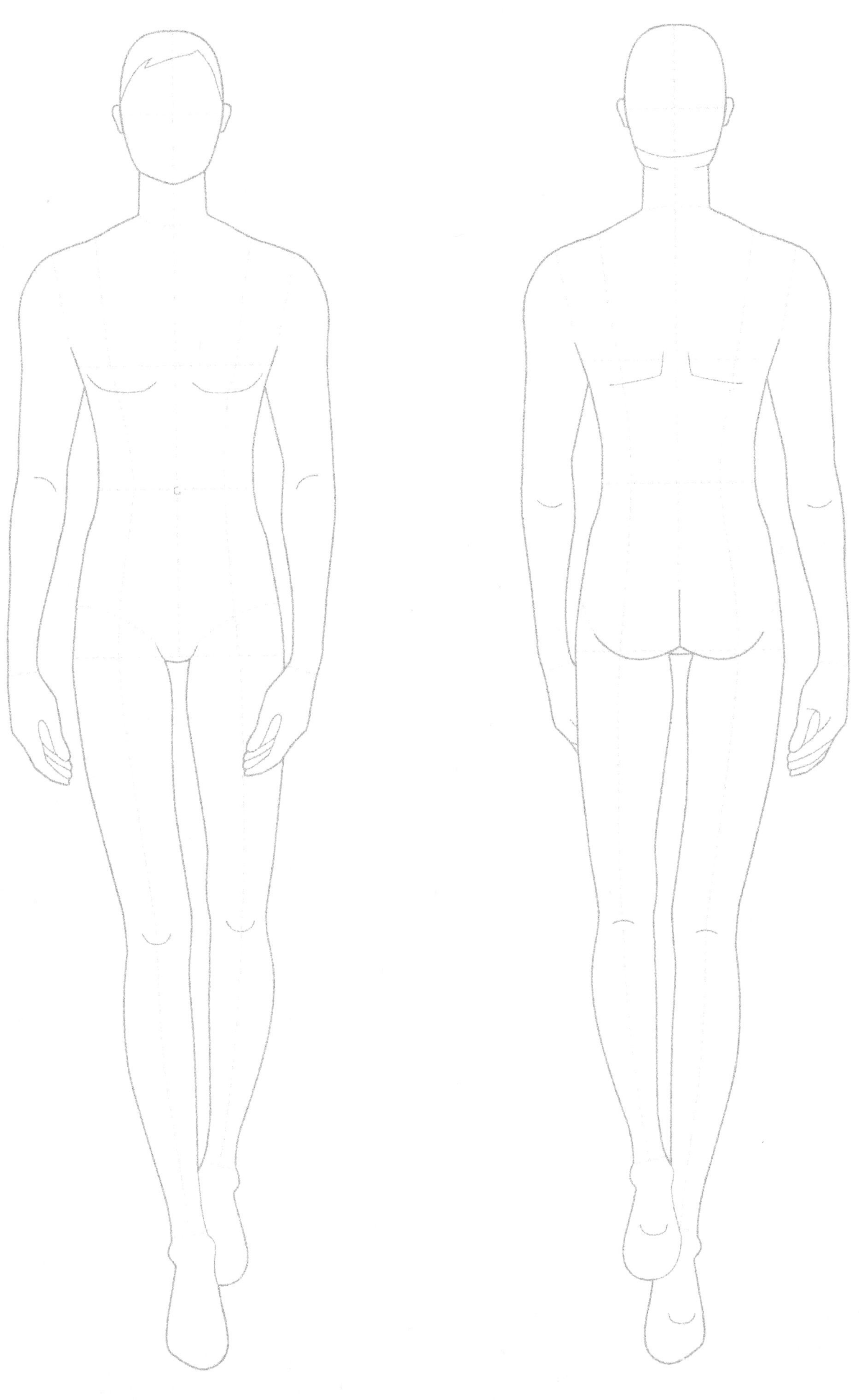

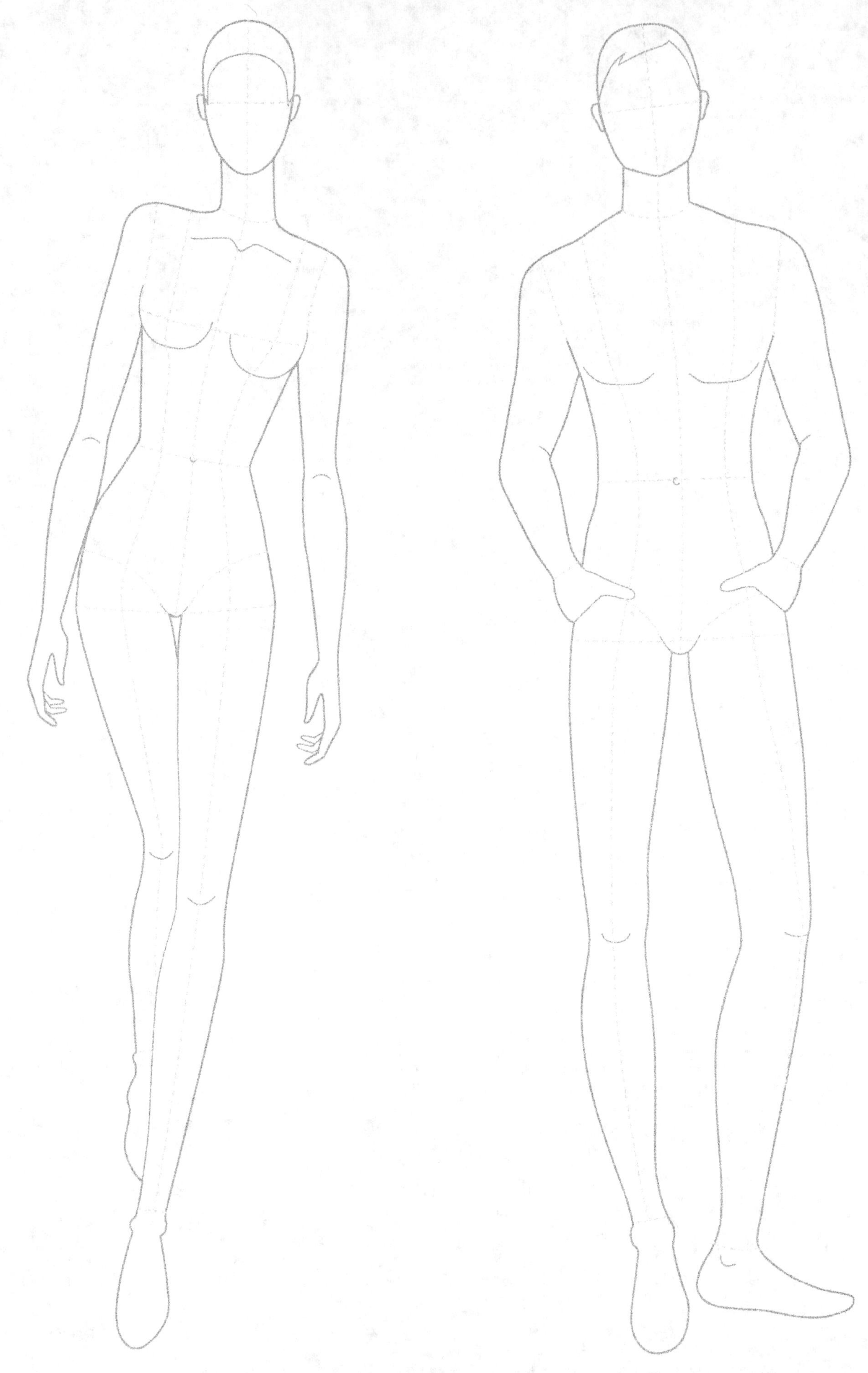

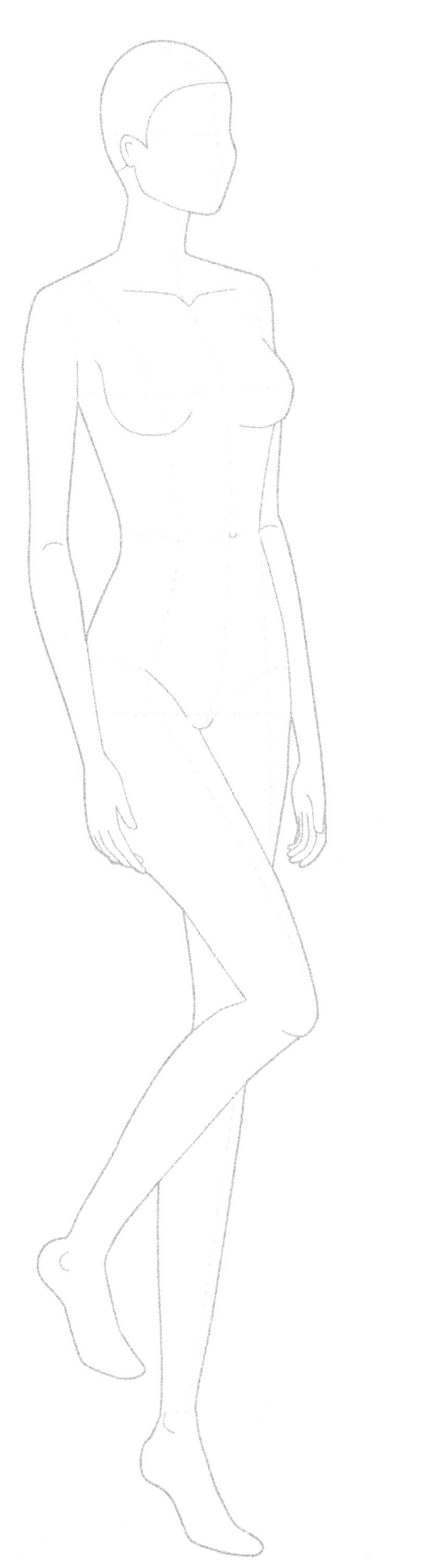
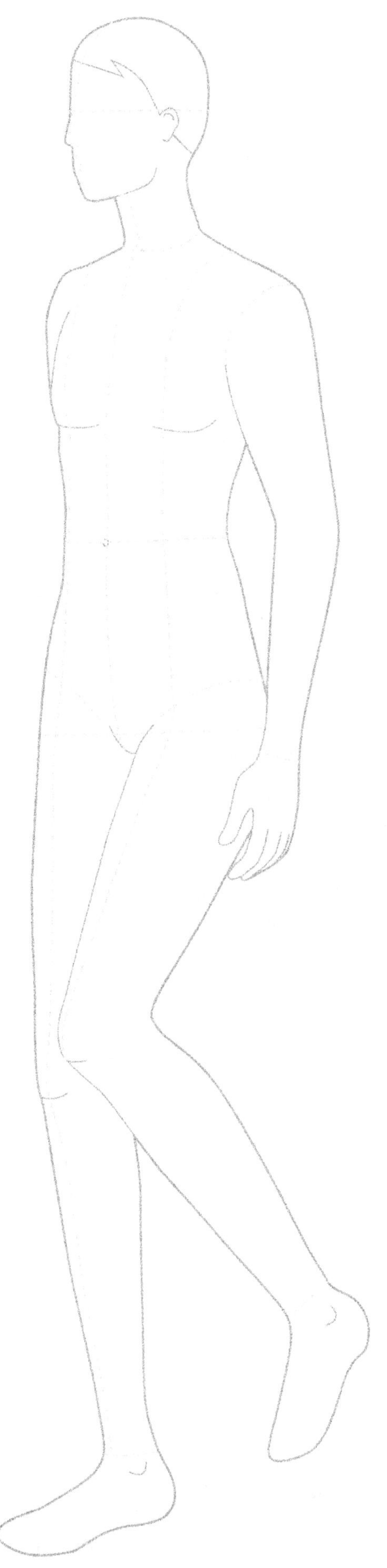

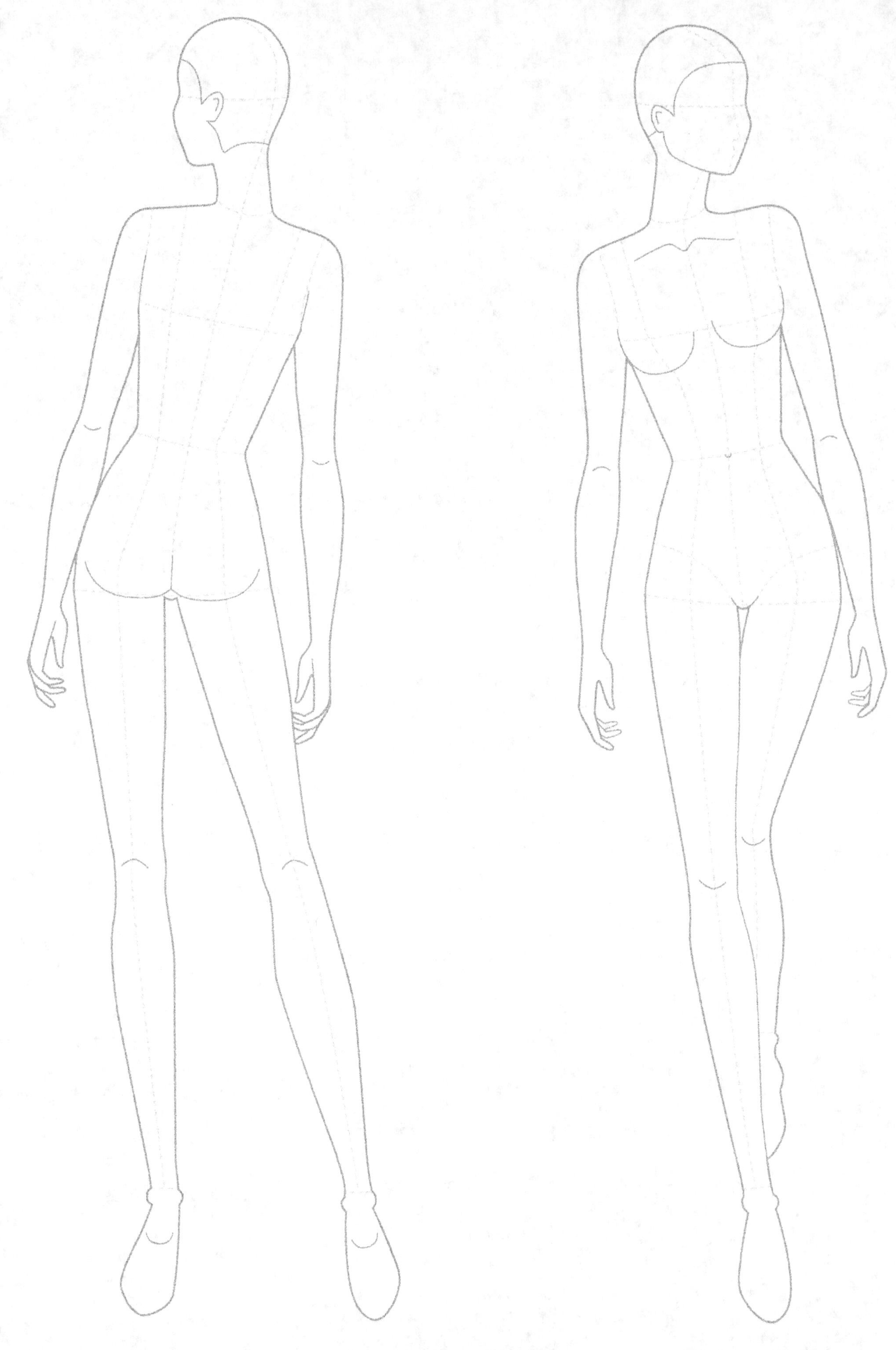

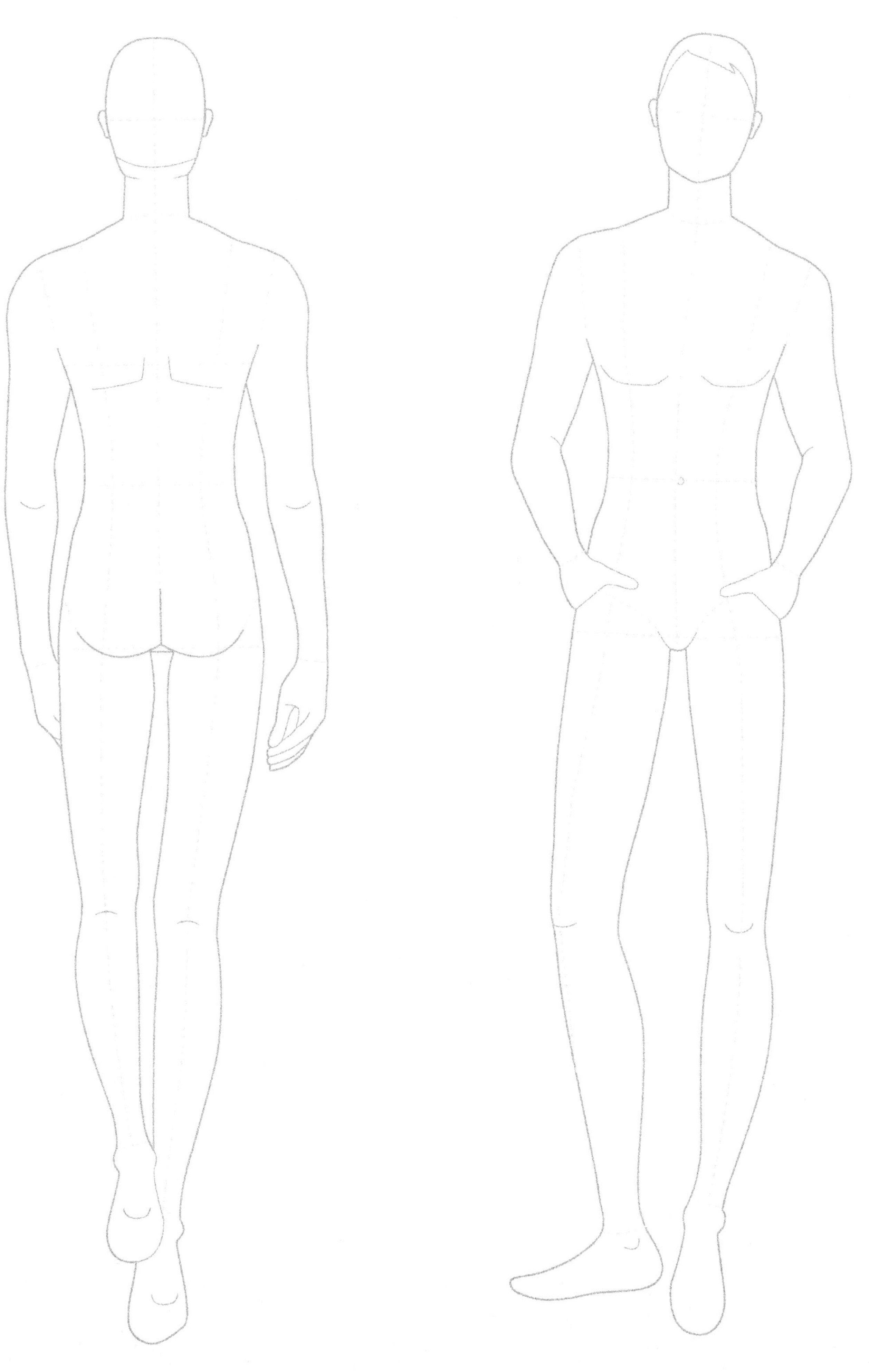

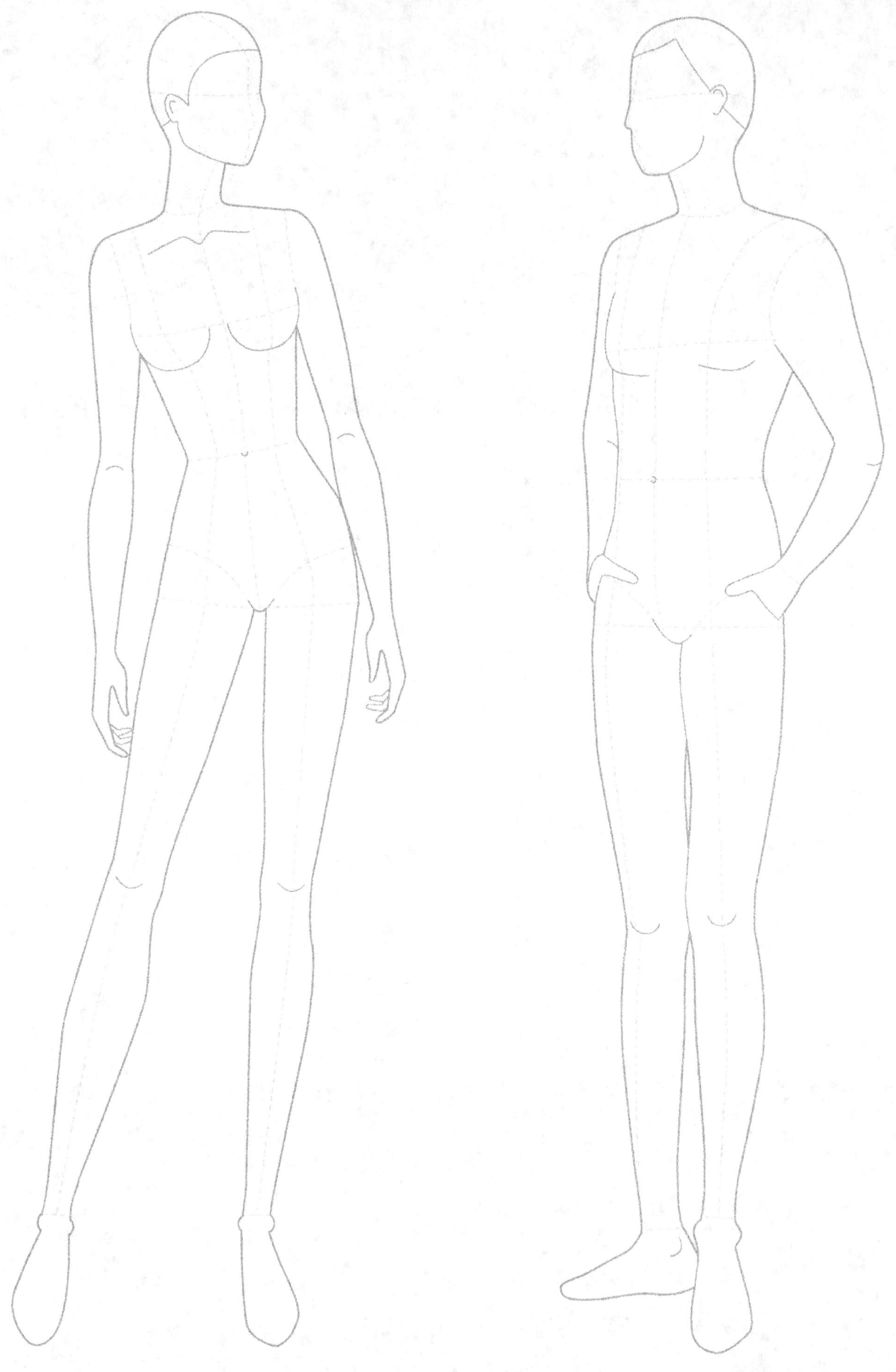

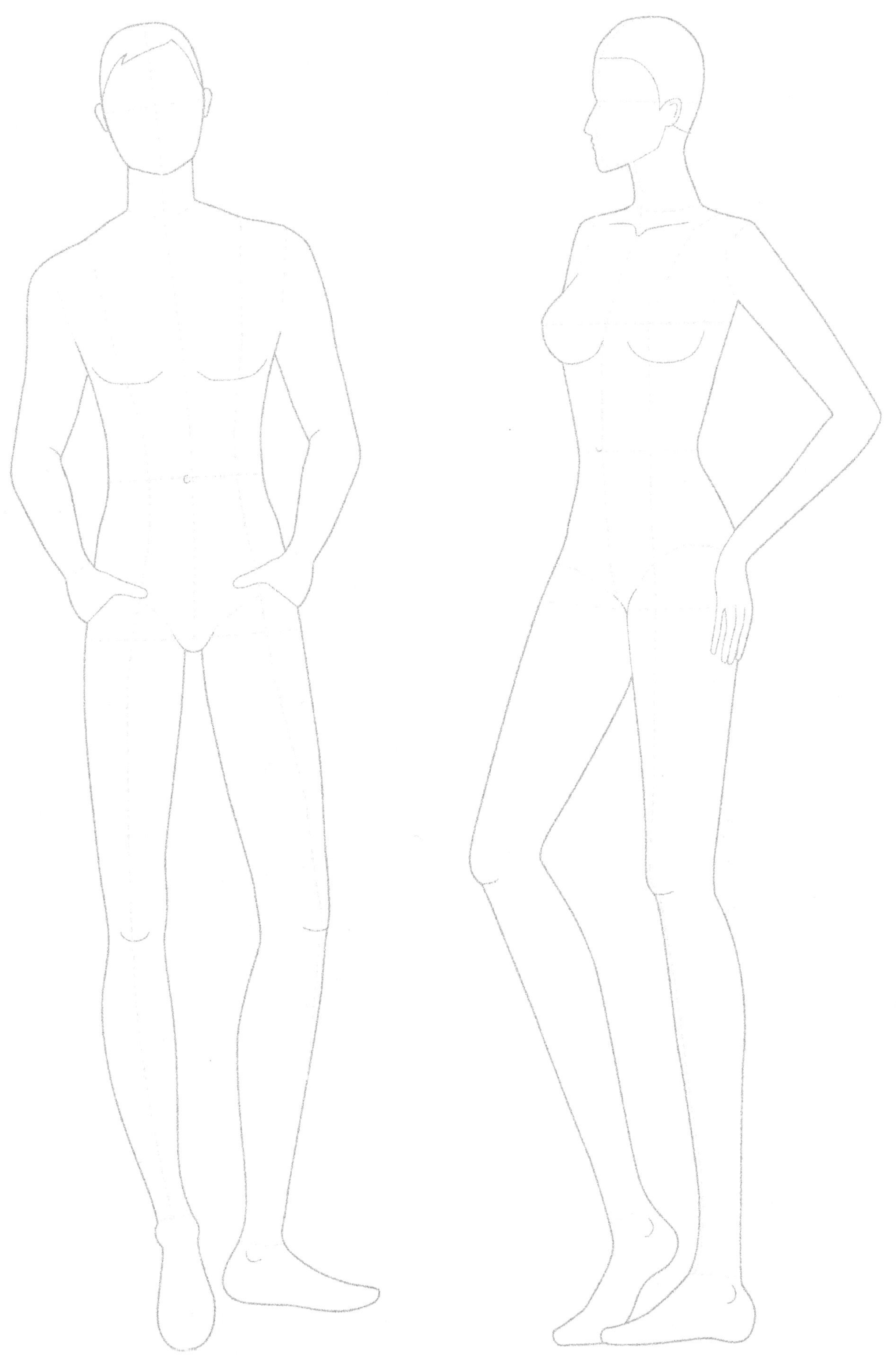

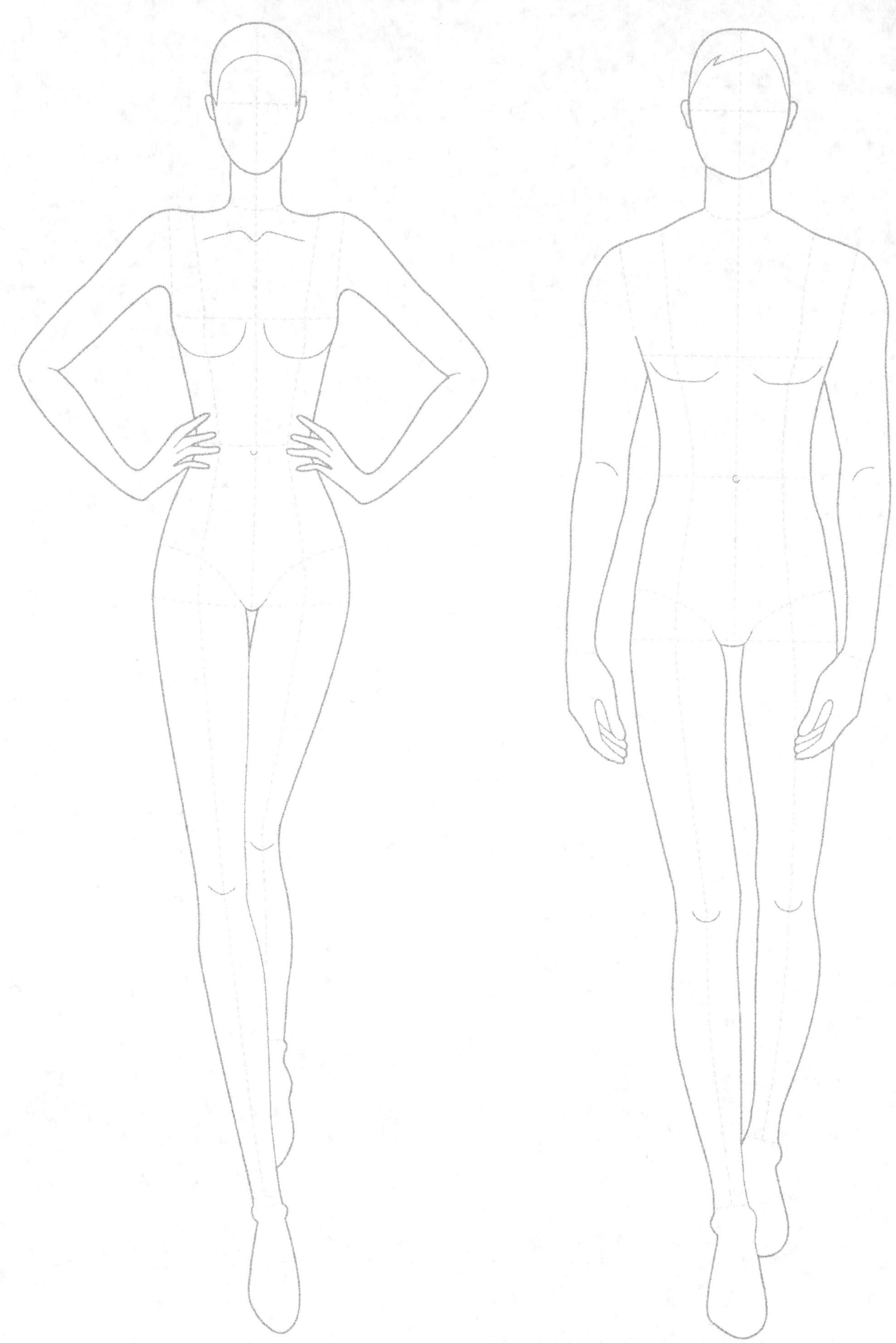

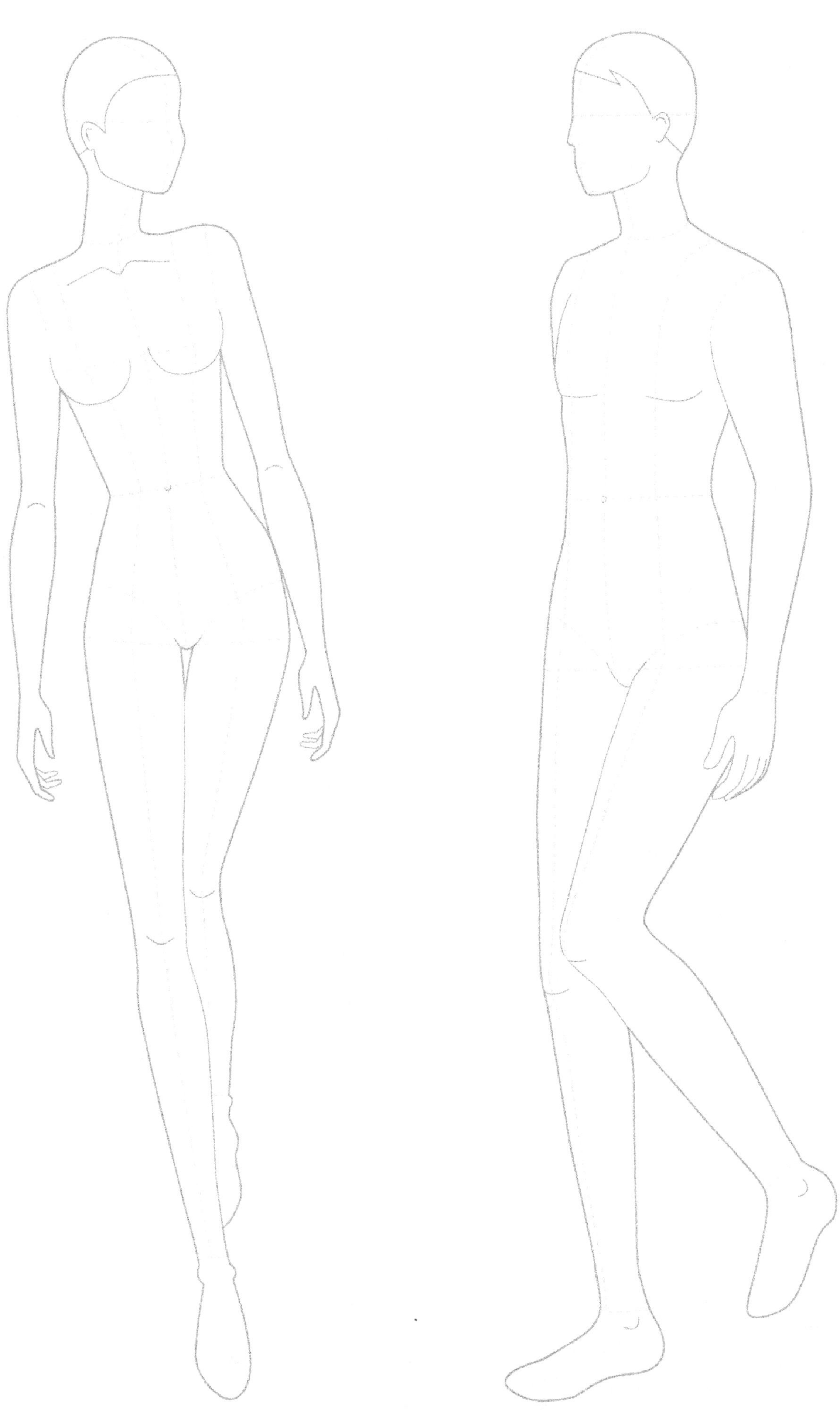

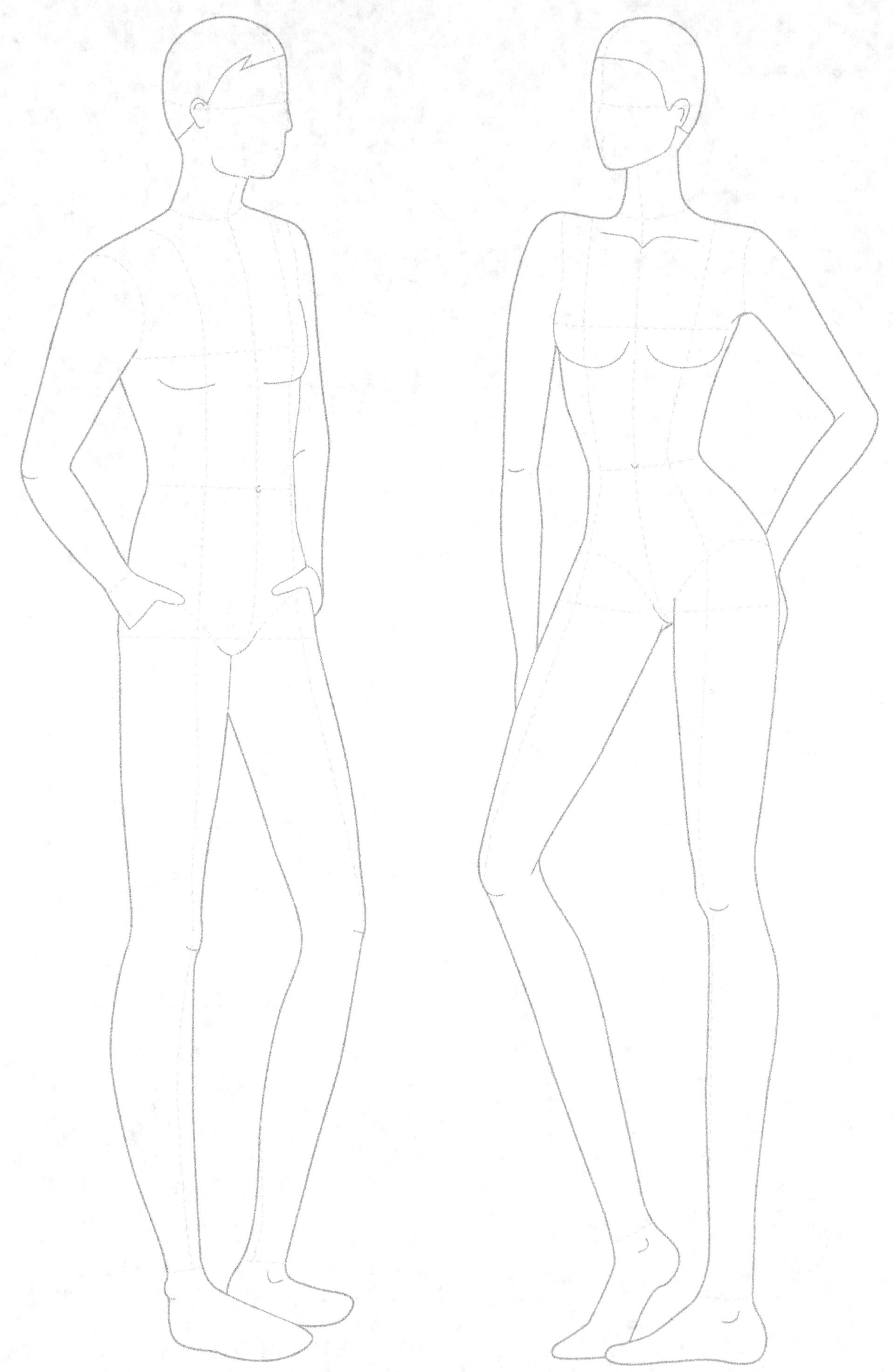

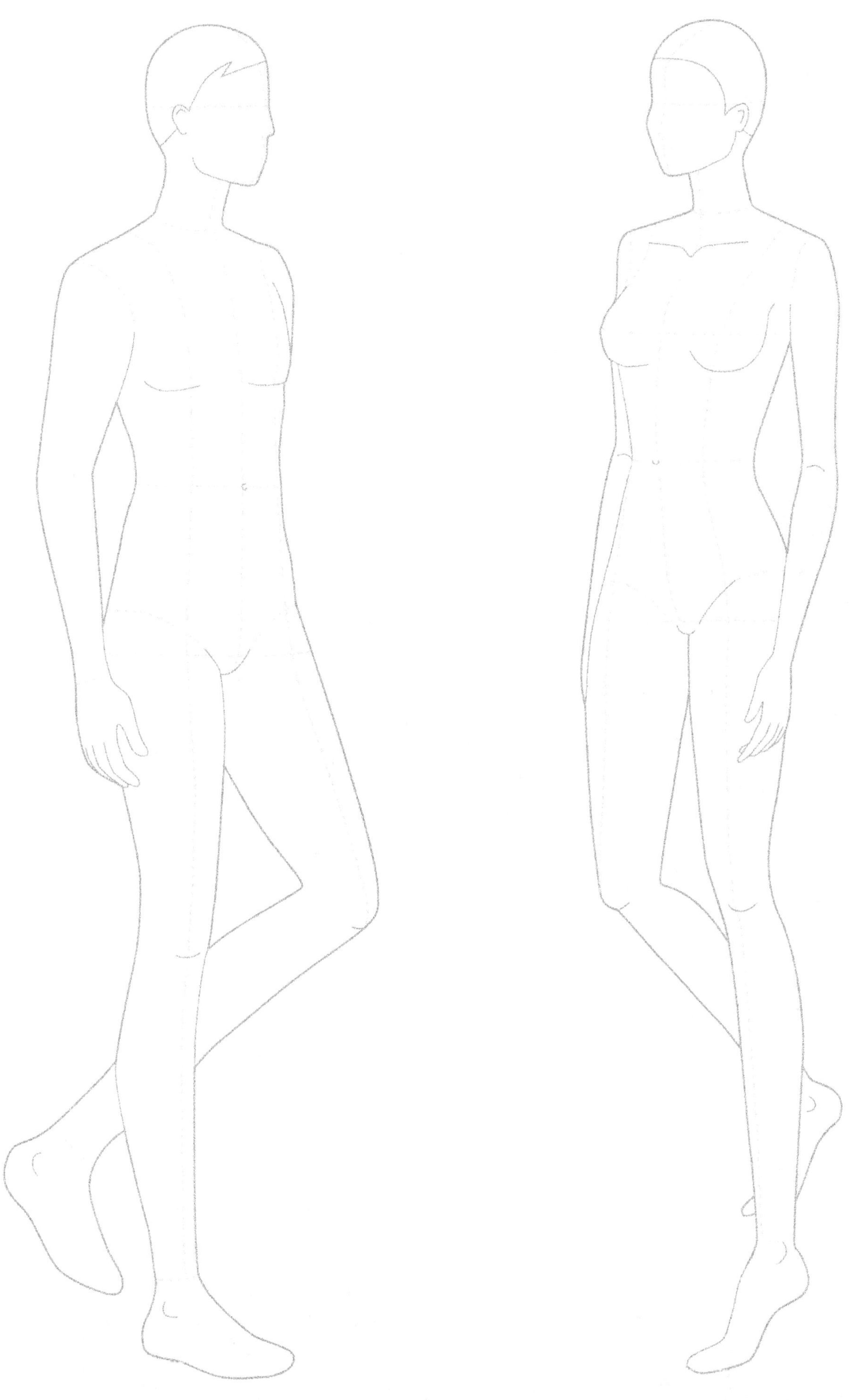

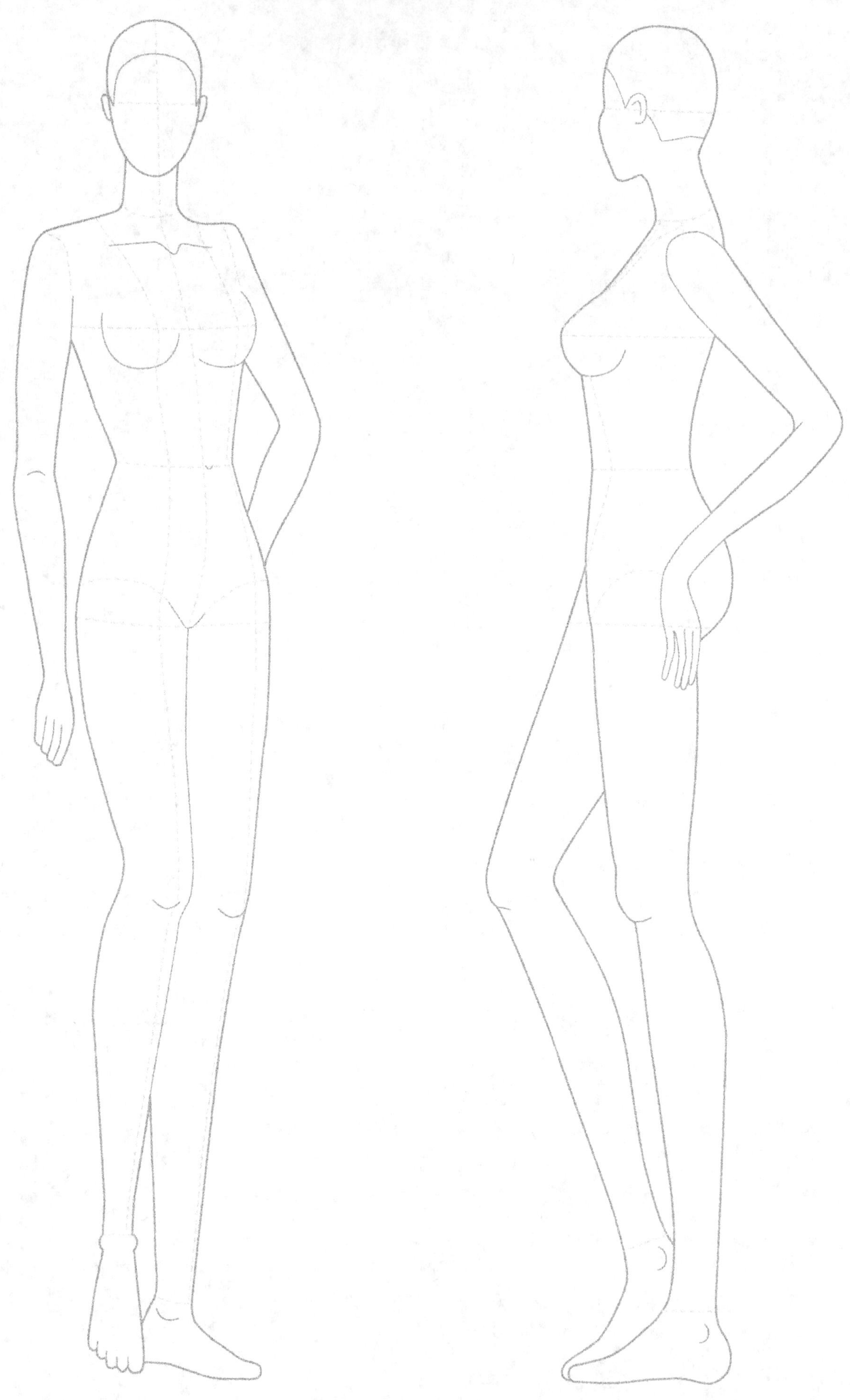

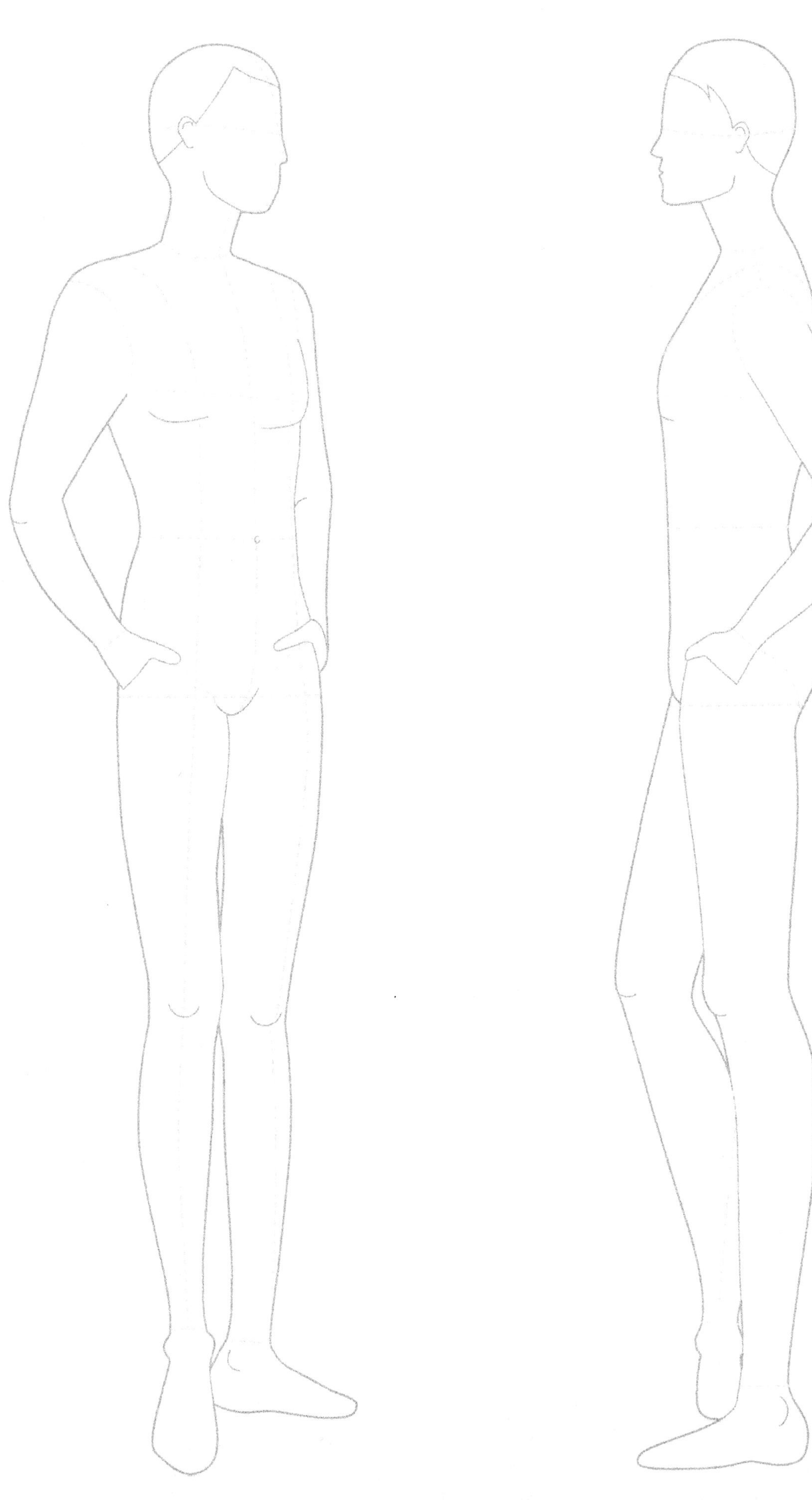

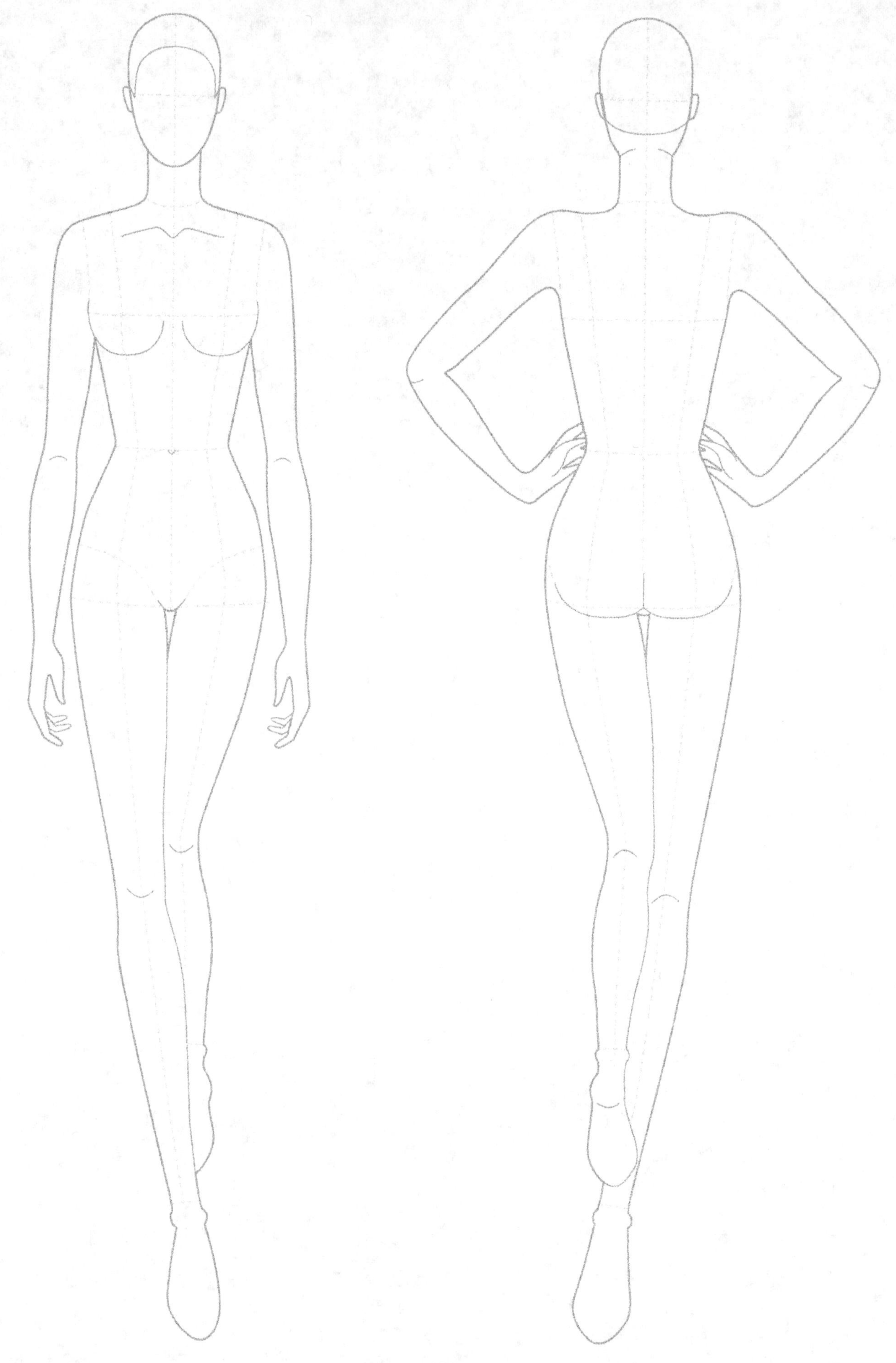

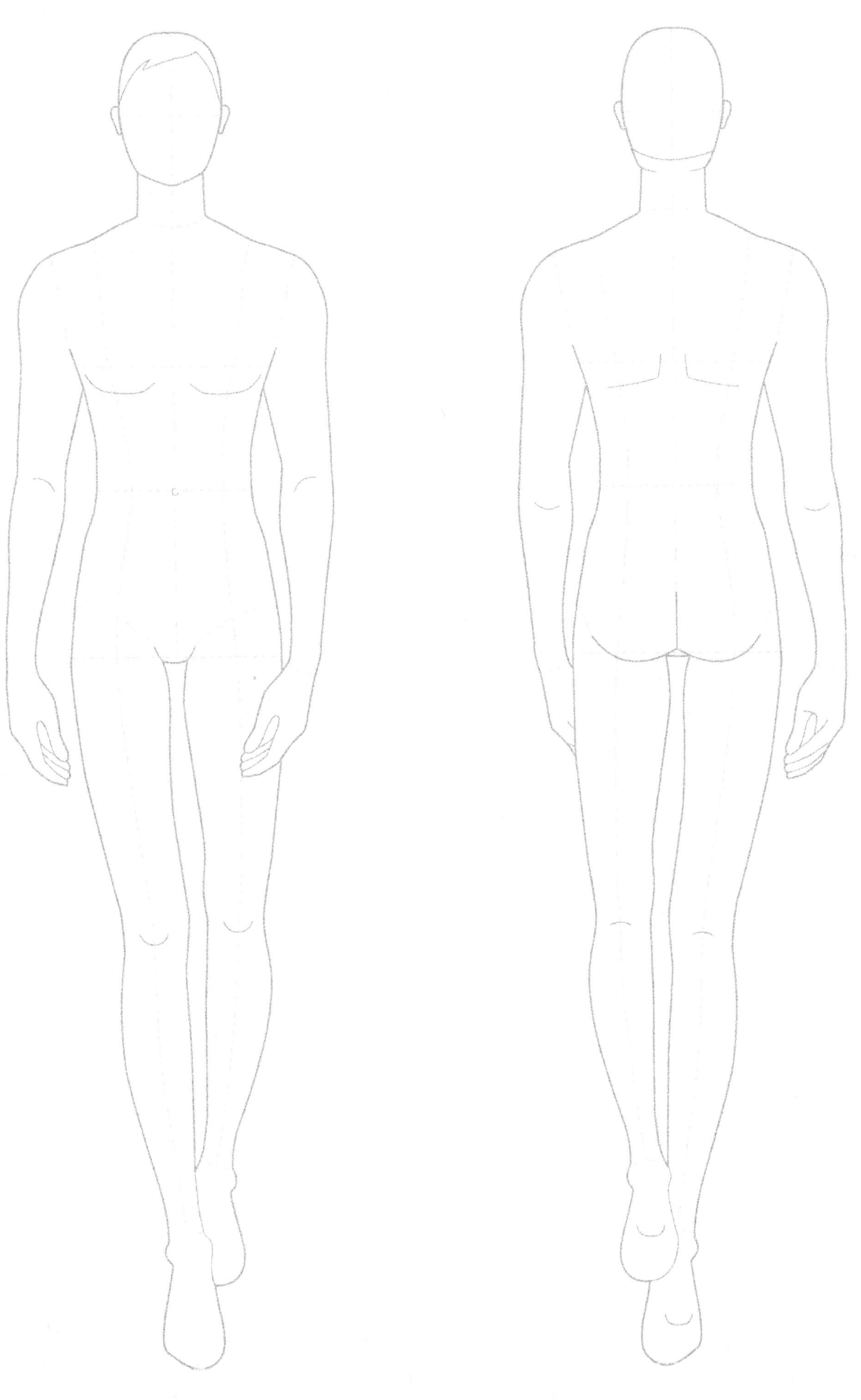

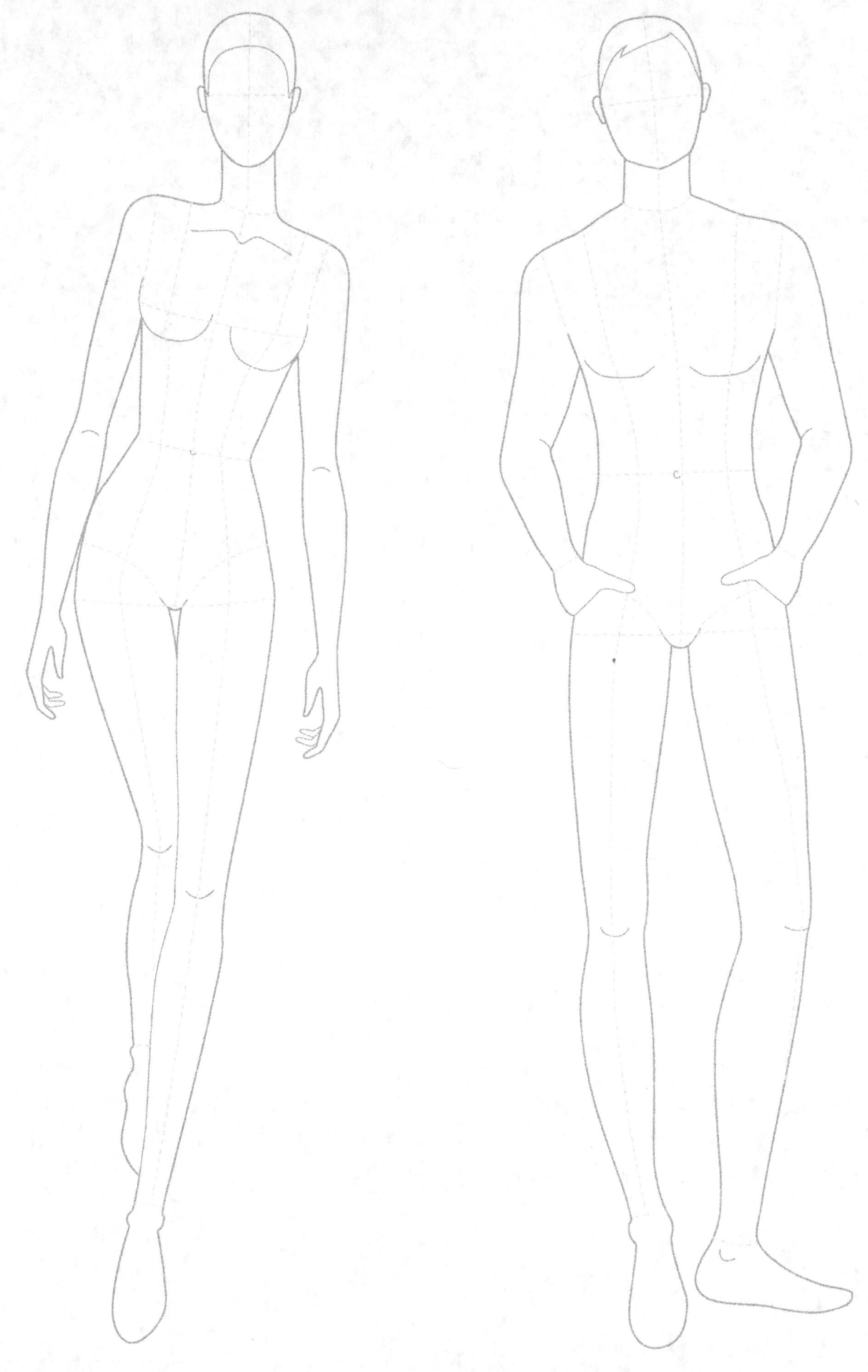

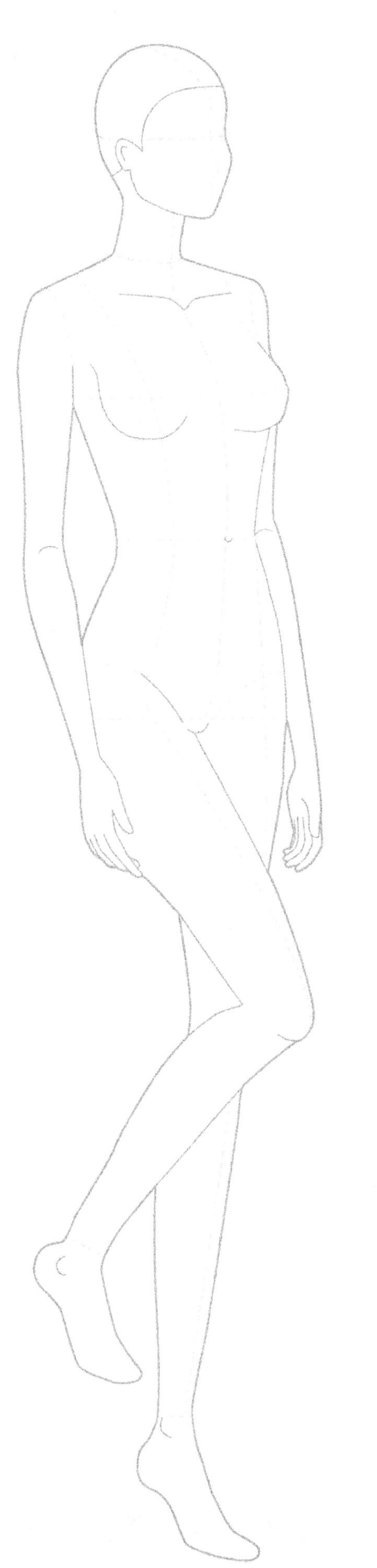
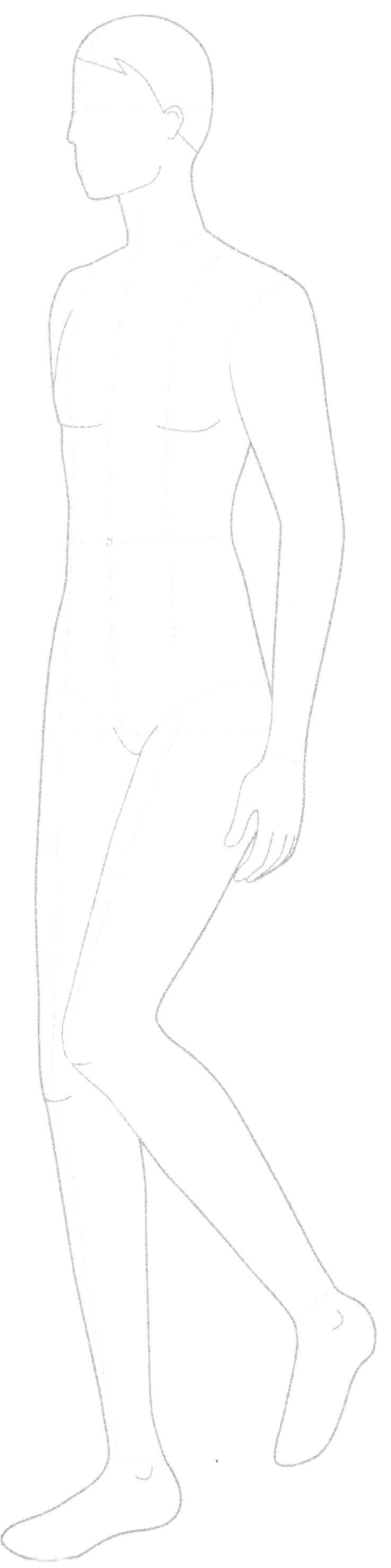

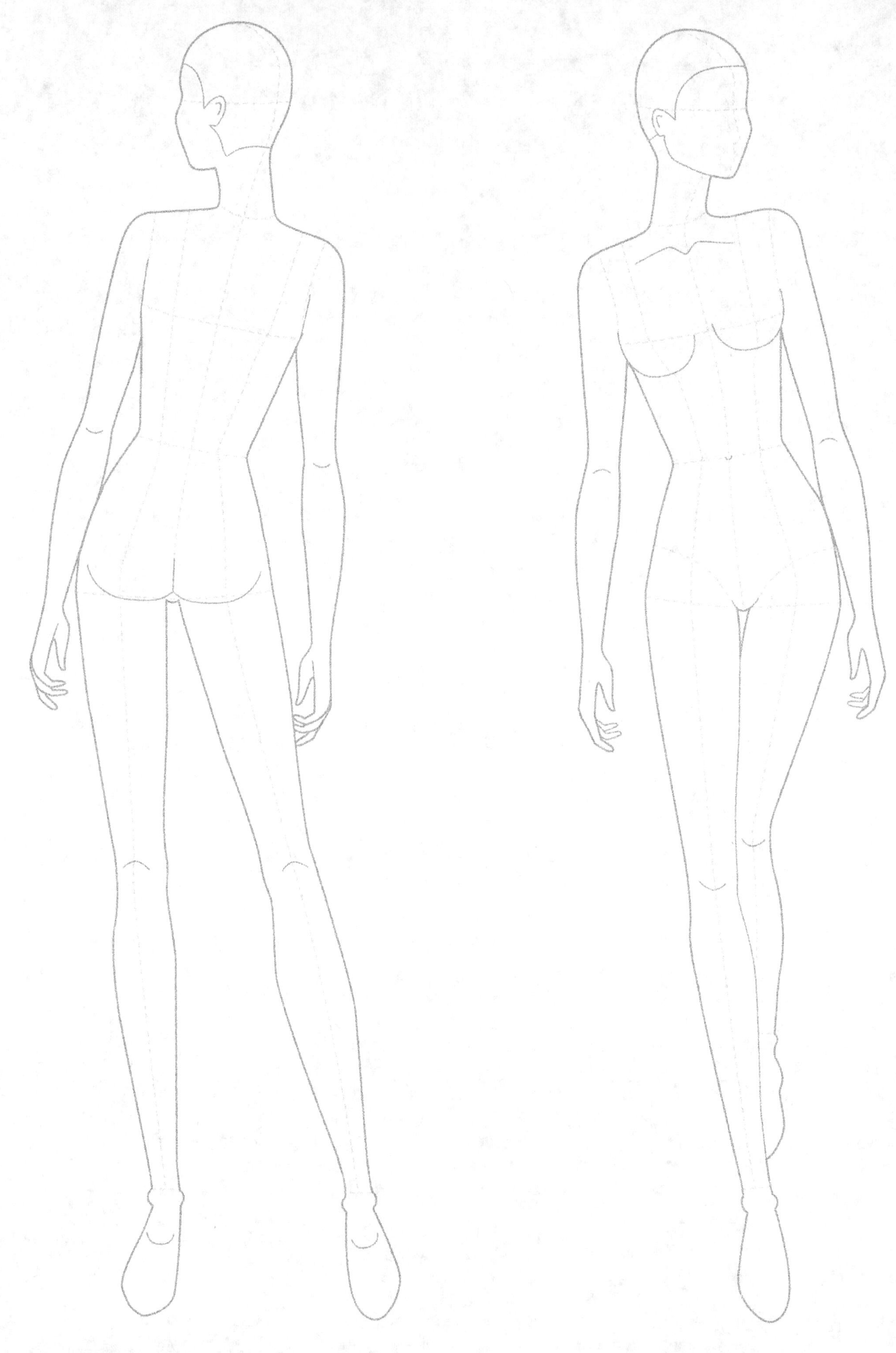

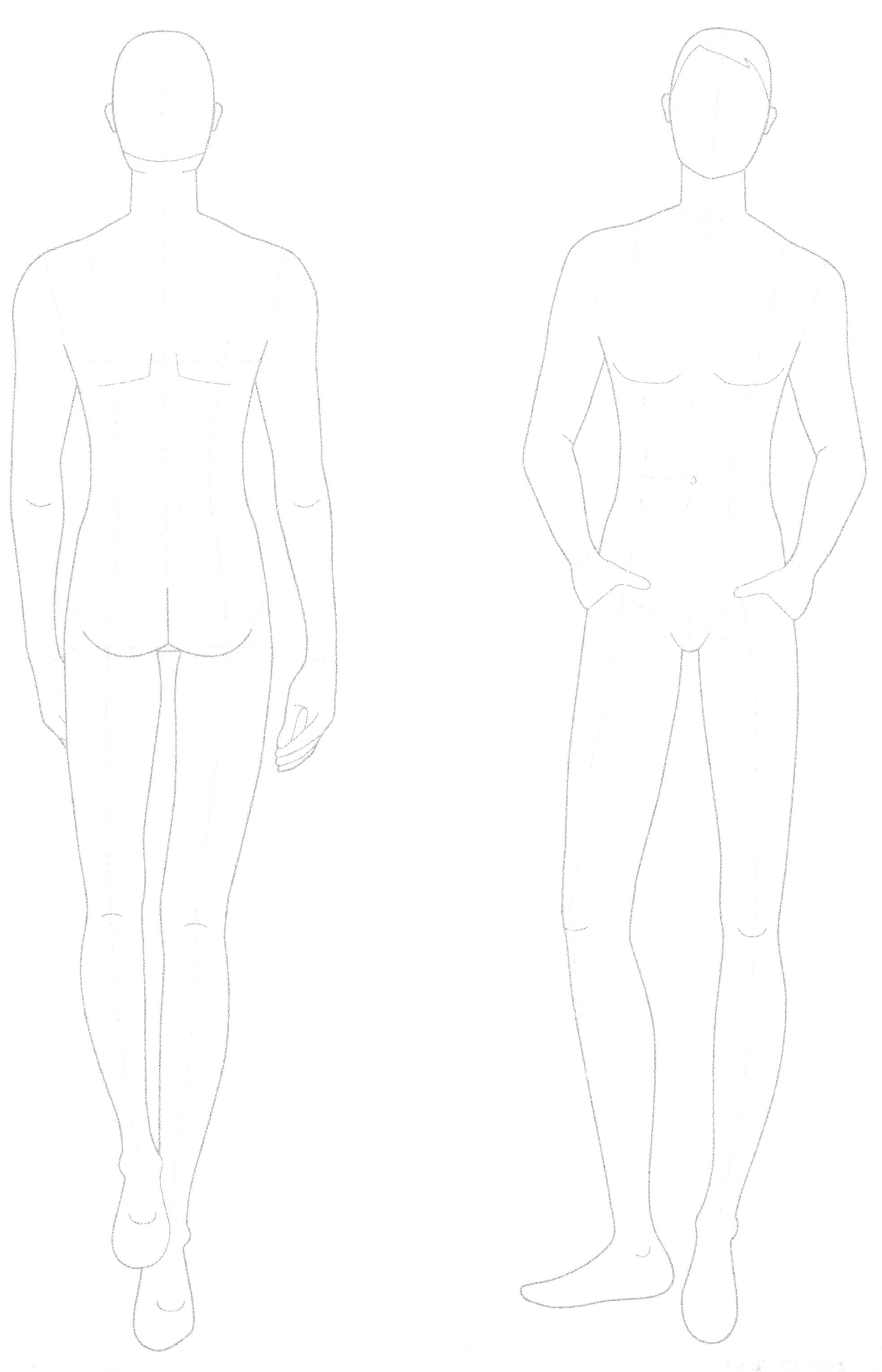